Let's Begin Reading Right
A Developmental Approach to Beginning Literacy

Marjorie Vannoy Fields
University of Alaska

Dorris M. Lee

Merrill Publishing Company
A Bell & Howell Information Company
Columbus   Toronto   London   Melbourne

Cover Photo: Merrill Publishing/Bruce Johnson

Published by
Merrill Publishing Company
A Bell & Howell Information Company
Columbus, Ohio 43216

This book was set in Bookman.

Administrative Editor: Jeff Johnston
Production Coordinator: Constantina Geldis
Cover Designer: Cathy Watterson

Library of Congress Catalog Card Number: 86–62017
International Standard Book Number: 0–675–20616–2
Printed in the United States of America
1 2 3 4 5 6 7 8 9—91 90 89 88 87

Photo credits: Merrill Publishing/Bruce Johnson photographs on pp. 49, 63, 69, 145, 212, and 220; Merrill Publishing/Charles Arbogast photograph on p. 203.

In loving memory of Dorris Lee, an inspiration for teaching and for living. She never wavered in her belief in children or in her efforts on their behalf.

Preface

My interest in effective reading instruction goes back to my own first-grade reading group. Invariably I was caught reading the more interesting stories at the back of the book when it was my turn to read aloud. As a result, it seemed I was always in trouble; however, I still couldn't keep my mind on the slow pace of the group lesson. I learned to dislike reading groups, but never to question them.

When I first became a teacher, I avoided reading groups by teaching kindergarten. Then I moved to a city where kindergarten was not taught, and I was assigned to a first grade. I thought I had no escape from boring reading groups. By chance, however, I took a reading course from Dorris Lee that summer and discovered a whole new vision of teaching reading.

As soon as I heard Dorris's description of effective reading instruction, I knew it was right. I knew it from my own experience of being a child and learning to read in spite of the way it was taught, and I knew it from my observations of the children I had taught. Starting with the language that children bring to school with them, building on the experiences they have already had, and teaching reading and writing simultaneously made sense to me.

So I boldly began teaching first grade without a basal text or any reading groups and, much to my relief, it worked beautifully. I told other teachers that the children seemed to be teaching themselves to read. Child after child experienced the "I can read!" breakthrough, and it was a thrill to get readable letters from "my kids" that following summer back in graduate school.

What I learned from Dorris and those first graders early in my teaching career became clearer to me as I studied more and continued to observe children. The basic principle was to assist children in learning the ways that are natural for them: a foundation principle of the early childhood education field. It became obvious to me that this concept of reading instruction for school-age children could be adapted to pre-schoolers. Studies of Piagetian theory regarding young children's learning confirmed this belief.

I saw that we could abandon the old debates over whether or not to teach reading to kindergarteners and preschoolers. Instead, we can acknowledge that children are learning about reading and writing, and a lot of other things, whether we are teaching it to them or not. When we pay attention to how youngsters learn on their own, we can be guided in how to assist those modes of learning and, therefore, be effective teachers. As long as we let children set their own style and pace, we have no reason to argue over whether reading instruction is good or bad for young children. Once we understand developmentally appropriate ways of helping children learn to read and write, we can feel comfortable about doing so.

The recent explosion of research on young children's writing development validated and extended my previous ideas and understandings about how children become literate. So much information is available about young children, learning, reading, and writing that I found I needed a book that would put it all together for my early childhood teacher-education students. Frustrated in my search and encouraged by my students, I contacted Dorris and convinced her to come out of retirement to collaborate with me on a book that would cover literacy development from preschool through the primary grades. I used it as a text in draft form, and my students responded well to it.

Dorris and I wanted this book to be useful not only as a text for prospective preschool and primary-grade teachers, but also as a reference for experienced teachers and as a guide for parents of young children. Since the home and family are so important to a child's overall education, many examples in this book are about home experiences. Since children begin to learn prior to entering school, infant and toddler years must be discussed too. Since written language and oral language are so closely intertwined, we cannot talk about one without the other. In fact, it is difficult to isolate any one stage or area of development from all others. We have attempted to focus on literacy, but to keep it in perspective with the rest of child development. Examples of actual teaching and learning behaviors are used liberally in hope of making this a practical book—one that is a guide to action as well as thought.

The book begins with an overview of child development theory and looks at it in relation to reading and writing. Next, an analysis of the early childhood education experience-based curriculum and its role in developing literacy is presented. Chapter 3 is a discussion of experiences with written language, describing how to support children's natural modes of learning as they explore written language in preschool, kindergarten, and first grade. Chapter 4 describes how second and third grade teachers can assist youngsters in discovering the full potential of their new reading and writing skills, while the book ends with a guide to decision making about reading curricula and materials for young children.

How to Use This Book as a Text

The topics covered in this book are organized in such a manner that the text can be used in either semester or quarter courses. In addition each chapter is divided into several parts, making it easy to assign parts of a chapter for each class session.

I spent three weeks on each chapter during the semester and had time for the discussions and activities which I have listed at the end of each chapter. Graduate students had time to extend their understanding by reading from the list of references provided.

Instructors who teach elementary reading methods can use this book as a supplementary text to provide coverage of beginning literacy, as most elementary reading texts don't do justice to that stage. Teachers whose colleges offer an early childhood language arts course but not a beginning reading course can use this book because of its integrated language arts approach. If you decide to skip a chapter, I suggest that it not be Chapter 1 since it provides the philosophical foundation for the rest of the book.

Acknowledgments

The guidance and inspiration of many wonderful teachers and enthusiastic children made this book possible. A special thank you goes to the teachers described in this book: Gretchen Reynolds, Chris Thomas, Kathy Hanna, Lynn Williams, and Nils Dihle (Mr. Larson). Many examples come from their classrooms; others are composite examples of effective teaching. Similarly, not all the statements attributed to them came from them, although they generously allowed me to use their names.

My appreciation also goes to my sister, Deborah Hillstead, and her five children, Mandy, Joey, Johnny, Amy, and Betsy, whom readers of this book will come to know. I have also learned a great deal from my own sons, Michael and David, who were lucky enough to have been taught by most of the teachers described. I also wish to thank my kindergarten and first-grade students from long ago and my students in the college teacher education courses I now teach. I have learned so much from you all.

The help of Kay Greenough, Gretchen Reynolds, and Katherine Spangler was essential in getting ideas on the page in a readable manner. I am grateful for their knowledge and their critical appraisal.

I am also indebted to Elizabeth Hoyser, Western Oregon State College; James Jackson, Southern Illinois University; Dan Kies, University of Texas at El Paso; Steven Reuter, University of Minnesota; and Salley Roberts, Western Illinois University, who reviewed the manuscript and provided insights that are reflected in the text.

The primary guidance and inspiration for this book and for my work in the field of education came from co-author Dorris Lee, who passed away before this volume was completed. I hope that the final product is a fitting memorial to her life's work on behalf of children and quality education.

Contents

1

Knowledge About Children That Affects Reading Instruction   xiv

2

A Developmental Approach to Literacy

3

A Natural Introduction to Written Language   102

5

Selecting Reading Programs and Materials   199

Let's Begin Reading Right
A Developmental Approach to Beginning Literacy

1

Knowledge About Children That Affects Reading Instruction

*One of the highest compliments
you can pay a good teacher
is to describe her as "child centered."*
(James Hymes, 1965)

Before exploring the topic of reading instruction for young children, we need to think about children themselves. We will be talking about children who are just beginning to read, from preschool through primary grades. This book explores how youngsters in these early childhood years learn and think differently from older children. These children are not only physically smaller and less competent than older kids, they are also different intellectually and emotionally. They perceive the world, its people, and events in a unique fashion.

Examining these differences is helpful in tailoring learning experiences to the needs of young children. Unless we make this effort, we run the risk of school becoming a place where children are fitted into teacher-made tasks rather than a place where they are helped to refine their views of the world and come to greater understandings of it and themselves. Our goal as teachers is to foster those kinds of understandings, not merely to train children in giving correct answers.

PHYSICAL DEVELOPMENT

First let's look at what is apparent—the young child's physical development. As children leave toddlerhood and prepare for a first school experience at age three or four, they are starting to lose their baby shape and babyish movements. They become taller and slimmer as they gain more adult-like proportions, and when they reach kindergarten, their little pot bellies are usually gone. As children's muscle coor-

dination increases, they become more sure-footed, agile, and fond of testing their new abilities.

Because physical development stages are observable, adults accept and understand them more easily than intellectual or emotional stages. No one questions that children sit before they stand, stand before they walk, or walk before they run. We have seen children progress through these stages and make gradual progress in specific skills, such as jumping and throwing. Our acceptance of immature efforts toward physical prowess can be our guide in acceptance of immature intellectual and emotional responses. Adults are less likely to expect youngsters to perform physical feats beyond their capacity than they are to expect youngsters to master advanced academic or social skills. For instance, a toddler throwing a ball isn't likely to be criticized for lack of good aim; yet, that same toddler is apt to be scolded for not wanting to share a toy with another child. Both achievements take time.

Physical development generally progresses from head to foot and from body center to extremities. Additionally, large muscle control, also called gross motor control, will precede the small muscle, or fine motor control. The neighbor's new baby, Betsy, could lift her head almost as soon as she was born, but months passed before she was able to control her hands to pick up a toy. She could pull herself around the floor by her arms—the "combat crawl"—before she could control her legs to stand or even crawl. Her first efforts at feeding herself will testify to the difficulty of fine motor control.

Teachers recognize these sequences in their planning of appropriate activities for young children. They do not present crafts projects requiring great finger dexterity to youngsters who still haven't mastered throwing a ball in the direction they desire. Early childhood educators allow the gross motor skills to mature before expecting fine motor skill; they expect hand dexterity, such as simple weaving, before they expect intricate feet movements, such as those involved in skipping.

The development of large and small muscle skills is necessary before academic work, such as making a pencil move in a desired direction; children must have ample opportunity to practice these skills in an early childhood education setting. Vigorous active movements—running, climbing, jumping, and lifting—develop strength and coordination of the large muscles in the legs, arms, shoulders, and back. (Stomach muscle strength can also be developed through appropriate exercise, but it lags behind the others developmentally. This explains why young children have difficulty standing on their heads or otherwise holding their torso rigid.) Children gain small muscle control, including eye-hand coordination, through practice with small manipulative materials such as Bristle Blocks, peg boards, and Legos. Additionally, painting and coloring experiences relate directly to the coordination required for handwriting.

We should supply materials and introduce open-ended activities which both increase children's skills and enable them to feel free of failure. Materials and activities which have no right or wrong response provide skills practice without failure. These open-ended learning experiences encourage participation at any level of skill or understanding. Closed activities and materials discourage those children most in need of practice. Their repeated failure to perform at a specified level eliminates their desire to try. The open-ended feature can make the difference between an activity which is developmentally appropriate and one which is inappropriate, between one which expects too much and one which encourages growth at a child's own level. While two tasks may require the same skill, the open-ended one allows gradually increasing levels of competence, while a closed task rewards only a certain standard of achievement. Painting at the easel is an open-ended activity, but being requested to paint a picture of your house is a closed one. Pounding nails at the workbench is an open activity, but following

directions to make an airplane figure is closed. Throwing a ball is an open activity, but playing catch is closed. What other activities and materials can you think of that are closed and may invite failure?

While children's muscles are gaining strength through being flexed, their senses also become more keen through use. Smelling, tasting, and touching, as well as hearing and seeing, are important ways of gathering information about the world. Many adults tell children not to touch things and not to put anything besides food in their mouth; yet, children need to exercise *all* their senses, just as they do their muscles. Children need to develop efficient listening skills in order to master the sound-symbol relationship used to read and write. (Screening out distracting sounds also is a necessary skill for children, as well as adults, in a noisy society.) We tend to emphasize vision as the major source of sensory input, but even though children rely heavily on what they see, they must master specific visual discrimination skills. For instance, they must learn which differences between letters are significant and which are not—whether an extra loop on a handwritten *a* or another crossbar on a *T* make them into different letters or not.

Screening for potential hearing, vision, and speech problems is a necessary part of the early childhood teacher's role. The teacher's own observations of a child is the first screening. As teachers notice a child who talks very little, one whose physical movements are awkward, one who is unusually passive, or another who is exceptionally active (you can't help noticing that one), they become alerted to the child's need for specific testing. All children should have a vision test as young as possible to insure they are using both eyes together and don't have a "lazy" eye. This is a common occurrence and easily correctable if caught at a young age.

As children develop increased physical competence, they become capable of many self-help tasks which greatly increase their independence. Timmy is able to get his own jacket zipped more often, Tanya can tie her own shoes, and Kelly can almost button the back of her favorite dressup dress. Hooks to hang clothes on, rather than hangers, and pullover paint smocks that don't need tying are examples of materials that foster the independence which is so important to children's feelings of self-worth.

Teachers can foster independence at snack time by providing children small pitchers and sturdy, wide glasses. Finger foods and other easily handled food also help, but it is always wise to keep a sponge handy. Showing children how to clean up spills and demonstrating an accepting attitude about occasional accidents further increase independence, confidence, and therefore skill. Child-sized chairs and tables also are helpful, as are child-sized toilet facilities. If the bathroom is the right size for young children, they are generally capable of taking full responsibility for toilet needs by preschool age. Expecting this independence at an earlier age is an example of expecting too much too soon.

Physical development is contingent upon basic physical well-being—freedom from disease, plus adequate nutrition, exercise, sleep, and sunshine. The school can guide families who need help or information to meet these basic needs. The immunization requirements for all schools are a positive step toward good health and should be linked to physical check-ups. Low income families may require information about how to make use of free health services.

The school program can provide a model for proper nutrition through the choice of foods for snack, especially if menus are published in class newsletters. Providing exercise and sunshine for children as part of the school program also models important values, as does providing adequate periods of rest. The teacher is in a position to notice when children's health needs are not being met and can assist parents who haven't learned how to meet them.

Additionally, schools themselves must be safe, healthy places for children. All hazards such as poisonous cleaning aids, sharp corners, accessible electrical outlets, and exposed heaters must be eliminated from an environment for children. Playground equipment must be surrounded by soft ground, and swing seats should be soft. Teachers need to remove broken or wobbly equipment, and must guard against splinters or exposed nails. Children should receive instruction in respon-

sible hygiene practices, with hand washing before meals and the disposal of tissues after nose blowing.

A strong, healthy body nurtures an inquiring mind. How then does that part of the child, the intellectual component, develop?

INTELLECTUAL DEVELOPMENT

The extensive research and writing of Jean Piaget provides insight into the mind of a child. Piaget discovered and described developmental stages in thinking and understanding, stages through which all children pass on their way to adult modes of knowing (Bybee and Sund, 1982). During the first stage, babies and toddlers perform their educational research by putting everything in their mouths and by grabbing anything that is not out of their reach. They are busily learning through their senses and are highly motivated to do so, no matter how many times they are told "no". Frustrated parents can only take comfort in the fact that all this activity is a sure sign of an inquiring mind. If the adults caring for children in this *Sensory-Motor Stage* of intellectual development keep them safely in a playpen or even restricted from the floor in a walker, they deprive the youngsters of stimulation necessary for intellectual growth.

The next stage of intellectual development—the one we will focus on throughout this book—Piaget calls the *Preoperational Stage.* During the preoperational stage, mental activity is not separate from physical activity or experience. This stage is more advanced than the sensory-motor stage because children use language in synthesizing the information they have gained through their senses. Most children move from the first stage to the second about the time they are two years old, and most stay in the preoperational stage until they are about seven years old. So you see, this stage encompasses all of preschool, kindergarten, and most of the primary grades. It is important to remember that individual differences determine the rate of change in this area of development, just as individual differences determine when a child walks or talks. Therefore, exact ages of moving through stages vary.

Even when children grow into the next stage of intellectual development, they are still not fully able to think about that which is outside their realm of experience. The third stage, called *Concrete Operations,* describes a time when children can deal with concepts or ideas which they have not directly experienced, but still are tied to those concepts which have some relationship to their own previous experience. Piaget uses "concrete" to mean real life happenings or things, and so the term "concrete operations" means abstract thinking about real things, or the ability to perform mental actions which reflect previous actual actions. It isn't until children are out of elementary school, if even then, that they can be expected to be capable of abstract thinking—or *Formal Operations.*

Piaget's Stages of Intellectual Development

1. Sensorimotor Period—approximately birth to twenty-four months
2. Preoperational Period—approximately two to seven years
   Child learns from experiences and interaction with real things (concrete)
   Child understands that which is discovered through personal experience rather than that which is explained (understandings constructed from within)
3. Concrete Operational Period—approximately seven to eleven years
4. Formal Operations—approximately eleven or older (if attained)

Source: From *The Origins of Intelligence in Children* by J. Piaget, 1963, New York: W. W. Norton.

This text describes children in the second of four stages of intellectual development, a stage significantly different from that of adults. What does this mean to us as teachers? Specifically, we must recognize young children's needs to personally explore their world. Just because they are no longer in the sensory-motor stage doesn't mean that they no longer need to learn through touching, tasting, smelling, hearing, seeing, and acting upon things. These are still their primary modes of intellectual input and provide them with the content for thoughtful analysis which leads to understandings.

Does this mean that firsthand experience with letters in workbooks is needed for learning? Or, does it mean that children should make cookies in the shape of letters to learn through their sense of taste? Should they trace the outlines of letters on sandpaper to learn through their sense of touch? Our answer is "none of the above." No matter what you do to letters, they are still abstract—very abstract. Letters are a symbolic representation of oral language, which itself is a symbolic representation system. For young children who rely on learning from real things, we don't recommend starting with letters in any form or flavor.

It is helpful to keep in mind that children start with understanding the real, or concrete, and only gradually develop the ability to think independent of real things. It may be useful to think of a baby learning to walk—first restricted to walking only where there is something to hold onto for support and gradually taking more and more steps independently before having to grab onto something again. Although the process of learning to walk without support may take only a few weeks, the process of learning to think without supports takes many years. This means parents and teachers need to be patient, not in a hurry, to wean youngsters from the concrete level learning, or children may fall flat intellectually just as the toddler would fall if deprived of support too soon.

Some people think that a concrete learning material is anything that can be touched and moved. They buy plastic letters in an effort to meet developmental needs. Others think that pictures of real things can be substituted for concrete level materials. They start visual discrimination lessons with workbook pictures instead of with actual objects, or they show pictures or films in place of actual experiences. Pictures are less abstract than letters and numerals; they are a symbolic representation which is closer to reality in that they are more easily linked to what they represent. Yet, pictures are not concrete, and teachers should not substitute them for action with real objects. Pictures can provide a useful link between the concrete and the abstract, however, especially if they represent something the child has actually

A Comparison of Abstract and Concrete Materials

Concrete Level	Semi-Abstract Level	Abstract Level
sorting shells	puzzles	name tags
peg boards	pictures	numerals
matching buttons	lotto games	alphabet charts

experienced. Perhaps they function like a mother's hand to steady the toddler who can almost walk alone.

Children Learn Through Concrete Experiences

Teachers of young children need to remember that their students require introduction to an idea at the concrete level through firsthand interaction with the environment. After this introduction, students can move to the semi-abstract level of looking at pictures or observing the actions of others. Only after sufficient time at each of these levels should teachers ask students to deal with the abstractions of symbols. We must remember that oral explanations are also abstract and generally of limited usefulness with preoperational stage youngsters.

The idea of a semi-abstract level, between the concrete and the abstract, brings up the issue of transition activities—those that help children make that bridge between the real and the symbolic. Pictures have been identified as being useful in this way. They can serve as links to the concrete when children match pictures with real things, such as when they use pictures on the toy shelves as a guide for where to put things at clean-up time. Pictures can be linked to the abstract, such as when they provide cues to word identification. When Mrs. Hanna encourages her kindergarteners to draw a picture of the designs they make with the geoboards or the pegboards, she is helping them make a transition from the concrete to the abstract. When Mrs. Thomas helps children to play a logic game with real objects before they play it with symbols on the computer, she is also assisting the transition.

Although no one argues that letters are unimportant in reading, we must advocate that we start at the beginning and help children work their way from concrete things to the abstraction of symbols. The first step is for the child to grasp the existence of symbol systems and to understand their purpose. This understanding of a series of intuitive concepts is not something that can be explained to children; they must discover it for themselves (Foreman and Kushner, 1984). Children can of course be taught to memorize letters and words, but recognizing the basic tools for a task is not the same as understanding the nature of the task itself. Adults take for granted the relationship between written symbols and the reality they represent, but they need to be patient while youngsters develop an awareness of that relationship.

Without awareness of the relation between symbols and reality, children cannot be expected to grasp the relationship between print and meaning. Without this insight, children can easily become mechanical decoders of a symbol system with little response to the message of the code (Cohen, 1972). Developing necessary understandings about symbolic representation takes time, raw materials, and encouragement. Unfortunately, schools often don't give children time to explore and to think; they keep youngsters busy filling in blanks or following directions of one kind or another. Additionally, the raw materials for creating symbols—clay, blocks, sand, and paints—are often not considered educational.

Yet, many early childhood teachers do provide appropriate learning experiences and materials for their students. When we observe in Mrs. Hanna's kindergarten class, we see Amy and Maria creating symbols for a variety of props needed in their dramatic play. When they make "pretend cookies" with clay, they are using symbolic representation. They are capable of letting a chair stand in for a baby stroller and a teddy bear represent the baby. In Mrs. Thomas's first grade we see Tyler's representation of a ferry boat which he has constructed with blocks. His actual experiences with ferry boats give him awareness of details which he has recreated symbolically through the medium of blocks. The process of communicating what he knows through blocks helps him clarify his understanding. When Tanya paints at the

easel and names her painting, this too is a step toward understanding of symbolic representation. She knows very well that the blobs of paint aren't really her pet dogs, but she is following the historic path of the cave dwellers and the sand painters in drawing images to represent meaningful aspects of her world.

Children Construct Their Own Knowledge

The children just described are discovering the concept of symbolic representation. If an adult attempted to explain this concept to them, they could not understand. But through their own experiences, they are capable of intuitive understandings of ideas too abstract for them to verbalize or to understand when verbalized by others. Piaget referred to discovery learning as "invented" understandings (Kamii, 1982). His research led him to the conclusion that children only understand that which they discover, or invent, themselves. Piaget cautioned adults against trying to teach by telling, since the telling keeps children from their own thinking process.

This characteristic of the young learner as someone who constructs his or her own knowledge from a series of hypotheses, experiments, and revised hypotheses is essential for the early childhood teacher to understand. If we didn't understand the learning process of the young child, we might think Ms. Reynolds is not a good teacher because she doesn't correct frequent misconceptions expressed by her four-year-old students. Ms. Reynolds knows that she needs to encourage children to think up their own explanations, to analyze and defend them, and to reject and replace them. If she is the authority for all knowledge, children will simply mimic her answers rather than develop their own thinking ability. When children are allowed to learn in the way that Piaget described as their natural way, they become thinkers instead of reciters and understand instead of just repeat.

When we adults already know an answer, we find it hard to be patient as children go through the process of figuring the answer out for themselves. We can admire and enjoy their intellectual activity if we understand it. It is crucial for teachers to realize that young children do not learn by having information fed into them, but rather by slowly adapting previous perceptions to fit with new experiences. In other words, learning happens from the inside out, not from the outside in.

If you do tell a child something, the best time is after she has made a discovery for herself but cannot yet verbalize the learning. Hearing an adult explanation at this point allows a child to understand because she already knows from experience that which is being explained; therefore, she will recognize it as true. An adult explanation at this point can give a child the words to describe what she already knows.

Given the opportunity, children discover much of what they need to know in order to read. Many of us know of children who seem to have taught themselves to read. These children usually have observed family or friends reading and writing, enjoyed being read to, received answers to their questions about the reading process, and received encouragement in their attempts at reading and writing. No one was working at making them learn, yet effective teaching was occurring in response to these children's interests. This natural way for children to learn suits their stage of intellectual development because it involves their own action in pursuit of knowledge they are interested in. If schools are to provide appropriate reading instruction for young children, (suited to the children's intellectual stage), they need to create learning environments which encourage this same kind of active discovery learning.

These learning environments will be "print rich" with posters, signs, books, and frequent use of written communication to extend oral communication. Such an environment allows children to discover for themselves the importance and use of reading and writing. These classrooms will offer open invitations for children to dictate their ideas to an adult who will write them down. Through such experiences children discover that what they say can be translated into print and can be read by others. Print-rich environments encourage children to write, whether their level of writing consists of pictures, linear scribbles, random letters, or actual attempts at letter-sound representations. Children will thus discover through their own actions the basic principles of writing, including phonics and other word recognition skills.

In print-rich environments teachers read to young children every day. Through hearing quality children's literature read by an adult who knows and loves the stories, children discover the joy of reading and the wonders to be found in books. In this type of classroom teachers keep track of what each child has discovered and help with appropriate questions and suggestions when a child fails to make a needed discovery without help. The critical element always will be the emphasis on the child's own actions and experiences, which are essential to discovery. Adults serving as models, resources, and guides are a vital element in these discovery processes too.

Sometimes when teachers plan for children's learning, they confuse watching with experiencing. Then they deprive youngsters of an essential ingredient of learning. Although children learn much from watching others, that learning doesn't become theirs until they have an opportunity to imitate or in some way recreate what they have observed. We are often amused at what little mimics young children are, but their mimicry is serious business in the learning process. Children need science experiments that they do themselves, instead of those they watch the teacher perform; they need field trips to the post office where they put mail items in specified spots and climb into delivery trucks, instead of just hearing explanations; and they need to write their own stories, instead of just seeing those written by others.

Teachers who understand Piaget's teachings and attempt to follow them don't adopt the traditional teacher role of telling children about the world and then questioning them to see if they remember what they were told. Instead of telling children information, they spend time listening to children and observing their explorations of the environment. Justin has been arranging and rearranging a set of cubes in different patterns at preschool today, and Ms. Reynolds stops by to ask about what he has been doing. Her questions are designed to promote thought and further inquiry, not to test specific knowledge. Her questions are open ended and have no right or wrong answer.

Piaget's writings say little about actual teaching methods; rather, they describe the factors involved in the child's movement from one intellectual stage of development to another. The four factors identified by Piaget are: maturation, action on the physical environment, social interaction, and *equilibration*—the desire to make sense of the world (Almy, 1976). Knowing how children learn guides teachers to adopt proper teaching methods at each stage of development. For instance, knowing that maturation is one factor influencing intellectual development guides teachers to select curricular activities which are age appropriate for their students. They will not accept portions of a curriculum designed for older children as a way of accelerating achievement.

Factors Involved in Intellectual Development According to Piaget

1. Maturation of the child
2. Action on the physical environment
3. Social interaction
4. Desire to make sense of the world (Equilibration)

Maturation works in conjunction with other factors to cause intellectual growth, but we should not rely upon it exclusively. As discussed earlier in this chapter, a child's action on the environment is necessary for the learning which maturation makes possible. Children's interaction with others is also necessary so their egocentric view of the world can be modified. Specifically, social interaction among peers as they compare their various hypotheses is an effective stimulant to young children's processes of constructing knowledge (Kamii and Randazzo, 1985). And finally, the drive of equilibration is necessary to make any of the other factors work. As fuel is necessary to make the parts of a car engine run, equilibration is the fuel that sparks a child's intellectual development.

Mrs. Hanna tries to create a kindergarten which nourishes all four intellectual growth factors. She carefully matches levels of abstraction with the maturation of her individual students; she provides various experiences and materials for exploration; and she encourages children to work and play together as they explore. Above all, she nurtures the natural questioning, seeking, and testing that exemplify striving for equilibration. She considers this the innate motivation to learn. She watches Zachary and Suzanne eagerly working with screws and screwdrivers as they take apart and put together some discarded door knobs donated to the class. Watching them, she realizes again how important it is for children to have this combination of concrete learning, personal activity, others to work with, and encouragement of curiosity.

Teachers of young children who attempt to use Piaget's theories have classrooms filled with activity and a variety of materials. Discussions, questions, and exclamations abound in such settings. These are not tidy, quiet, classrooms with children working sedately at their desks using paper and pencil.

EMOTIONAL DEVELOPMENT

Providing for optimum intellectual growth also fosters emotional health. Intellectual and emotional development contribute to and depend upon each other. Even Piaget, who spent his life studying intellectual development, commented extensively on the ''affective domain,'' or emotional realm of learning. Certainly, the equilibration factor in intellectual development seems more emotional than intellectual—an emotional feeling that drives intellectual pursuits. Sadly, we have seen people of all ages who appear to have lost that drive, and we are struck by the emotional side of their loss. The lack of striving to know and experience often is associated with low self-esteem. Low self-esteem in turn is characterized by lack of self confidence and fear of failure which conflict with people's ability to learn.

Self-Esteem

Obviously if we educators want to be effective in the classroom, we must help children to be teachable, and that means we must be concerned with self-esteem. *Self-esteem* is sometimes used interchangeably with *self-concept,* which actually has a broader meaning. Self-concept refers to an individual's idea of who she is, while self-esteem results from perceptions of how acceptable that self image is (Dinkmeyer, 1965). These perceptions are heavily influenced by feedback the child receives from others—whether parents make the child feel loved, whether teachers make the child feel important, and whether peers make the child feel accepted. Although adult feedback is most significant for the young child and peer response is most significant for older children, children as young as preschool age are deeply hurt by peer rejection. Perceptions of self-worth are also influenced by success or failure as the child attempts new accomplishments. Each success encourages more ambitious attempts; each failure discourages more attempts.

How can teachers influence self-esteem? Activities can help a child develop a self-concept, or knowledge of oneself; but self-esteem occurs on a more subtle level. Traditional preschool and kindergarten activities such as tracing the outline of a child's body on a large piece of butcher paper and encouraging the child to color and cut out the figure, or using photographs of each child and his or her family in a study of families provide help with self-awareness. Self-concept activities can be planned, but self-esteem builders must pervade the entire classroom environment. They are a part of every interaction between teacher and student, and part of every interaction between children. Encouragement or discouragement of self-esteem is the result of every activity and experience offered in a curriculum.

Ms. Reynolds has a special way of making every child in her class feel important. She gives her undivided attention to each child who speaks to her. She doesn't respond with a stock ''that's nice'' to what a child says; instead, she makes a thoughtful comment or asks a

relevant question. She places great importance on listening to children and makes time for that ahead of other more traditional teacher roles. Of course sometimes she must attend to something more pressing, but at these moments she doesn't ignore a child or just pretend to listen. Instead, she quickly arranges with the child a time when they can talk uninterrupted. This is an example of "respecting" children. The adult-child ratio of one to five in her cooperative preschool allows much more attention per child than when she taught kindergarten with twenty-five or thirty youngsters by herself. She thinks that usual public school kindergarten class sizes provide unhealthy emotional environments.

The respectful way that Ms. Reynolds treats youngsters in her class provides a model for positive social interaction among the children. However, learning how to be a friend is a hard job, and some children need help. For several days now Caleb has been going up to Kelly pretending he was a big bear, growling and making threatening motions at her. Kelly has run away leaving Caleb behind. Ms. Reynolds thinks that maybe Caleb would like to play with Kelly but doesn't know how to start. When she asks Caleb if that is what he wants, and he says it is, Ms. Reynolds suggests another approach and helps the two children find a play topic they both enjoy. This type of intervention is important to keep socially unskilled children from developing low self-esteem due to social rejection.

Mrs. Hanna is careful to provide various activities so each child can find one where he excels. She knows that self-esteem is based on cognitive competency, social competency, and physical competency (Harter, 1982) and that children may be helped to achieve in one area when they have difficulty in another. She is quick to call attention to the accomplishments of each child. She focuses her comments on how good the child feels about the feat. Helping children tune into the intrinsic rewards of doing well, whether at pumping a swing or completing a puzzle, provides a base for gaining personal satisfaction from accomplishments rather than relying on the judgments of others. Mrs. Hanna rarely says, "You did a nice job," but more often says something like, "You must feel proud of yourself," or "How did that make you feel?" She uses praise sparingly since she wants children to be self-motivated rather than rely on her judgments of their behavior.

Besides providing for curriculum variety in helping all her students experience success, Mrs. Hanna also matches the level of difficulty in a task with the child's level of competence. This doesn't mean that she asks children to only try what they can easily do. Rather she prepares activities that are challenging without being excessively difficult. She knows from years of teaching kindergarten that children who experience success continue to strive for more challenge. Often children will create their own variations on an activity in order to have greater challenges. Although she hasn't time to plan totally separate activities to match each child's level, neither does she group her students and assume homogeneity within a group. She provides choices—choices between activities and choices of ways to complete a task. Children generally are drawn to choices which are appropriate developmentally for them. If a child consistently chooses that which is too easy or too difficult, Mrs. Hanna recognizes that either choice may indicate a lack of self-confidence, and she guides her students toward more realistic choices.

Mrs. Hanna's kindergarten is set up into various learning centers to provide children with choices. These centers may contain activities which accomplish the same curriculum objective, but they are appropriate for different ability levels and encourage different interests. Mrs. Hanna attempts to provide open-ended tasks as often as possible so children will seek their own level of challenge. She has set aside a time today for reading skills, with a special emphasis on visual discrimination. Billy and Maria are working and talking at a table as Billy sorts through a bag of pebbles to find similarities and differences while Maria matches shells with others of the same type. Nearby Christy and Jennifer are discovering the various ways in which the "attribute blocks" can be sorted. Elsewhere several children are engrossed in putting together puzzles. Sitting beside Zachary and Suzanne, Amy is at the listening center reading along with a tape of a favorite story. Jennifer and Jamie are both working in the writing center, where Jennifer is writing a letter to her grandmother with near-standard

spelling, and Jamie is drawing pictures telling about a movie he saw. Although Jennifer and Jamie are at different levels in their writing, both are making appropriate use of the writing center. Mrs. Hanna moves among the children asking pertinent questions, making suggestions, answering questions, and keeping activity constructive.

Mrs. Thomas provides as much choice as possible for children in her first grade class. She wants children to make decisions and do things for themselves. Making decisions will give them a sense of power which reduces their feelings of helplessness and increases their feelings of competence (Maccoby, 1980). She involves her students in such decisions as setting class conduct rules and individually choosing reading materials. Mrs. Thomas also encourages feelings of competence through realistic standards of performance. When Becky generously allows a classmate to hold her special ''adopted'' doll, Mrs. Thomas compliments her without mentioning that Becky wouldn't let the other child change the doll's clothes. Similarly, when Michael manages to tie his own shoelaces, Mrs. Thomas doesn't notice that the shoes happen to be on the wrong feet. Or, when David writes his first story, she doesn't try to correct his creative spelling.

Probably the most important thing that Mrs. Thomas, Mrs. Hanna, and Ms. Reynolds do for the self-esteem of their students is to accept and enjoy each one of them, regardless of how they are performing or who they are. Carl Rogers (1983) calls such acceptance *unconditional positive regard.* Of great importance is the teacher's own positive self-image which allows her to relinquish some of her own power to the children she teaches. These children will in turn experience enhanced self-esteem.

Emotional Development Stages

A strong determinant of self-esteem is whether a child experiences success or failure while passing through the emotional development stages which Erik Erikson describes (Erikson, 1963). Generally if children satisfactorily complete developmental tasks at each stage, they will have positive self-esteem. If they have not, children will have negative self-esteem.

The first stage occurs in infancy and involves the development of *trust*—belief that someone cares about you and can be counted on when needed. The old idea that it spoils babies to pick them up when they cry has negative consequences for trust development. Fortunately this notion is becoming less prevalent. A baby left to cry only learns that no one cares and that his or her desires are unimportant. The baby will eventually learn not to cry, but only because of becoming convinced no one cares. Infants' attachment to those who care for them is another part of their developing trust. This explains why continuity of care givers in child care settings is important. If babies have different persons meeting their needs rather than one or two consistent ones, they have difficulty in developing attachment and learning to trust. If the development of trust is not accomplished in infancy, lack of trust often persists throughout a person's life and hampers the success of close relationships.

Autonomy, the second stage, occurs during toddlerhood. The time often called the "terrible twos," this stage is characterized by a drive for independence. "No" and "Me do it" are common responses during this stage of a child's development. Toddlers have gained the independence of walking around alone and have begun to exercise control over their bodies including bowel and bladder control. They are eager to assert their independence and to accomplish as much as possible for themselves. Wise adults provide ample opportunity for toddlers to make choices and do things for themselves in appropriate circumstances. This independent action will help the child better accept those situations when the adult must make decisions affecting the child. For instance, a toddler can decide whether to wear the blue coveralls or the red ones, whether to eat the corn or the applesauce first, or whether or not to share a beloved toy with a friend. Allowing a child to make these decisions will help him accept the adult decision that he will play in the yard and not in the street, that he will go to bed now and not later.

Erikson's Stages of Emotional Development

1. Trust vs. Mistrust—infant
2. Autonomy vs. Shame—toddler
3. *Initiative vs. Guilt*—early childhood
   Increasing sense of power and desire to prove self
   Ability to work cooperatively and accept adult guidance
   Developing sense of responsibility and self control (Beware of over-emphasis on self-control)
4. Industry vs. Inferiority—middle childhood
5. Identity vs. Role Confusion—adolescent
6. Intimacy vs. Isolation—young adult
7. Generativity vs. Stagnation—prime of life
8. Ego-Integrity vs. Despair—old age

Source: From *Childhood and Society,* by Erik Erikson, 1963, New York: W.W. Norton. Copyright 1963 by Eric Erikson. Adapted by permission.

Although a child should have completed the trust and autonomy stages before preschool, teachers need to understand these stages in order to assist those youngsters who have not successfully completed those tasks. These children will require special attention. The teacher's unconditional positive regard, referred to earlier, assists a child in continued trust development, as do fair and consistent rules and discipline approaches. Freedom to make choices, previously recommended for enhancing a child's feelings of power to assist self-esteem, also encourage increased autonomy.

Most preschool children will be in the stage Erikson calls *Initiative* and therefore eagerly seek to prove themselves on ever new frontiers. They are developing an increasing sense of their own power and ability to make things happen as their physical and intellectual capacities mature. Eager to learn and work cooperatively, they willingly accept the guidance of teachers and other adults. Although they are developing a sense of responsibility and self-control, Erikson cautions this can be over emphasized and turn into guilt, inhibiting activity. Children are still so inept at this age, that many of their attempts at constructive activity turn into chaos. An adult can easily focus on the mess that a child has created instead of good intentions or positive results. Understanding adults will take care to emphasize the positive and assist the child in ever-increasing feelings of competence.

Children in this stage want to do work—real work, not just pretend. They want to help make the cookies and help wash the dishes. They want to rake leaves and shovel snow. We need to put aside our standards of achievement long enough to allow youngsters the ego-strengthening satisfaction of real work. Hendrick (1984) suggests a number of meaningful tasks which children can find productive and pleasurable in the school setting. Among them are: loading sand in a wagon to be carted to the swing area and shoveled under the swings after a rain, cleaning the aquarium, mixing paint, cutting fruits and vegetables for snacks, puttying up holes drilled in the wood working table, hammering in loose nails for safety, and oiling tricycles when they squeak. Try to think of other useful tasks that pertain to your own situation.

The desire to be productive and contributing grows into the stage of emotional development called *Industry*. This stage corresponds to elementary school age and involves learning to be a worker, earning recognition by producing things, and mastering the use of tools. One of the basic tools is literacy, another is mathematics, and another is interpersonal skill. The child must not only learn the basics of academics but also the basics of cooperation. Erikson (1963) says that feelings of inferiority result from failure to achieve the developmental tasks of this stage.

If previous emotional needs have been met and the child feels loved, secure, and confident, then that child is in the best possible position to succeed in mastering this new set of skills. Maslow's hier-

archy of needs indicates that it is only through having basic physical and emotional needs met, that a person is free to achieve the next higher need described on the pyramid.

LANGUAGE DEVELOPMENT

Most children can talk quite well by the time they reach preschool. How extensive is this ability? How did they acquire it? The teacher of young children finds these questions significant.

A Hierarchy of Needs

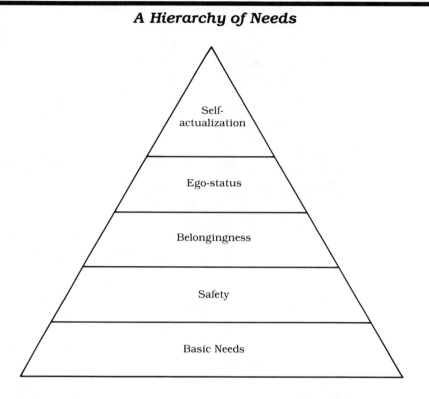

Source: From Motivation and Personality by A. H. Maslow, 1970 New York: Harper & Row

The extent of preschoolers' language ability is amazing. Early in life they mastered the idea that speech is a means of communicating with other human beings—a way of expressing their desires, sharing their feelings, and explaining their experiences. Then they went on to master the complexities of accurate communication. When they were only about six months old, they imitated intonations, so that their speech sounded as if they were creating sentences. They still had to work on the specific sounds involved. Before their first year was over, they had sorted from all the possible sounds, the ones that were significant to their parents. Before long, they began making these sounds in combinations that meant something specific. As soon as they acquired this ability to say words, they began stringing them together for even greater results.

As they began using words in combination, they put them together in ways matching the grammatical rules of their language. English-speaking children put the subject before the verb and, when they became more sophisticated, the object after the verb. Later, they learned to use grammar rules such as adding an *s* to make the plurals in *feets* and *mouses* and added *ed* for the past tense in *runned* and *digged*. They were motivated to increase their vocabulary and incessantly asked the names of things.

By the time teachers see them in preschool, most children seem to be proficient with language. They are generally able to make themselves understood to others and are good at understanding what others say to them. How did they learn so much in such a short time? They did not learn it by being drilled in the sounds and grammar of their language.

An old joke says if we taught children to talk the way we teach them to read, there would be a lot of non-talkers. Yet, few people seem to turn the joke around and suggest that if we taught children to read the way we teach them to talk, we wouldn't have many non-readers. That is precisely what this book is suggesting teachers do.

Let's look carefully at how a child learns to talk. Watch the neighbors' new baby, Betsy, as her parents bring her home from the hospital. Already there is communication between Betsy and her parents. Mostly, she makes random noises and crys to express her discomfort; however, her communications bring responses from her parents, sisters, and brothers. People babble to her in imitation of the sounds she makes, or someone feeds or changes her in response to her cries. She discovers the power of communication.

When Betsy's dad bathes her, he talks to her about how warm the water is, about how slippery the soap feels, and about what cute little toes she has. When her mother dresses her, Betsy hears about her dry diaper, the snaps on her jump suit, and her sweet smile. When her big brother, Johnny, plays with Betsy, he shows her all his toys and tells her what is happening as he drives his toy trucks around her baby seat. Johnny makes her laugh.

Betsy hears language, both that directed to her and that surrounding her, as her family goes about its daily life. She likes to participate in the conversation, and soon she is uttering strings of sounds which make her family stop and listen. These sounds are much like "real" language, but close attention reveals that there are no words in Betsy's sentence. More and more, the sounds she makes are the sounds she hears. One day she makes a "da" sound, and her dad suddenly pays attention, bending over her repeating, "Da da."

When Betsy is about a year old, she is able to make several sounds that get a specific response from her family. She may make the same sound to mean different things, which she indicates by her tone, facial expression, pointing gestures, or other nonverbal clues. For instance, "Ma ma" can mean, "Where is Mama?" or "I want my Mama!" or "There is my Mama." Soon she begins adding action words to nouns

and communicates in two word sentences. Again, these two-word sentences can mean different things, depending on the context in which they occur. Already Betsy knows that the meaning is not inherent in the words alone, but also in the mutual understanding between speaker and listener. This interpersonal aspect of communication remains true even after Betsy has mastered adult-sounding sentences.

As Betsy's knowledge of words and ability to create sentences increases, her previously "good" grammar seems to deteriorate. Her big sister, Mandy, is concerned because Betsy says, "I goed to the store." Mandy patiently corrects her and says, "No, you *went* to the store." "That's right," says Betsy happily as she wanders off. Their mother comforts Mandy by explaining that Betsy will talk correctly before long, that she makes mistakes because she is trying to make sense of grammar right now. Obviously Betsy's mistake is an overgeneralization of the rule for the past tense form. Mandy's mom asks her not to correct Betsy for fear of discouraging Betsy from practicing language. She also cautions Mandy not to imitate Betsy's incorrect grammar, for Betsy may mimic her speech and continue speaking incorrectly.

Betsy's mother knows that "babytalk" will also disappear by itself if no one corrects it or imitates it. Betsy just finds it hard to make all the sounds in her language, even though she is three years old. She still can't make *l* or *r* or *s* sounds because they take more coordination than she has yet mastered. But, although she may say *tore* instead of *store*, she gets upset if someone else says these words incorrectly.

As Betsy becomes more proficient with language, she has much she wants to say and speaks eagerly. Betsy's resulting rush of words sometimes trip over themselves. Her uncle thinks that she is stuttering, so he says, "Slow down Betsy. Start again and say it slowly." While =0this may appear to be sound advice, Betsy's mother asks him not to interrupt her or call attention to the problem. Uncle John gets a lecture on *normal nonfluency* and how it isn't stuttering but can become stuttering if a child is made nervous about it. Betsy's mother tells him that the best help he can give Betsy is to give her his undivided attention. Then she won't feel rushed. Betsy's mother has learned about language development with her four older children.

As Betsy's family helped her learn their language, they didn't have to be told about most of the important things they did to help her learn. They naturally reinforced her language attempts with response and imitation and adjusted how they spoke to her according to her changing ability to understand. Apparently an unconscious accommodation to a child's emerging language ability guides the length and complexity of adult speech to children (Schachter and Strage, 1982). Therefore, adults tend to automatically simplify their grammar, limit their vocabulary, repeat words often, and speak slowly with clear enunciation when speaking to young children.

Betsy's parents, like many other middle-class parents, respond to her speech by adding to what she has said and extending her immature sentences. So, at Betsy's first birthday when she says, "Ma ma!" her mother might say, "You want Mama to come pick you up?" At two years when she says, "Daddy gone," her mother would reply, "Yes, Daddy is gone to work now." And at three years when she says, "See me riding," her dad says, "Look at Betsy riding fast on her speedy red tricycle!" These expansions of her speech help Betsy toward increasing complexity in her own language.

The amount and kinds of Betsy's experiences, also influence her language complexity. When she plays outside and feels the prickly softness of the grass as she rolls on it, she experiences the smooth hardness of the driveway where she rides her trike, and she squeals with delight at the flying sensation when she swings. What a great many things she has to talk about now, and what a great many words she can add to her vocabulary if someone listens and extends her speech as she tells about playing outside.

Not all children have such an ideal language environment. Some are ignored when they make sounds or even when they cry. Some are spoken to only a little or do not have their questions answered. Some come from families where adults simply do not talk a great deal, or where the adult sentences are short and lack complexity and specific-ity. Some children lack coordination to create speech, some can't hear language to imitate it, and some are too fearful to speak. These children

need more time and ample opportunity to experience the kinds of language stimulation that are a part of Betsy's everyday life.

Even children from optimal language environments have much to learn about language when they reach preschool. They may sound quite mature, but their vocabulary is still limited, as is their ability to deal with different grammatical structures. They can become confused about a new word or one with several meanings. They can also become confused by the difference between "ask" and "tell." Have you ever told children they could ask questions after a guest speaker presentation? They don't ask the speaker questions; they tell their personal experiences! They get confused by questions in general since questions turn around the natural order of a sentence. Passive forms also turn around the familiar sentence patterns and result in miscommunication. For instance, when we say, "Betsy was given a tricycle by her dad," children look at us quizzically and wonder why Betsy's dad would want a tricycle.

Generally children do learn a huge amount of language in a short time. When they get to school, they must be allowed to continue their language development in the way that has already proven successful for them. Then they must be encouraged to learn written language using the same active and interactive ways they learned oral language—through observing and experiencing others reading and writing, through having their own attempts at the process encouraged, through adult patience when children make wrong assumptions as they construct their own understandings, and through continued life experiences to provide meaning to both oral and written language. Subsequent chapters will include more detailed discussions about how teachers can promote these active and interactive experiences.

READING DEVELOPMENT

Children learn oral language without formal instruction but are bombarded with assistance in learning to read. Ironically, oral language is actually the greater intellectual feat of the two (Loban, 1963). Learning to read is less difficult than learning to talk, as reading merely builds on what the child has already learned about language. In acquiring oral language, children must first discover the existence and purpose of language, then master its sounds and structure, and finally learn the multitude of oral symbols which constitute vocabulary. In learning to read, children can build on their previous knowledge of their language as they figure out the written symbol system used to represent it.

Few of us can remember the experience of learning how to talk, but many can remember the experience of learning how to read. Sometimes an examination of these memories helps our understanding of how to teach effectively. If you have memories of failure and frustration, remembering what caused those feelings may help you avoid those experiences for your students. If you have memories of pride and accomplishment, you may be able to recreate for other youngsters the experiences which led to those wonderful feelings. Think about when you first realized you could read and how you felt then. Think about what learning experiences you associate with getting to that place.

Many adults have a vague memory of phonics lessons at the time they were learning to read, but they tend to remember not having any idea that phonics was associated with reading. One young man didn't discover until his college-level teacher training classes that phonics was connected to reading. Another student, a young woman, thought that she was to learn the letter sounds merely to please her first grade teacher so that she would get rewarded by being taught to read. Although most adults do not connect phonics lessons with learning to read themselves, many believe that they can teach children to read by starting with lessons on the sounds of letters. So much knowledge about the written language system is required to make sense of such instruction that this approach is wasted upon most young children. As Schickedanz says, this attempts "the impossible—getting children to hear what the teacher knows." (1981)

Learning to Read and Learning to Talk

If we consider written language an extension of oral language, then we can reasonably compare learning how to read and write to learning how to talk. Carol Chomsky's (1972) extended research on this subject indicates that this comparison is valid and that, indeed, children do acquire ability with written language through much the same process as that with which they acquired their ability to speak. The research of Chomsky and other psycholinguists (Graves, 1982; Read, 1971; Goodman and Goodman, 1983) has shown that young children learn written and oral language the way Piaget said they learn many other things—through constructing their own rules and relationships rather than by being told about them. Chomsky's research also demonstrates that children exhibit much the same drive to discover what books and other writing can tell them as they showed in trying to discover what spoken language was about. Chomsky's recommendation is that children be allowed to direct their own process of learning to read, just as they directed their learning to talk. Does this mean that we simply leave children alone to learn to read? No, it means that adult assistance in the process should closely resemble the type of adult assistance given children as they learn to talk.

When we help a baby learn to talk, do we conduct lessons on the sounds of words and then try to get the baby to blend those sounds together to make language? Did Betsy's family only allow her to say words that she could pronounce properly? Did they restrict her speech to vocabulary-controlled topics or to sentences which she could form properly? Of course not. They encouraged her to experiment with language in any way she chose, and they rejoiced with her at each discovery. They provided Betsy with models of rich language and helped her learn through her own observation and experimentation as she tried to join in oral communication. In short, they included her in the oral interaction of the family at whatever level she was currently capable of participating.

Learning to Read Through Social Interaction

Adults can act as models, advisors, resources, and cheerleaders to children when they learn to read just as they did when children learned to talk. Older children can also assist younger ones in becoming literate just as they helped them with other language acquisition. Betsy's four older brothers and sisters don't realize that they teach the younger ones, but they do a fine job. The younger children in the family always want to do whatever the older ones are doing. When they see their older siblings reading, they want to read, too. At first they only know that reading involves looking at the book or newspaper or cereal box. (Remember the initial photo of Betsy's sister, Amy, at age two with the

newspaper propped beside her morning cereal?) Then they discover that there is a message contained in books even beyond the fascination of the pictures. When big brother Joey was in second grade, he would invite his three younger brothers and sisters to sit on his bunk bed and entertain them by reading library books.

When Joey was at school, two-year-old Amy would ask her four-year-old brother, John, to read to her. John couldn't read actual words, but he could tell a story, turn the pages, and admire the pictures with Amy. Both Amy and John were learning a great deal about reading through these sessions. Amy was learning that books were a source of information and pleasure; John was practicing the idea of getting meaning from a book. He was aware of the print and its relationship to the content, but couldn't yet decipher it. At this point in his development, John tried to put together a cereal box prize toy. He was having trouble, so his visiting grandma offered to help, saying, "Let me read the directions." John replied, "I already did." Grandma persisted, "Let me see if you missed anything." John handed her the direction sheet which contained both illustrations and printed instructions, saying matter-of-factly, "I missed the words."

You might ask, "Does this family have a television?" So often television is blamed for people not reading. The parents in this family enjoy books, but they also enjoy television and think that it isn't necessarily bad. Like many parents, they know children learn new vocabulary words from shows and through television are exposed to a vast array of ideas and information. Also, like many parents, they are often uncomfortable with some of this new learning. They use what they believe is both the good and the bad on television for helping their children grow intellectually and emotionally.

Mealtime discussions often focus on favorite television shows, with the youngsters taking turns explaining why they like certain programs. These parents encourage their children's critical thinking skills by posing questions about what specific things make a show good or bad. They try to make even weekly situation comedies and commercials educational this way.

During the many trips chauffering children to various activities, their mother, Deborah, often allows them to tell about something they have seen on T.V. Instead of merely gritting her teeth during endless, disjointed dialogues, Deborah helps with language and communication skills by asking, "Who do you mean when you say 'he'?" or "Why did that happen?" Other favorite discussion topics revolve around the nature of T.V. characters. "Who would you like to be and why?" is one favorite. When Deborah asks her children which person on a specific show they think they are the most like, she gets fascinating insights into their self-concepts (Figure 1.1) .

While the family watches a show together, the parents encourage their children to predict outcomes. Sometimes the older ones make a game of seeing who was right. Always the emphasis is on why they believe what they do: "What makes you think it will end that way?" Deciding who is the bad guy and who is the good guy is an interesting topic, as is a subsequent discussion of what makes a person good or bad. Another topic is whether a show is real or pretend and whether it attempts to show real people. Younger family members sometimes get confused watching cartoons, followed by space shows, followed by murder mysteries, and then the news. Discussions along with television viewing are wonderful practice in critical thinking.

Sometimes Deborah's children see things on television that oppose the family's value system. Rather than turning off such a program, Deborah and her husband often use these situations as a basis for discussions. Sensitive issues brought up on television such as death, child abuse, divorce, or even sexual relations are discussed at whatever level of interest and understanding a child has. Deborah may leave the room if there is much violence in a show and express her horror. Her actions are effective expressions of a value, more likely to cause children to reject violence than if she turned off the television. Deborah has observed that children whose family censors their television watching become fascinated with that which is forbidden. Those kids come to her house and are glued to the television.

When adults make television viewing an active rather than passive experience, viewing can be a source of language, critical thinking,

I watched Return of the Jedi. The best part
was that I saw the pit. Then R₂ D₂ popped out
the light saber. Luke caught it. Then Luke
turned it on and then he started to fight all the
bad guys and he knocked them in the pit.

Figure 1.1   An example of dictated writing stimulated
by television.

and values transmission. Television can provide a valuable background for literacy, but when families use it as a substitute for talking, thinking, and family interaction, it has negative consequences.

Learning to Read Naturally

The children in this family are learning to read naturally, just the way they learned to speak. This family doesn't plan it, but they teach reading in a powerful way—through example. The process of learning to read seems to start for each child as soon as that youngster can talk, even before preschool. Yet, no one makes a child sit down for a lesson disguised as a game. Deborah laughs at advertisements for materials for teaching babies and toddlers to read. She thinks the idea of trying to teach those little ones about reading with an artificial presentation of pictures and letters is silly. She knows that a child has to discover first the existence of reading and its purposes. Then if it looks like something of interest, each child will explore the subject and refine his or her understanding of it gradually, just as they did with speech. Deborah knows that children start with the whole and gradually examine the parts when they learn new things. She gets upset if one of her children's teachers violates this principle by drilling on isolated letters and sounds before children are reading, thereby turning the natural order around and putting the parts before the whole.

The work of Carol Chomsky would validate Deborah's right to be upset. The teaching of reading by pronouncing the sounds of letters is described by Chomsky as a teaching method which might be appropriate for teaching a foreigner who does not speak the language (1976). She considers it a totally inappropriate method which contradicts the purpose of obtaining meaning from what is read. Piagetian scholar, Constance Kamii, also says that the common practice of teaching phonics in kindergarten is based on an erroneous assumption of how children learn (Willert and Kamii, 1985). Chomsky and Kamii are among many researchers who advocate doing away with phonics workbooks and worksheets. Instead, they encourage children to write with invented spelling as a way of learning to read.

Learning Phonics Through Writing

Writing with invented spelling seems to be the natural mode for children to learn phonics principles and to unlock the rest of the written language system. Consistent with their hypothesis-experiment approach to learning, children try to discover which letters represent the sounds they hear in a word. This approach maintains the whole to part sequence because the child starts with the idea to express, formulates the desired sentence, considers the individual words of the sentence, and isolates the sounds of those words. Of course this sequence also

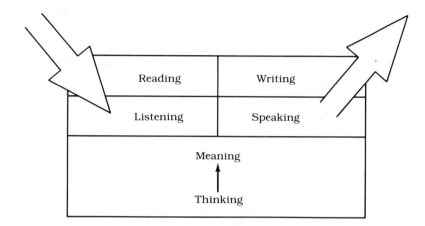

| Reading | Writing |
| Listening | Speaking |

Meaning

↑

Thinking

At the base of all communication is, of course, meaning. Meaning is received in or sent from the mind as a result of thought. It is incomplete to describe the communicative acts without the foundation of meaning and thought.

Source: From *Language and Learning: An Integration of the Process.* Unpublished master's thesis by M.C. Tarlow, 1980, Berkeley, CA: University of California. Reprinted by permission of the author.

emphasizes the meaning of the written symbols and therefore preserves their communication intent. When children are freed from the fear of misspelling, they spontaneously experiment with writing. In the process, they learn more from their own experience with print than a teacher could ever tell them. Allowing this experimentation to occur naturally, according to the child's own time line, ensures that the child will first attain sufficient maturation and prerequisite knowledge.

Parents often need to have invented spelling explained to them (Figure 1.2). Eric's dad called Mrs. Thomas to ask why she wasn't paying attention to how kids spelled in her first grade class. The father was concerned that Eric would think that "bird" was spelled *brd* or that "church" was spelled *hrh.* Mrs. Thomas had to explain to him that this was a stage that Eric was going through on his way to spelling correctly, just as he went through a stage of babytalk on his way to more adult speech. She emphasized the importance of the invented spelling process for Eric's understanding of the sound-symbol system and for learning to read and write in general. Mrs. Thomas also explained that Eric's continued exposure to correct spelling and his desire for others to understand what he has written would assist him in gradually modifying his own spelling to conform to standard spelling.

Figure 1.2   Child's invented spelling. (Blue bird, blue bird, fly through my window. Buy molasses candy.)

(Similarly, his exposure to his parents' speech assisted him in gradually matching his speech to adult models.) Mrs. Thomas assured Eric's dad that although as an educator she accepts and values Eric's invented spelling, she does not imply to the youngster that it is correct, standard spelling. Mrs. Thomas then described some teaching strategies, such as the individual word files, which she uses to help children learn the correct spellings of words they use often. As soon as she finished talking to Eric's dad, Mrs. Thomas wrote an explanation of invented spelling for the class newsletter, realizing that she didn't have time to explain this individually to each parent.

Mrs. Hanna has a similar issue to explain to parents in her news-letter this month. Although some of her kindergarteners are ready to try invented spelling, most are still doing much of their writing with the aid of a "secretary." Because Mrs. Hanna records children's ideas exactly as they dictate them, these compositions are often ungrammatical. The resulting ungrammatical sentences and phrases make some parents uncomfortable. In her newsletter Mrs. Hanna first states the purpose of writing down children's dictated ideas, experiences, and stories. She explains that children learn the relationship between talking, writing, and reading when their own words are written down and can be read back. She further explains that children learn much about writing by watching how writing is done. When they see their own words being written down, they know what those words say and are able to make direct connections between the written word and the spoken word. However, children cannot discover those connections unless the teacher writes their exact words. So, Mrs. Hanna writes, "Me and my daddy go hiking" as part of Billy's account of summer fun. She knows from past experience that Billy's parents might be worried about that sentence unless she explains that Billy wouldn't be able to read it if she had changed his sentence and written "My daddy and I go hiking." It would have confused him in his attempts to make the important discoveries about reading and writing. Mrs. Hanna assures parents that the ungrammatical speech will change if it doesn't match adult speech at home. In the meantime, children will have learned to read, starting with reading their own dictated sentences (Figure 1.3).

The Fish Story

Me and my daddy go hiking. My dad has big boots that go up to his belt. He has a fishing pole and he has some eggs, too! I don't get fish, my dad catches 'em. That's what we do goin' fishin'!

Figure 1.3   Child's drawing and story, including ungrammatical constructions dictated to the teacher.

Both Mrs. Hanna and Mrs. Thomas notice that their students discover reading principles as they participate in writing activities. Both teachers base their approach to educating children on what they have learned about intellectual development from Jean Piaget's research. With that research as their guide, they try to present concepts at the concrete level rather than the abstract level which young children cannot understand. These teachers believe the active process of writing is more concrete than reading and that writing is a good introduction to reading.

Learning Style

Allowing the child to initiate composition through dictation or through invented spelling is consistent with Chomsky's (1976) recommendation that each child be the director of his or her own reading acquisition. Not only does this approach guard against teachers prematurely presenting material or concepts, it respects individual learning rates and individual learning styles. Educators now understand that variations exist among children in their preferred learning environments and their preferred learning modes, but they have difficulty both determining individual styles and catering to such diversity.

Some children prefer to work in the midst of noise, people, and activity; others must have quiet and freedom from distractions in order to concentrate. Some youngsters learn better when they can move around or lie down to work, while others thrive on a straightback chair behind a desk. Some must see a visual representation of an idea in order to grasp it; others must hear someone explain the idea, and still others require some physical action to retain an idea. There are young people who thrive on ambiguity, enjoying the pursuit of an illusive idea; while others require closure, a definite result, when exploring an issue. How can a teacher discover which children are which? Then how can one teacher possibly plan for and teach to that many individual differences?

Allowing children to take the initiative in their own learning will help solve the problem of learning styles as well as that of maturational appropriateness. Given some choice of activities and the freedom to make mistakes, children will usually select the learning experience which is most appropriate and beneficial to their own stage and style of learning. So, when we visit Mrs. Thomas's first grade class, we see various activities. A group of children are talking, laughing, and debating proper spelling as they make up and write their own ghost stories to share at the Halloween party next week. Several children work in individual nooks around the room: some children have chosen desks facing the wall with partitions on the sides to shield out distractions, and a few children are curled in decorated packing boxes outfitted with cushions and a "skylight." Knowing that individual preferences vary from activity to activity and from day to day, Mrs. Thomas allows children to choose if they wish to work at tables with others, work at desks near others, work on the floor with or near others, or work in the private spaces described. Children can switch freely as their needs change. Mrs. Thomas only requires that children be constructively involved. She moves among the groups and individuals providing encouragement, assistance, and guidance as needed.

How Good Readers Read

All this effort at providing a stimulating yet flexible environment as children enter the reading phase of their language acquisition stage is aimed at achieving one result: a good reader. What is a good reader? Can we get some clues about how to create good readers by examining one?

Betsy's oldest sister, Mandy, is one such example. Her teachers describe her as an exceptional student and a good reader. Mandy likes to read and spends much time with library books. She often chooses to read over other activities. Mandy's choice is fine with her mother if she chooses reading instead of watching television, but Mandy's mother worries if her daughter chooses to read rather than play outside. Fortunately, Mandy has many interests and does get adequate fresh air and exercise. Interestingly, when she is reading, Mandy is oblivious to everything else around her. Her younger sisters and brothers get upset because they can't get her attention away from her book. Good readers freely choose to read and tend to concentrate as they read.

This year Mandy is reading horse stories. She got hooked on the *Black Stallion* series, and when she finished those, she started reading every other horse story she could find. Although she doesn't have a horse and has rarely been on one, Mandy knows about horses from her reading. When she reads, Mandy can pretend that she owns a horse that carries her galloping over sand dunes or green meadows. Mandy's cousin, David, is reading another type of book—the *Choose Your Own Adventure* type of reading excitement. Both Mandy and David read mainly for pleasure, while David's brother, Michael, has always chosen to read for information. Michael became an expert on marine mammals through his reading in grade school, and then in junior high he switched to reading about hunting and camping. He uses the information he has gathered from reading for his weekend expeditions. Good readers find pleasure and purpose in their reading.

As we watch Mandy read, her eyes flash across and down the page. How can she possibly see every word, let alone every letter on the page? She doesn't. If she were to read slowly enough to see each letter, the process would be so laborious that she would not find pleasure in

reading and would not often choose to do so. If she had learned to read thinking that she was supposed to sound out each letter and blend words together, she might have continued to look at each letter and never have become a good reader.

What about reading all the words? Mandy knows exactly what the story is about; she can tell you details and will speculate excitedly about what might happen next. But, she does not labor over individual words. If she comes to a word that she doesn't know, she can usually skip over it and still get the meaning from the rest of the sentence. After a few times of skipping over the same word and getting meaning from the context in that manner, she has an idea of what the word means even if it isn't part of her general vocabulary. If the printed word is part of her spoken vocabulary, eventually she will discover what it is from a combination of phonics clues and context clues.

Frequently, when children have some phonics or word analysis skill, they combine that information with an idea of what word would contribute to the meaning and come up with the right one. If the word is not one with which they are familiar, they can use context clues to select a familiar word of similar meaning. Thus, reading continues and the child gains satisfaction from the process. Having to stop and find the "right" word would destroy the reader's train of thought and frustrate her. If Mandy misreads a word, changing its meaning, she quickly realizes something is wrong because her word doesn't "fit" with the rest of the story. She then checks to find the error and makes sense out of what she is reading.

When Mandy reads something at an easier level, where she knows all the words, she can really fly. She isn't aware of the physical process, but her eye often identifies the words merely from their general outline or configuration. These configuration clues serve as shortcuts to identifying sight words and increase reading speed.

An observer might describe Mandy as a youngster who doesn't see most of the letters or many of the words she reads, and even reads books with words that she doesn't know. Is Mandy typical of good readers? Research tells us yes.

We have looked at how reading ability develops and examined how a good reader reads. A detailed discussion of the teacher's role in developing and nurturing good readers follows.

SUGGESTED FOLLOW-UP ACTIVITIES

1. Observe in a preschool and in a primary grade classroom. Contrast the levels of physical development and the small muscle dexterity you see in these settings.

2. Spend a few minutes visiting with a two-year old, a four-year old and a six-year old on separate occasions. Note the rapid change in ability to communicate, vocabulary, and sentence constructions.

3. Observe a teacher's interaction with students. Note teacher responses which enhance a child's self-esteem and those which might diminish self-esteem.

4. Observe a child engaged in a self-selected activity and one engaged in an adult-selected activity. Compare the levels of the child's absorption and the length of the child's attention span.

5. Visit a preschool, a kindergarten, or a primary classroom. Analyze the materials and activities available for children in terms of whether they are concrete, abstract, or transitional.

6. Watch television with children. Engage them in critical thinking as described in this chapter.

DISCUSSION TOPICS

1. Many parents of preschoolers want to help their children learn to read. What are appropriate ways for parents to assist the beginning literacy process?

2. Many early childhood programs still include worksheets or workbooks. How can a teacher who doesn't believe they are appropriate deal constructively with working in one of these programs?

REFERENCES AND RESOURCES FOR FURTHER READING

Books

Almy, M. (1973). *Young children's thinking.* New York: Columbia University Teachers College Press.

Baghban, M. (1984). *Our daughter learns to read and write: A case study from birth to three.* Newark, DE: International Reading Association.

Boegehold, B. D. (1984). *Getting ready to read.* New York: Ballantine Books.

Bos, B. (1983). *Before the basics.* Sacramento, CA: Cal Central Press.

Britton, J. (1980). *Language and learning.* New York: Penguin Books.

Bybee, R., & Sund, R. B. (1982). *Piaget for educators.* Columbus, OH: Charles E. Merrill.

Cazden, C. (1981). *Language in early childhood education.* Washington DC: National Association for the Education of Young Children.

Chomsky, C. (1972). *Language and mind.* New York: Harcourt Brace Jovanovich.

Chomsky, C. (1979). Approaching reading through invented spelling. *Paper Presented at the Conference on Theory and Practice of Early Reading.* Hillsdale, NJ: Erlbaum.

Clay, M. M. (1977). *Reading: The patterning of complex behaviour.* Exeter, NH: Heinemann Educational Books.

Cochran-Smith, M. (1984). *The making of a reader.* Norwood, NJ: Ablex Publishing Corporation.

Cohen, D.H. (1972). *The learning child.* New York: Random House.

deVilliers, P.A., & deVilliers, J.G. (1979). *Early language.* Cambridge, MA: Harvard University Press.

Dinkmeyer, D.C. (1965). *Child development: The emerging self.* Englewood Cliffs, NJ: Prentice-Hall.

Donaldson, M. (1978). *Children's minds.* New York: W.W. Norton.

Elkind, D. (1978). *A sympathetic understanding of the child: Birth to sixteen.* Boston: Allyn and Bacon Inc.

Erikson, E. (1963). *Childhood and society.* New York: W.W. Norton.

Flinchum, B. (1975). *Motor development in early childhood.* Saint Louis: C.V. Mosby Co.

Forman, G.E., & Kuschner, D.S. (1984). *The child's construction of knowledge: Piaget for teaching children.* Washington DC: National Association for the Education of Young Children.

Genishi, C., & Dyson, A.H. (1984). *Language assessment in the early years.* Norwood, NJ: Ablex Publishing Corporation.

Graves, D.H. (1982). *Writing teachers and children at work.* Exeter, NH: Heinemann Educational Books.

Hendrick, J. (1984). *The whole child.* St. Louis: Times Mirror/Mosby.

Holdaway, D. (1979). *The foundations of literacy.* New York: Ashton Scholastic.

Kamii, C. (1982). *Number in preschool and kindergarten.* Washington, DC: National Association for the Education of Young Children.

Lee, B., & Rudman, M.K. (1982). *Mind over media.* New York: Seaview Books.

Loban, W. (1963). *The language of elementary school children.* Champaign, IL: National Council of Teachers of English.

Maccoby, E.E. (1980). *Social development: Psychological growth and the parent-child relationship.* New York: Harcourt Brace Jovanovich.

Maslow, A.H. (1970). *Motivation and personality.* New York: Harper and Row.

Miller, G.A. (1977). *Spontaneous apprentices: Children and language.* New York: Seabury.

Pearson, D. (1984). *Reading and research.* New York: Longman.

Piaget, J. (1963). *The origins of intelligence in children.* New York: W.W. Norton.

Rogers, C. (1983). *Freedom to learn for the 80's.* Columbus, OH: Charles E. Merrill.

Rudolph, M., & Cohen, D. (1984). *Kindergarten and early schooling.* Englewood Cliffs, NJ: Prentice-Hall.

Saunders, R. (1984). *Piagetian perspective for preschools: A thinking book.* Englewood Cliffs, NJ: Prentice-Hall.

Schacter, F.F., & Strage, A.A. (1982). Adults' talk and children's language development. In S.G. Moore & C.R. Cooper (Eds.), *The young child: Reviews of research: Vol.3.* Washington DC: National Association for the Education of Young Children.

Smith, F. (1982). *Understanding reading.* New York: Holt, Rinehart & Winston.

Taylor, D. (1983). *Family literacy.* Exeter, New Hampshire: Heinemann Inc.

Wadsworth, B. (1984). *Piaget's theory of cognitive and affective development.* New York: Longman.

Periodicals

Almy, M. (1976). Piaget in action. *Young Children, 31* (2), 93–96.

Brocker, M. (1981, December). Reading is 90% inspiration. *Early Years* p. 41.

Bussis, A., Chittenden, E., Amarel, M., & Coutney, R. (1982, Fall). Two paths lead to reading success. *Developments*, pp. 5–9.

Carbo, M. (1982, February). Be a master reading teacher. *Early Years*, p. 39.

Chomsky, C. (1976, March). After decoding what? *Language Arts, 53,* 289–294.

Chomsky, C. (1971). Write first, read later. *Childhood Education, 47,* 296–299.

Dillon, D. (1983). Language and learning, learning and teaching. *Language Arts, 60,* 549–552.

Duckworth, E. (1973, October). Piaget takes a teacher's look. *Learning Magazine*, pp. 22–27.

Elkind, D. (1972, March). Misunderstandings about how children learn. *Today's Education, 61* (3), pp. 90–91.

Genishi, C., & Dyson, A.H. (1984, Winter). Ways of talking: Respecting differences. *Beginnings*, pp. 7–10.

Goodman, K.S., & Goodman, Y. (1977). Learning about psycholinguistic processes by analyzing oral reading. *Harvard Educational Review, 47,* 317–333.

Goodman, K. & Goodman, Y. (1983, May). Reading and writing relationships: Pragmatic functions. *Language Arts*, pp. 590–599.

Graham, T.L., & Knight, M.E. (1983, August/September). How to promote a positive self-concept. *Early Years*, pp. 40–41.

Hart, L. (1981, March). Don't teach them; Help them learn. *Learning*, pp. 39–40.

Harter, S. (1982). The perceived competence scale for children. *Child Development, 53,* 87–97.

Honig, A.S. (1984, Winter). Why talk to babies? *Beginnings*, pp. 3–6.

Hymes, J. (1965, March). Being taught to read. *Grade Teacher, 82,* 88–92.

Kagan, J. (1980, December). Jean Piaget's Contributions. *Phi Delta Kappan, 61,* 245–246.

Kamii, C. (1985). Leading primary education toward excellence: Beyond worksheets and drill. *Young Children, 40* (6), 3–9.

Kamii, C. & Randazzo, M. (1985, February). Social interaction and invented spelling. *Language Arts, 62,* 124–133.

Kirkland, E. (1978, February). A Piagetian interpretation of beginning reading instruction. *Reading Teacher, 31,* 497–503.

Manning, G., & Manning, M.A. (1981, January). Talk, talk, talk it up. *Early Years*, pp. 26–29.

McCartney, K. (1984, Winter). Caregivers talk to children. *Beginnings*, pp. 11–13.

Miller, S.R. (1983, August/September). Behavioral indicators for self-esteem. *Early Years*, pp. 44–45.

Pellegrini, A.D. (1981). Speech play and language development in young children. *Journal of Research and Development in Education, 3,* 73–80.

Read, C. (1971). Preschool children's knowledge of English phonology. *Harvard Education Review, 41* (1), 1–34.

Schickedanz, J.A. (1981). Knowledge children need in learning to read. *Young Children, 37,* 18–27.

Shrier, D.K. (1981, Winter). Helping preschoolers reach optimal development. *Day Care and Early Education, 8* (2), pp. 21–36.

Smith, F. (1975). The role of prediction in reading. *Elementary English, 54,* 305–311.

Smith, F. (1976). Learning to read by reading. *Language Arts, 53* (3), 297–299, 322.

Snow, C.E. (1983). Literacy and language: Relationships during the preschool years. *Harvard Educational Review, 53,* 165–189.

Tarlow, M.C. (1980). *Language and learning: An integration of the process.* Unpublished thesis, University of California, Berkeley.

Taylor, J.E. (1977). Making sense: The basic skill in reading. *Language Arts, 54,* 668–672.

Thibault, J.P., & McKee, J. (1982, November). Practical parenting with Piaget. *Young Children, 38* (1), pp. 18–27.

Thomas, K.F. (1985, September). Early reading as a social interaction process. *Language Arts, 62,* 469–475.

Voyat, G. (1972, February). Thinking before language? A Symposium. *Childhood Education, 48,* pp. 248–251.

Willert, M.K., & Kamii, C. (1985). Reading in kindergarten: Direct vs. indirect teaching. *Young Children, 40* (4), 3–9.

Woodward, M. (1983). The development of thinking in young children: The problem of analysis. *International Journal of Behavioral Development, 12,* 441–460.

Wolfgang, C.H. (1983). A study of play as a predictor of social-emotional development. *Early Child Development and Care,* pp. 33–54.

Zenhausen, R. (1982, February). Right and lefts and how they learn. *Early Years,* p. 51.

Children's Book Series

Choose your own adventure series. New York: Bantam Books. (Authors and dates of publication vary.)

Farley, W. *The black stallion.* New York: Random House, Inc. (Sixteen more books about him.)

2

A Developmental Approach to Literacy

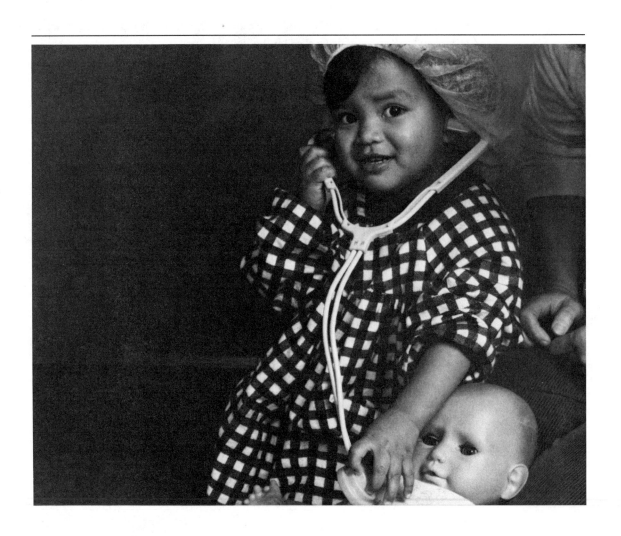

Educational programs for young children traditionally include opportunities for children to play, to run and jump and climb, and to explore the world they live in. These activities bow to the inclinations of young children in allowing them to be who they are, but sometimes adults have provided these activities without realizing their inherent teaching potential.

Parents and teachers of young children answer their questions, encourage them to talk, and read their favorite stories over and over. Yet, sometimes adults overlook the educational value of these activities. Those parents and educators who understand the value of these experiences, to which young children are irresistibly drawn, will defend such activities as basics in early childhood curriculum planning. They will resist supplanting such developmentally appropriate activities with educational experiences designed for older children.

Let's review the educational value of such childhood activities in relation to the task of learning to read.

LEARNING TO READ THROUGH PLAY

> When a child creates with blocks,
> when he communicates with paint,
> when he uses his body freely
> as a means of expression,
> he is being taught to read.*

---

*From "Being Taught to Read" by J. Hymes, March, 1965, *Teacher*, pp. 88–92. Copyright © 1965 Macmillan Professional Magazines. Used by permission of the Instructor Publications, Inc.

Traditionally, society has considered play the opposite of valuable work and therefore the opposite of learning. This assumption causes problems in the education of young children since play is their work and also their principal means of learning. Prejudice against play in school settings can hamper the effectiveness of early childhood education. Teachers of young children need to understand exactly how play helps youngsters learn, and they need to be able to explain that idea to parents, administrators, and school boards. Teachers generally know that young children learn best when at play, but teachers need to become more knowledgeable and eloquent in defending play.

Let's take a close look at children playing to see what they are learning. What do we mean by play? Sometimes what looks like work to an observer feels like play to the participant; sometimes what looks like play can feel like work. What makes the distinction? Generally, work is that which we must do in order to attain something of value or avoid something unpleasant, and play is that which we choose to do because it is inherently interesting or pleasurable.

Usually we would consider digging a ditch to be work, yet Timmy is having a wonderful time digging a ditch to drain a big puddle on the playground. Since he chose to do this and is enjoying it, digging a ditch becomes play for him. Now we see a group of children in a kindergarten who appear to be playing with a set of blocks of various colors and shapes. Their teacher is directing the activity, requesting that they all find a red triangle and add it to their block structure. Several of the children appear restless and have to be reprimanded to pay attention. Since this block play is not self-selected or motivating to these children, it cannot be classified as play.

Exploratory Play

Timmy's ditch digging is a type of play in which children explore their environment and seek to understand it through manipulation. Sand and water play are in this category, as are other exploratory activities which cause youngsters to "fiddle around" with almost anything they can get their hands on. Obviously teachers want to provide a variety of acceptable things with which young children can experiment. Children can then indulge their curiosity yet not endanger themselves or damage their surroundings.

How can we explain to Timmy's parents that digging a ditch is an educational activity and shouldn't be interrupted for a *real* lesson? Watch as he struggles with the shovel: He isn't having much luck digging deeply into the ground, so he changes the way he is holding the shovel and tries again. He will discover principles of physics such as leverage while he solves the problem of how to shovel effectively. When he does get a little of the ditch dug, he sees that the water isn't going

into it. He stops and ponders the problem, discovering that his ditch is uphill from the puddle. With amazing patience, Timmy locates the lower side of the puddle and begins again. What better lesson in gravity could be taught? What better experience in problem solving could be devised? When Timmy succeeds, what a boost to his self-esteem!

As he digs, Timmy will encounter the properties of dirt. It seems hard and solid where packed, but he can loosen it into powder. Where water mixes with it, the dirt becomes soft and squishy. When the dirt turns into mud, it no longer brushes off his hands and clothes, but sticks to him. Timmy may find that it contains rocks or even something as interesting as worms. Timmy's discoveries become a foundation of knowledge which he draws upon as he goes on to discover new concepts. Timmy's discoveries will also provide new or added meaning to specific words which relate to his experience.

Dramatic Play

Now let's watch Kelly who has a long scarf tied around her waist to simulate a skirt. Banging pots and pans around the play house, she admonishes two dolls propped at the table. "Hurry up and eat," she says. "We'll all be late. I have to get to work on time." When Scott wanders in, she adds, "You be the dad, and then we'll get divorced." She hands him one of the dolls and tells him to get the baby dressed. But Scott wants to cook. He drops the doll and says, "I'll fix the dinner." Kelly gets visibly upset, yelling, "No! I have to go to work now. It's morning." Scott continues to try to mesh his goals with Kelly's and suggests, "Let's pretend you came home now, and I fix your dinner." Reluctantly, Kelly agrees but insists that she has to leave first and then come back.

An observer of the dramatic play just described immediately notices the amount of language the children have used. We can tell at once that dramatic play enhances language development. The give and take in attempting cooperative play also provides children an excellent opportunity for practice in social skills, especially in becoming less egocentric. As children find out that others might not see things their way, their drive to play with another child causes them to compromise their initial position. Discovering that theirs is not the only view of a situation represents intellectual as well as social growth. Additionally, dramatic play provides children an opportunity to play out personally important themes and cope with anxiety stemming from those themes. When Kelly pretends about divorce, moving, or illness, she can put them in a controlled situation for practice with the feelings. Dramatic play also allows children to try various roles and see how they feel. Feeling the power of being grown up can counteract a young child's consistent feelings of powerlessness. The potential for emotional development through dramatic play is significant.

Dramatic play also fosters intellectual development. Piaget (1962) tells us that play is a child's way of thinking through things. Since they cannot retain ideas in their head to mull them over as an adult might, children play them out. If Kelly wants to understand her mother's

impatience of that morning, Kelly is helped by reenacting it. The scarf that Kelly has tied around her waist also represents practice in an intellectual feat. She is using one thing to represent another. Representation of this nature is the essence of our written language. Using a scarf to represent a skirt, a block for a telephone, or beads for pretend food helps Kelly understand that a set of squiggles can be a symbol for a word, which in turn is a symbol for an idea.

Block Play

Let's look at what Michael and David are building in the block area. When we come to watch, they begin to work even more diligently. They have created an elaborate set of roadways and are attempting to add bridges and ramps. They are testing the set-up with small cars and trucks. When David drives a truck under the bridge that Michael has just put up, he knocks the bridge down. Both are concerned about how to make the bridge bigger, and they search for different blocks, discussing their needs. They are so engrossed that they do not want to stop at lunch time. As other children comply with the teacher's requests to clean up, the two boys continue with their project. Finally, the teacher says they must stop for lunch, but encourages them to leave their project where it is and make a sign asking that no one touch their highway. Following lunch, Michael and David return to the block area.

These boys are concentrating on their task and surely are increasing their ability to pay attention for extended periods. Their teacher showed respect for their involvement and concentration when she valued it over immediate compliance with her clean-up request. Michael and David's pride in their work was also enhanced by the respect their teacher paid it by allowing the structure to stay up for awhile. Creative activity such as block play offers special opportunity for personal pride and consequently for increased self-esteem.

What are Michael and David learning? The fine quality unit blocks these boys are using are designed so that the smallest ones are exactly half as long as the next larger size, which in turn are exactly half as long as the next larger, and so on. Additionally, triangular shaped

blocks fit together to exactly match square or rectangular shaped blocks. Half circle pieces fit into arches and cylindrical pieces are the same length as some rectangular ones. These features assist children in making observations about relationships in size and quantity. Michael can say that his highway has seventeen long blocks and twenty-five short ones; then he can say that if he had used all short ones, it would be fifty-nine blocks long. If David runs out of rectangles for the road, he can substitute two triangles which represent the rectangles sliced either lengthwise or sideways. When he builds a bridge, the nature of the blocks assists him in measuring the distance he wishes to span.

Building bridges or spans of any sort with blocks provides practice in perceptual skills such as determining size and distance. Blocks also naturally lead into practice with balancing and stabilizing. The various shapes and sizes of blocks make them excellent classification materials—especially when they are stored according to size and shape. Block play also involves significant symbolic representation. The blocks can become whatever the child desires—bricks, houses, roadways, towers, or bridges. They can even be people, cars, or furniture. Children need frequent experience with symbols to represent other things before their teachers can expect them to accept letters to represent language. Michael and David had sufficient understanding of written language to accept that a sign on their structure would communicate to others. They also had sufficient skill to be able to make the sign with some teacher assistance.

When children use blocks to represent other things, their play generally involves a theme from which dramatic play flows. Props such as miniature people, doll furniture, small animal figures, or small cars and trucks can extend block play ideas as well as assist the dramatic play element.

The Teacher's Role

Do children outgrow dramatic play and block play when they leave preschool? Certainly not. The block builders previously described were in first grade, and the dramatic scene in the play house was in kindergarten. Mrs. Hanna knows that five-year olds need many opportunities to extend their language and thinking skills through dramatic play. They need practice in learning to cooperate and discovering that other children don't always see things their way. Additionally, Mrs. Hanna welcomes the symbolic representation involved in this type of activity. She wants her students to thoroughly understand this concept as she guides them in their transition from concrete learning to dealing with the abstraction of symbols.

Mrs. Hanna provides dress-up clothes, a variety of props, and a play house area in her kindergarten classroom. Because of limited space, she designed a structure which creates a cozy reading loft on top and a play house underneath. She also encourages dramatic play through her presence as an observer, and sometimes as a participant when invited. Observing dramatic play has the added value of providing important diagnostic teaching information. By watching her kindergarteners in the play house or in the block area, Mrs. Hanna gains valuable information about children's interests, their experiences, and their level of understanding about those experiences. She also can pick up clues about possible emotional problems if she sees a child who replays one theme over and over again or if she notices a child who seems unable to participate in this type of play.

Were you surprised to find a block area in a first grade class? Most people expect all these things in a preschool and even in a kindergarten but expect big changes as the child enters first grade. However, the first grade child is still in the preoperational stage of intellectual development and continues to require concrete experiences for meaningful learning. Mrs. Thomas makes sure that her first graders have those concrete experiences and manipulative materials to help them in their thinking and understanding. She has several children in her class this year who are repeating first grade. They came to her "turned off" about reading but excited about opportunities to play. Mrs. Thomas believes that they were stopped short in their play and must have some of their needs met through play before they can go on.

She believes blocks are such important learning tools for six-year olds that she managed to make room in her classroom for a fully equipped block area. Plenty of blocks are available so that children will not run out while in the middle of a project. Mrs. Thomas made sure there were shelves for storing the blocks; she knows that dumping them into a bin makes it impossible for children to find the block they need and that bin storage may damage the blocks. She labeled the block shelves with the outline of the size and shape blocks that are to be stored in each section. This labeling assists children in clean-up and calls their attention to classification categories. Mrs. Thomas further enhances the block play environment by frequently watching or admiring what is happening there. She gives her students the message that she thinks their block building is important.

Mrs. Thomas's efforts are rewarded with wonderfully intricate and innovative block structures. She considers it a shame that schools generally deprive children of this type of play just as they attain enough maturity to really create with raw materials. When she took her turn as a parent helper in her children's preschool, she saw that three-and four-year-old youngsters played with blocks more in an exploratory manner, messing around with what could be done with blocks. Frequently, they got out the blocks and just spread them around. When she taught kindergarten, she saw that with previous block play expe-

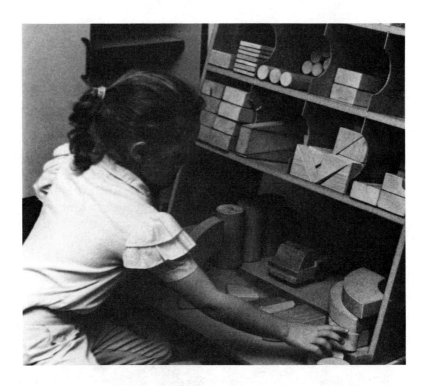

rience plus added maturity, her students were beginning to realize the potential of the blocks. Her first graders are becoming sophisticated in their block building. Also, block play experience and the feelings of accomplishment that come from it provide interesting topics for discussion and writing.

Mrs. Thomas attempts to provide as many play opportunities for her first graders as possible. She knows that they are still in the "golden age" of dramatic play and still emotionally and intellectually need that mode of dealing with ideas. Therefore, a play sink and stove are part of her room, plus dress-up clothes and other props which can be used for various themes. Her students often use desk tops covered with a cloth to represent tables for playing house. Mrs. Thomas understands the continued need for water and sand play too, so she never hurries children as they wash paint brushes or hands at the sink. Also she never tells them not to play in the puddles or or not to get dirty on the playground. She purchased a water play table for the class this year, and sometimes she fills it with rice or beans or sand. She provides further experiences with a variety of substances through frequent classroom cooking activities.

Both Mrs. Thomas and Mrs. Hanna value play as an integral part of their curriculum just as much as Ms. Reynolds does in her preschool. None of these fine teachers views play as a break from learning, but rather as an essential mode of learning. Outdoor play is considered equally as important as indoor play and work. These teachers take children outdoors even when the weather is a little rainy or cool. They just make sure that everyone is comfortably dressed.

These three teachers don't stop teaching while their students are outside the classroom. They continue to supervise closely, not only to ensure children's safety, but also to ensure maximum advantage from learning situations as they arise. They never dominate or try to lead children's play but remain available as consultants to answer questions or to make suggestions which could enhance the play experience. They find that observing youngsters in an outdoor setting often provides additional insights about their students since many children act more naturally out of the classroom.

The Parent's Role

All three teachers work hard at helping the parents of their students understand the value of children's play. They encourage parents to spend time observing and helping in their classes, and the teachers send newletters home which describe school activities and explain their educational objectives. Mrs. Reynolds posts a list in each activity area of her preschool telling the value and purpose of that activity. Since she teaches in a cooperative preschool with different parent helpers daily, she also posts guidelines for assisting children in gaining the most from each activity. Parents learn how to enhance their child's development from helping at school as well as learning what the teacher is attempting to do. This knowledge makes them into strong supporters of the teacher and the school.

The newsletters that these teachers send home to parents contain hints to aid parents in their role as their child's most important teacher. These newsletters routinely mention the value of providing versatile materials which can become different things according to a child's current play theme. For instance, a scarf not only can be a fancy skirt, it can also be a super hero cape, a baby blanket, or a prop for creative dancing. Purchasing each of these props separately would be expensive, but the real cost would be in depriving the child of the opportunities for creativity and problem solving. Versatile use of materials also increases symbolic representation experiences for the child.

The value of raw materials in general for play is apparent to all of these teachers as they watch their students. They see children taking boards, barrels, and tires and creating an ever-changing set of play equipment which engrosses them much longer than the permanent swings and slide. The teachers are especially upset by the proliferation of advertised play props which allow no creativity and require no thought. For example, parents may purchase complete costumes— from spacesuits, to princess dresses, to Indian outfits. Toy stores also have ready-made play wigwams, starbase tents, or plastic playhouses with windows. These teachers remember the fun and challenge of making tents with old blankets over tables or strung between chairs when they were little. They don't want to see today's children deprived of that type of experience. They are afraid that heavily advertised play props plus television will put children into such a passive mode that they will lose their ability to think creatively.

These three teachers understand the value of play and play materials. They also understand how play meets the physical, emotional, and intellectual needs of their students. Mrs. Thomas, Mrs. Hanna, and Ms. Reynolds use play as an effective teaching method as they assist children to grow strong and proud in the control of their bodies. They use play to assist children to grow in self-confidence, eagerness to learn, and social skills. They use play to assist children to grow from understanding only the here and now, to a gradual ability to think about abstract ideas and use symbols for recording their thoughts.

LEARNING TO READ THROUGH PHYSICAL ACTIVITY

When a child uses his whole body—
two eyes, two hands, two arms,
two legs and knees and feet—
to pull himself up a scary slanted climbing board,
he is being taught to read.

(James Hymes, 1965)

Physical skills are one component in the process of becoming literate. Reading involves sophisticated coordination of eye movements, and writing involves an intricate combination of eye-hand coordination. Unless children have adequate opportunity to develop this type of coordination, they will be hampered in their attempts at reading and writing. Teaching reading without including these skills is unreasonable. However, these skills are built upon many prerequisite skills which also must be developed.

Teachers of four-, five- or six-year olds can expect that their students will have mastered many skill prerequisites. How much mastery will vary not only with the age of the child, but also from child to child. A teacher's knowledge of stages in physical development will assist her in determining how far each child has progressed and what experiences each requires next. This knowledge gives teachers realistic expectations of children and serves as a guide for logical sequencing of physical skill activities.

Classroom Examples

Ms. Reynolds knows that most of her preschool students will be good runners and fairly good climbers, but she knows that most of them still struggle with fastening buttons and snaps and have difficulty controlling their paint brush while at the easel. Although she expects competency with most large muscle skills, Ms. Reynolds realizes that some children will be deficient compared to others of their same age and will need extra encouragement. She also realizes that preschoolers who are competent for their age with large muscle skills still require ample opportunities to practice and extend these skills.

Ms. Reynolds has arranged the preschool where she teaches so an area is set aside for large muscle activity. There is plenty of space for running without getting hurt, a sturdy climbing tower, trikes, large blocks, a rocking boat, and a continually changing variety of other

interesting equipment. Ms. Reynolds provides time for outdoor play too. When she taught children in a day care center, Ms. Reynolds was even more careful about outdoor time since she had the children with her all day. She assumes that her preschool children will have further chance to play outside at home in the afternoon.

In Ms. Reynolds's school the area for small muscle skill practice is located in the adjacent room. This keeps the noisy, rambunctious work separate from that requiring closer concentration. In the small muscle area Ms. Reynolds puts out manipulative materials representing various levels of difficulty. This way each child will be able to find an appropriate challenge. She has these beads, blocks, puzzles, pegs, playdough, markers, and pencils stored neatly on open shelves to be readily accessible to youngsters. The storage shelves are next to a long, low table at which children can use the materials. Because not all the materials are available to children at once, some storage space is for the teacher's use and is not accessible to children.

A nearby art area provides easels and paint always ready for use and features daily art exploration challenges. These opportunities for painting, drawing, cutting, and pasting are directly related to fine muscle and eye-hand coordination skills which children must use in reading.

Kindergarteners in Mrs. Hanna's class will find much the same type of materials when they come to school. Mrs. Hanna knows that these five-year olds are still developing their large muscle skills and have a long way to go before mastering the finer coordination skills. She expects that most of them will still have difficulty skipping, although they are proficient at running and jumping. She knows that many will still have trouble tying shoes, and that making a pencil or crayon go where they want it to can cause most of her young students great frustration.

Mrs. Hanna's kindergarten provides a gradual transition from preschool. Children are not expected to sit still for a long time, and they may still often choose among activities. This freedom of choice is essential to ensuring that each child has the appropriate balance between quiet and active work. The right balance varies significantly from child to child, and children themselves are usually the best judges of how long they can sit still. Mrs. Hanna observes her kindergarteners carefully to discover what skills each possesses and what level each is ready for next. She learns about their individual temperaments and their individual tolerance for high levels of activity and for sedentary pursuits.

By the time children reach Mrs. Thomas's first grade, they have made progress in both large and small muscle coordination. However, Mrs. Thomas does not expect complete mastery and continues to provide opportunities to enhance coordination skills for all the youngsters. Additionally, she provides a unique set of activities for Alice, who is being mainstreamed into this class in a wheelchair. Activities for Alice are designed to assist her in developing perceptual abilities despite inability to move her body as she desires. Mrs. Thomas has worked with preschool and kindergarten youngsters as well as first graders and so has an excellent perspective on her students' developmental levels.

Mrs. Thomas's classroom is not large enough for students to run, ride tricycles, and scale a climbing tower, but she makes other provisions for large muscle activity indoors and encourages active outdoor play at recess. She would never consider keeping a child in from recess as punishment or in order to complete other work. Mrs. Thomas understands the importance of vigorous movement for proper development. Frequently, she will take youngsters outside at unscheduled times for special activities with large rubber balls or with a parachute.

Her kindergarten classroom has space for a balance beam and a safe chinning bar. Students may use this equipment throughout the day, along with various small muscle materials. Yes, this first grade still has blocks for building, beads to string, playdough to squeeze, and

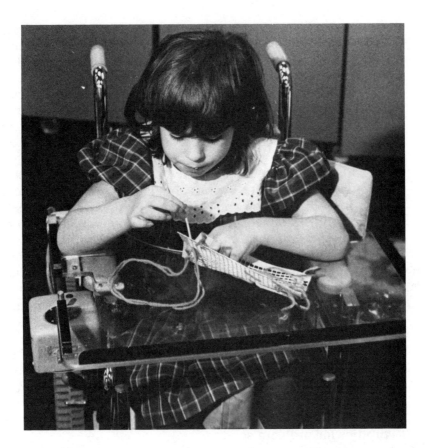

puzzles to assemble. Mrs. Thomas knows that children in her class are now mature enough to experience greater success with these materials and to be creative rather than merely exploratory. She firmly believes these activities assist students in the process of learning to read.

Large Muscle Activities

Children in preschool through primary grades require similar types of large muscle opportunities. Children vary not in their need for them but in their levels of mastery. They all should have opportunities for lifting and shoving, for crawling through things, for climbing, for balancing, and for hanging from bars. They need to continuously test and increase their strength and skill.

Children also need to bounce balls as well as throw and catch them. They need to try hitting or batting a ball on a rope and kicking balls of all sizes. Activities which get children to roll or crawl or even climb stairs may be missing from their experience unless teachers encourage them. Skipping is appropriate for first-grade children, but will be difficult for most younger ones. Hopping, the first step toward skipping, can gradually lead to hopping on each foot alternately, which can then lead to skipping. Many teachers report a high correletion between ability to skip and readiness to read.

Arnheim (1979) refers to a category of activities which cause a child to be airborne. These include swinging on swings or bars to create an airborne sensation, as well as bouncing on a mattress or inner tube. Trampoline bouncing is not recommended due to the extreme danger involved.

Equipment for all these activities must be safe. Climbing structures should be stable, swings should have soft seats in case of contact with a head, tricycles and wagons must have their wheels and pedals intact, and no sharp points or splinters should jut from equipment. Schools should use quality equipment and see that it is maintained properly. Wooden surfaces must be sanded and varnished as needed, wooden and metal toys should be stored away from moisture at night, and wooden outside toys must be used on the grass or other soft surfaces, rather than on cement which will splinter them. Children can be involved in watching for dangerous splinters and in caring for equipment.

Not all equipment needs to be expensive. Some of the best large muscle equipment consists of raw materials such as barrels, boards, cable spools, sawhorses, rubber tires, and even cardboard boxes. These have the advantage of being multi-use and movable. The versatility that results frees children's imaginations and provides excellent opportunities for problem solving.

Creative dance or other rhythm and movement activities provide for further large muscle development. Teachers can encourage children to greater body awareness through suggestions such as, "How much of you can you get in the air at once?" or "Can you fit your body inside this space?" Different music rhythm speeds and patterns can encourage various rhythmic movements. Additionally, the natural rhythm in movements such as swinging or walking can be matched with music.

Large and small muscles are involved in relaxation and tension-relieving activities. Educators should not overlook these, especially as more and more adults are striving belatedly to learn them in order to cope with a hectic pace of life. Children too are susceptible to stress and need help in learning to relax. Teachers can combine exercises in which children tighten and relax specific muscles with creative movement activities. Children can flop like a rag doll or stiffen like a tin soldier. When children are helped to feel the difference, they can learn to control the amount of tension in their muscles. How is this related to learning to read? Think of how much you profit from an educational experience when you are tense.

Gardening involves raking, hoeing, shoveling, and bending to plant and weed. These are valuable large muscle activities, especially in light of what they can help children learn about the world.

Small Muscle Activities

Most people see that fine motor coordination activities are related to reading skills. These activities have been more welcomed into the school rooms of young children than gross coordination activities. That is, until first grade. After that, it is less common to find the manipulative materials that we found in Mrs. Thomas's first grade classroom, and even less common to find them used as a vital part of the program. More commonly schools relegate manipulative materials to be time fillers, after workbook or work sheets are completed.

This arrangement of priorities shows a lack of understanding about how young children develop and learn. Manipulative materials should continue to be an essential part of young children's education through the primary grades. Children continue to require practice for refining their small muscle coordination and their eye-hand coordination. Additionally, many manipulative materials, such as puzzles, simultaneously provide practice in visual discrimination, which can assist in discrimination between letters and words.

Many interesting manipulative materials are available in school supply catalogs catering to preschool, elementary, and special education. Toymakers have created an amazing variety of shapes for children to stick together. Each manipulation requires a slightly different set of movements to make the pieces stay together and allow the child to construct a three dimensional object. Most small muscle activities also require careful eye-hand coordination to get the desired result. In addition to small construction objects, other materials such as peg boards, beads and strings, puzzles, drawing materials, and art materials of all types enhance fine motor control.

Some commercial fine motor materials provide artificial practice in life tasks. Sewing cards, bolt boards, dressing frames with laces, zippers, and buttons are examples. Real life sewing, woodworking, and dressing and undressing experiences not only are important life skills for children to practice but also inexpensive for the teacher to provide.

Other life experiences which provide small muscle practice include cooking projects and helping to serve snacks. Pouring, measuring, and stirring opportunities during food preparation can also be made available to children when they work with sand and water and use kitchen utensils as props.

 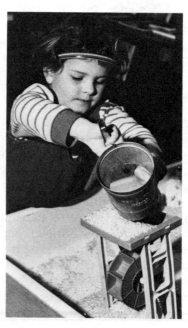 

Teacher's Role

Although the physical environment and the materials in it are important elements for children's physical skill development, the emotional environment is just as important and apt to be overlooked. The teacher's attitude creates an environment which either encourages or discourages certain types of activity. Activities valued by the teacher in a specific classroom are generally what children in that class are most involved in. A teacher who gets nervous when children make noise or when they run around will not provide many opportunities for large muscle activities. Likewise, a teacher who sees the real business of school as children working in their seats will only tolerate a small amount of large muscle play as a break from learning. Subtle indicators, such as what activities a teacher pays most attention to or gives recognition for, will influence children's choices.

A teacher who views large muscle activity as a vital part of learning, rather than as a break from learning, will not only provide adequate space and materials to foster this type of play but will provide plenty of time and teacher attention for it. A teacher who values active vigorous movement will naturally stimulate it in youngsters; a teacher who values experimenting with clay or blocks will stimulate that type of involvement. Teachers of young children need to understand the value of using a wide range of activities which promote growth in all developmental areas.

Children are able to explore uses for equipment and develop challenges to their physical skills more readily if their teacher is flexible about their using equipment in different ways. A teacher who is tolerant of the mess and noise which are natural byproducts of many large and small muscle activities such as fingerpainting, water play, and woodworking also encourages children's creativity.

A wise teacher further assists children through providing a balance of active, noisy experiences and restful, quiet ones.

Curriculum Integration

Often when teachers design activities to develop large and small muscle coordination, those same activities will provide children with experiences to enhance their intellectual development. Ensuing discussions may enhance their language development. For example, the large muscle activity of moving a barrel allows children to discover physical properties in our world: What shaped objects will roll, and over what surfaces will they roll best. The child who makes these discoveries will find them a delightful topic of conversation.

Conversely, we find that activities designed to expand children's knowledge base such as gardening, cooking, and field trips will also provide opportunities to enhance physical skills. Hendrick (1984) points out the varied possibilities in a simple tricycle expedition around the block during which children are allowed to stop and observe things which interest them.

Most important is the interrelatedness between children's large muscle skill development and their self-esteem. When Joey manages to climb up the rope ladder, his sense of pride fills him with self-confidence. This confidence will carry over to his attitude about learning to read.

LEARNING TO READ THROUGH ORAL LANGUAGE ACTIVITIES

> When a child hears good adult language,
> and when he has the fullest, freest
> chance to use his own language,
> he is being taught to read.
>
> (James Hymes, 1965)

As we help children learn to read, we must keep in mind the relationships between oral and written language. Oral language symbolizes experiences, ideas, and feelings; written language symbolizes oral language. The learning sequence begins with experience, moves to oral language, and then moves to written language. Reading instruction must be based on a foundation of oral language, which in turn must be based on a foundation of experience.

What are some ways we can build these foundations for reading? Let's observe as Ms. Reynolds assists the language development of her preschoolers. She values the language learning that her students have already acquired, so she continues and extends the processes which have proven successful in their past learning. Ms. Reynolds definitely reinforces children's communication efforts in this preschool.

Adult Conversations with Children

Ms. Reynolds pays close attention to children as they talk to her, and she tries to squat or sit at their eye level for the best possible communication. She not only listens respectfully, she asks questions which encourage the children to think and use additional language. Frequently she makes comments which extend a child's statement, elaborating on the idea and incorporating new vocabulary words. When Blair tells her that she got a puppy, Ms. Reynolds asks Blair to tell her more about the dog. After Blair's enthusiastic description, she comments, ''I think you are going to have a wonderful time playing with that cuddly puppy.''

Sometimes teachers experience difficulty giving individual attention to children when there are so many of them at preschool. Ms.

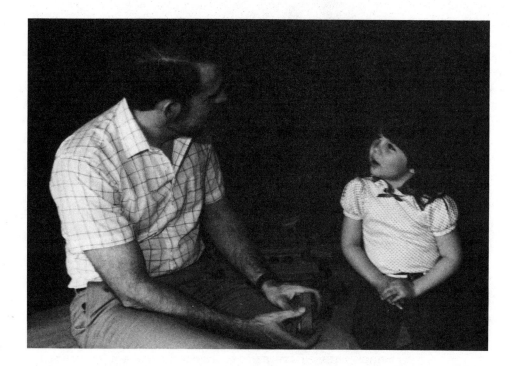

Reynolds believes that two minutes of her undivided attention is worth more to a child than two hours of her attention when that child is part of a group. She strives to build trust and rapport with her students through these one-to-one encounters, knowing that trust and rapport are necessary for effective communication. She makes a point of initiating conversations with those children who make no effort to talk to her. Since reading a report several years ago (Monaghan, 1974) indicating that teachers generally talk most to the more verbal children, who need it least, she has been especially sensitive to that issue. She has noticed, however, that some quiet children seem to feel overwhelmed by language from very verbal persons. Sometimes she makes it possible for a child just to be with her and works on trust before conversation.

Much of Ms. Reynolds's individual conversations with children occur incidentally—as they arrive at school or while she is assisting them with boots and coats for going outdoors. Other opportunities arise as Ms. Reynolds circulates among her students while they are engrossed in their various chosen activities. She teaches the parent helpers how to encourage children's language also. Yet, she knows that the relationship with the one teacher who is there every day is most important to her children. She makes herself available to more children by keeping herself free to circulate, while assigning the parent aides to supervise specific activities such as baking blueberry muffins or creating collages.

When Ms. Reynolds converses with children, she herself says little. Instead, she stimulates children's thinking and expression of thoughts. She carefully does not give feedback which turns off conversations. She never makes a judgmental response, such as, "That wasn't a nice thing to do," when a child confides in her. She rarely gives information or a quick answer to questions either. Rather, she prolongs the conversation through questions such as "Why do you think that happened?" or simply, "What do *you* think?" Her responses indicate acceptance of what is said and frequently seek to verify communication through paraphrasing what she heard. For instance, if a child says, "My baby bad," Ms. Reynolds might say, "Your baby has been doing something wrong?" Then the child would know what message Ms. Reynolds received and might elaborate on it by saying, "Yes, he cry all night. But he just little." This information, in turn, could be elaborated on for further conversation. The information could also result in a topic for a dictated story.

Conversations Between Children

Snack time offers an excellent chance for conversation. The parent aides and Ms. Reynolds each sit at a table with about five children. The adults eat with the children, modeling table manners and mealtime conversation manners. They take care not to monopolize the conversation and encourage children to talk among themselves even more than to the teacher. In this preschool, opportunities abound for children to talk with one another. They talk while they paint, they talk while they work puzzles, they talk while they climb the climbing tower, and they talk while they act out dramas in the play house area or pretend to be their favorite television hero.

In addition to informal conversation among children and between teacher and children, teachers plan many activities to enhance language. The changing props in the play house, which suggest a store for awhile, a doctor's office next, and a fishing boat another time, all are designed to enhance language. Additionally, the many stories, songs, poems, and fingerplays which children experience daily in this preschool have language development as their primary purpose. Actually everything children do, from fingerpainting to playing with the pet gerbil, enhances their language development by providing motivation and content for speech.

In her kindergarten class, Mrs. Hanna also provides a rich foundation of experiences to assist the language development of her young students. She continues the stories, dramatic play, and other language development activities which most of them encountered in preschool or day care programs. She doesn't repeat what children have already experienced. Instead, she builds on what they have experienced. Since children have had different experiences, she must approach their language development in various ways.

Mrs. Hanna also continues the practice of encouraging children to talk among themselves as they work at learning centers. She knows that talking with others about what they are doing increases children's understanding. This type of social interaction is one of the essential ingredients for intellectual development as described by Piaget: When children compare their perceptions with those of their peers, they try to figure out which view is correct. When an adult's perception is different from a child's, the child naturally assumes the the adult is right, whether or not the adult view makes sense to the child. With peers, children assume that their own ideas are of equal value, and they will explain and defend those ideas, which requires their careful analysis. With peers, children do not automatically assume the other person is right; instead, they go through the valuable process of analyzing the other viewpoint, comparing it to personal understandings, and modifying or solidifying previous views (Kamii and Randazzo, 1985).

Listening and Diagnostic Teaching

Mrs. Hanna finds that by being a careful listener she not only encourages more communication from children but discovers a great deal about their level of language development. This guides her in planning appropriate educational experiences for each of her students. When she discovers that some children are using more sound substitutions

than normal for their age or that some are confusing words which sound somewhat alike, she knows she must provide auditory discrimination practice for those children.

She doesn't become concerned when children say, "Is this aw wite?" or when someone asks to hold the "nake." She knows that production of the *l,r,* and *s* sounds will come with maturity. But if children continue to confuse other sounds in kindergarten, perhaps they aren't hearing them properly. Once she has determined that no hearing problems exist, Mrs. Hanna engages those children in rhyming word games, shows them the set of sound matching cans, or helps them notice various sounds on the playground. Many children enjoy when the teacher gathers together a small group and has them hide their eyes. Then one child is tapped to say something, and the others guess whose voice they heard. Careful attention to subtle sound differences is needed as children begin to learn the sounds of letters in words.

Mrs. Hanna never corrects children's speech, even though she makes it a point to notice speech problems. She knows that the most effective way to increase language ability is through practice, and she doesn't want to stop anyone from practicing because they fear she will correct them. Children do practice in her classroom. This kindergarten is not one where the teacher says "shh" to children; instead, children talk to the teacher, to each other, and to themselves.

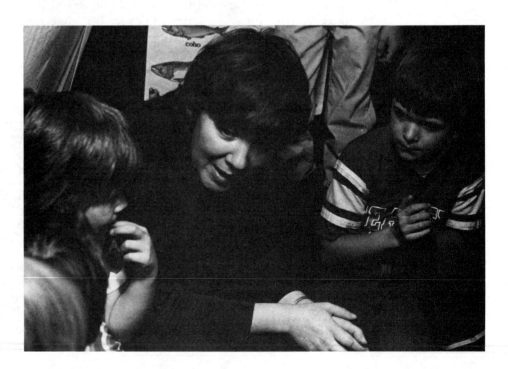

Children can learn from talking to their peers and imitating one another, but sometimes they don't know how to start a conversation with another child. Then Mrs. Hanna will help with a comment such as, "Zachary, have you told Jennifer about your new kitten? I think she has a black kitten too." Sometimes Mrs. Hanna will bring a small group together for a discussion. These group discussions have specific purposes, perhaps planning a cooking project or naming the new class rabbit. These situations provide excellent practice in group discussion skills, with Mrs. Hanna guiding the students in taking turns and being sure everyone is heard, but never dominating the conversation.

Occasionally, the whole group is brought together for a discussion that affects everyone. However, these children are not ready to function well as a group of twenty-five. They get too squirmy and bored sharing the limelight and the teacher's attention with so many others. Mrs. Hanna finds it more valuable to divide the group at least in half, with a parent helper leading one group discussion, or with the rest of the class engaged in independent activities. She keeps in mind James Hymes's (1981) guideline which says that the right size group for a child has no more people than that child has had birthdays.

Language Differences

Sometimes a child will come to kindergarten who does not speak standard English or any English at all. Although Mrs. Hanna knows that this child will eventually need to learn standard English to succeed in American schools, she values whatever language a child speaks. Her main concern is that the child uses language to communicate, not what kind of language that child uses. She believes that accepting a child's language is part of accepting that child and that child's background. If the child speaks a language Mrs. Hanna doesn't understand, she works with the school district to bring in an aide who does speak that language. If the difference is merely a dialect of English, she does not feel hampered in teaching. In fact, her method of teaching reading allows all children to learn to read and write initially in their own dialect.

Classroom Examples

Have you guessed by now that Mrs. Thomas also encourages talking in her first grade classroom? This approach may be quite a change from your experience with first grade. Mrs. Thomas knows that her students haven't finished their language development and that they still need practice. She is also aware of the significant role social interaction plays in the intellectual development of her students. Mrs. Thomas not only makes sure that students get play opportunities which encourage language but also provides for collaborative discussion while students pursue more academic kinds of learning. Youngsters in this classroom talk together as they compare the stories they have read, plan a puppet show, or discuss proper spelling while they write.

Mrs. Thomas also brings children together in groups for discussions. With first graders, she sometimes feels comfortable working with the total group, but she sees they still function best in smaller units. When she brings the whole group together, she does so for short periods and for specific purposes. As the children begin to gather, she leads the group in conversation, singing, or acting out a fingerplay. This ensures that those already sitting are involved, instead of bored. This technique rewards those who cooperated in coming to the group, instead of the more usual approach of rewarding with attention those who are not cooperating. Going ahead with the action also tends to get laggards to the group more quickly than nagging or cajoling them.

Today the topic for discussion is class rules. Mrs. Thomas knows that children can be more free when they know the limits of that freedom. Yet, she also knows that people most respect rules which they determine themselves. She creates a language development opportunity as she guides the students in discussing essential, reasonable classroom regulations. Mrs. Thomas records everyone's ideas for rules as they suggest them. Tomorrow she will assist the children in selecting two or three ideas which will help everyone live and work together in that classroom harmoniously. Mrs. Thomas doesn't encourage the children to complete the entire task in one session. She wants the discussion to stop before sitting still and taking turns in a large group becomes unpleasant for the youngsters. Children leave with a better feeling about joining the group discussion next time.

After the group disbands, Mrs. Thomas briefly confers with a parent volunteer about the session. The parent tells her about a fascinating informal discussion which had been going on simultaneously with the formal one: Two girls were debating the pros and cons of a rule about interrupting someone who is reading to ask for help with a word. This information helps Mrs. Thomas since she had been wondering whether or not she should have allowed that sub-discussion to continue. This information reinforces her belief that the most important discussions may not be those planned by the teacher.

By the end of first grade, most sound substitutions and overgeneralized grammar rules have disappeared from children's speech. Not due to any specific lessons or drill to correct the problems, this development is a natural process resulting from children's maturation plus their continued imitation and analysis of the language around them. As youngsters mature, they become more able to duplicate the sounds of their language. Through continued exposure to the language patterns of their culture, they naturally discover the exceptions to grammar rules as well as the rules themselves. Mrs. Thomas listens carefully to students to determine if any of them are still having difficulty and should be considered for special speech help.

Schedule for Speech Development

3 years	About 300 word vocabulary
3½ years	B, *m, p, v,* and *h* sounds develop
4 years	About 900 word vocabulary
4½ years	D, *t, n, g, k, ng,* and *y* sounds develop
5½ years	F sound develops
6½ years	V, sh, za, and *l* sounds develop
7½ years	S, *w, r, th,* and *wh* sounds develop
7 to 8 years	Sentence foundation mastered (pronouns and prepositions)
8 years	All sounds are developed and speech should be intelligible

Until the end of first grade, or about seven years of age, much immature speech is developmentally normal and requires no remedial intervention. Although alert to children who require special help, Mrs. Thomas does not correct their speech. She considers the rapport established with her students to be so significant to their language development that she is unwilling to jeopardize that rapport with a critical response to a child's communication.

All three of the teachers previously described believe that children's language is a personal extension of the child, and that to reject the child's language is to reject the child. These teachers believe that children's language is based on their experiences, and that a child with meager experience will be a child with meager language. Therefore, the teachers make great efforts to enhance the experience base of all their students. Through these experiences, youngsters in their classes gain subjects to talk about, motivation to talk, and an increased vocabulary. Finally, all of these teachers believe that children must talk in order to develop language proficiency as well as increased intellectual growth. None of their classrooms are quiet places. These teachers know that they are dealing with children in their language acquisition years.

As they help children develop oral language proficiency, early childhood educators help children build the foundation of understanding required for the next step—mastering symbolic language: reading and writing.

LEARNING TO READ THROUGH EXPERIENCES

When a child looks ever so carefully
at the scale in the store
or at the life in his aquarium,
He is being taught to read.
When his year is a series of
mind-stretching, eye-filling trips,
Helping him know more solidly his world,
He is being taught to read.

(James Hymes, 1965)

Children and adults need to bring meaning to the printed page in order to get meaning from that page (Lee and Rubin, 1979). Without some relevant experience or some personal meaning, much of the message that one reads will be lost. Written words can extend our understandings, but they must build on an existing understanding. Most adults have begun to read an article which was too technical—in other words, dealt with unfamiliar facts and concepts—and have soon put the article aside. On the other hand, adults tend to enjoy reading about the adventures of others which are similar to their own.

Even more than adults, children need to build on personal experience in their encounters with written and oral language. What we know about how young children think and learn, thanks to the work of Jean Piaget, tells us that children are much less able than adults to conceptualize ideas from mere words. As explained in Chapter 1, the pre-operational stage child requires concrete level explorations to develop understandings. When youngsters manipulate or interact with real objects, they begin to develop concepts (*Foreman* and Kuschner, *1984*).

Educators must make the distinction between learning concepts and learning facts. An adult can tell a child facts, and that child can memorize and repeat them. However, this performance does not imply understanding or necessarily involve thought. Although facts are part of a concept, they are not the same thing (Cohen and Rudolph, 1984). A concept is a broader principle derived from analysis of a series of facts or events. That the leaves turn bright colors in the fall is a fact, but the concept of leaves turning color involves an understanding of the cyclical nature of the seasons and their relationship to regeneration in nature. Concept development requires thought rather than memorization. This type of thought can only occur for the young child through first-hand experiences and observations which allow the hypothesis and experiment cycle of constructing knowledge (Piaget, 1973).

Sometimes adults get in a hurry for children to learn. Adults try to speed the learning process by substituting second-hand experiences for first-hand ones. They confuse passive exposure through pictures or films or lectures with the active learning mode which Piaget tells us is especially necessary for children under eight years old. When these short-cut approaches result in a veneer of superficial knowledge, some adults think that the children have learned a great deal in a short time. However, knowing specific words and understanding what they represent are not necessarily the same thing. Just observe the results of youngsters' overexposure to television. These young children are able to talk about a number of things about which they understand little.

The first-hand experiences and observations take time. Betsy has to pour the water from one container to others over and over, on many different occasions, before she can understand that water will conform to the shape of its container or that a short, wide container can hold the same amount as a tall, narrow one. Even then the concepts she develops are only beginnings. Sometimes she will even temporarily develop an incorrect concept due to her incomplete experience and her immature understandings. What a temptation it is to rush in and explain to her that she is wrong and to tell her the "right" answer. Knowledgeable teachers and parents resist that temptation; they know that Betsy can never discover what she has been told and that she only understands what she discovers for herself. These adults know that if they tell Betsy that her perceptions of reality are wrong, Betsy only learns to distrust herself as a learner. When a child's immature view of the world tells her that the tall, narrow container holds more than the short, wide one, no amount of telling her otherwise will help her understand. She will believe the wise adult and believe that she is wrong, but she will be confused and cease to trust and learn through her observations.

This type of shortcut to teaching causes children to rely on adults rather than to think for themselves. In a world with ever changing facts and various views of truth, children must learn to think for themselves. Learning the process and developing the confidence for life-long learning is more important than learning specific information at age four, five, or six. Parents' and teachers' over-zealous attention to correct information may destroy the child's learning process.

When teachers and parents have encouraged children to explore and experiment with their environment, the children build a foundation of understanding. They have experiences to think about, talk about, and write about; they expand their vocabulary with meaningful words related to their experiences; and they can relate personally to what others write about similar experiences. Additionally, children gain practice in "reading"—or bringing meaning to a wide variety of experiences. They learn to "read" people's moods from their expressions or to "read" the weather from the color of the sky (Lee and Allen,

1963). Children learn to "read" symbols, such as the "golden arches," which relate to their experience. Additionally, they learn to read printed symbols with which they have had experience, such as the letters on the red sign that say STOP.

Home Experiences

Much of a child's experience occurs before preschool age, and once a child enters school, much of his experience continues to occur outside school. Some parents provide ample opportunity for their offspring to investigate pots and pans, plants and animals, and various textures, tastes, and smells. Other parents either do little to encourage their children to explore or prevent children from investigating due to safety concerns. Some families take young children on walks and excursions, while others don't realize the importance of such trips.

Betsy's home is ideal for exploring. Her mother understands that babies need the intellectual stimulation of moving around and touching, tasting, and smelling. Betsy's mother uses the playpen to put dangerous or delicate objects in, not to put babies in. She keeps pins, needles, and other dangerous objects off the floor and covers electrical outlets so that little people can explore in safety. Despite having plenty of commercial toys in the playroom, Betsy's mother, Deborah, knows that babies don't learn much about the real world from manipulating brightly colored plastic. Deborah learned after reading materials by Magda Gerber (1979), a noted infant education specialist, that a large scarf can be one of the best toys possible for a baby. Amazing things about object permanancy are learned as the baby uses the cloth to cover and uncover first the object and then herself.

Older children in the family expand their learning experiences beyond toys by helping with chores. A two-year old can put away canned food when groceries are unpacked, a four-year old can sort and mate socks when laundry is folded, and a six-year old can help a toddler get dressed. All the children get to help in cooking at some time, even though their help means more work for their mother.

Betsy and her brothers and sisters have a large yard for play. Their yard includes a paved area for riding tricycles, grass to run barefoot in, and dirt to dig in. Fruit trees, a vegetable garden, and pet rabbits in a cage also are in Betsy's back yard. The children in this family may choose from a variety of outdoor experiences: They are allowed to pick and eat the fruit when it is ripe and washed, they can eat fresh peas out of the pod or pull up tender young carrots to see if they are mature, and they can gently pet the soft, furry bunnies. On warm days, the children add the delightful sensory experience of water play when they get to fill the plastic swimming pool.

The family van has enough space, seat belts, and baby seats to take all five children safely and comfortably on errands or outings. These children go to the grocery store, the fabric store, and the hardware store. They get to ride along to pick up Aunt Marjie at the airport and to bring Mandy home from her ballet lesson. Along the way, they see bridges, trains, and construction work. Of course, they don't just stay in the van; they get out and explore the grocery store, learning to identify products on the shelves and vegetables on display. They get to watch the planes land at the airport and they get to pull the luggage off the baggage belt. These children are storing up many understandings to bring to oral and written language.

This family's everyday activities also provide the children meaningful experiences with written language. The younger ones watch as their mother writes the grocery list, and they suggest items to include. Those who can write make note of grocery items which they notice are running low, such as their favorite juice or lunch dessert. The schedule for various car pools is written and posted for daily reference. The children realize the importance of writing down the complicated plan for getting Joey to and from karate, getting Amy to and from swimming lessons, and getting Mandy to and from ballet. Another printed item posted prominently on the refrigerator door is the school lunch menu. The school-age children check it daily to decide whether to pack a lunch or buy one at school. Those who can't read the menu and don't yet need to are nevertheless aware of the significance of reading this notice.

School Experiences

Because not all children have these experiences at home, Betsy's pre-school teacher tries to create a school environment which provides many similar experiences. Ms. Reynolds consciously plans experiences to help her young students find out some answers to their constant questions of "why?" She recognizes the intellectual curiosity of preschoolers and works at satisfying that curiosity in ways that will be meaningful. She knows children the age of her students must learn through all their senses, not just through hearing. The preschool setting which she has prepared for youngsters is a series of invitations to experiment with various materials—sand and water, paint and paste, blocks and puzzles, magnets and magnifying glasses, fish and guinea pigs, large muscle and fine coordination challenges, and props for trying out roles seen in the real world.

Ms. Reynolds makes sure that her students regularly have new, stimulating experiences, both in and out of the classroom. She changes the standard classroom offerings with new props or variations on a theme as she observes children becoming ready for new challenges. The water table might be set up for float and sink experiments for awhile, then another time contain funnels, hoses, and pumps for moving water in different ways, and yet another time have detergent added for blowing bubbles with straws. The sand area may contain toy trucks and road building machinery, then at other times contain toy dinosaurs or zoo animals, and yet other times allow the combination of water and sand play for a different kind of sand experience. Props in the dramatic play area change to reflect current child interests or field trips recently taken. Ms. Reynolds rotates puzzles and manipulative materials, presenting increasingly difficult ones, to vary the children's routine and to challenge them.

Still, Ms. Reynolds knows that children learn much outside the classroom, and she wants her preschoolers to be exposed to other environments. She plans excursions to visit the boat harbor, the fish processing plant, and the neighborhood grocery store. She takes advantage of unplanned opportunities such as when the house across the street was being spray-painted and when a nearby street was dug up so workers could replace some pipes.

Planning Outings

Generally Ms. Reynolds likes to plan excursions well in advance. She visits the site first to decide how many children can be accommodated at one time, to acquaint herself with potential hazards, and to analyze the potential for first-hand experiences. If a guide will lead the children on a tour, Ms. Reynolds makes certain that the guide will not spend much time talking, but will show children things and let them touch whatever they safely can. She emphasizes that these young children will not learn everything about the operation they are observing, but will learn a little now and more later. Past experience has taught her that this caution is necessary as part of keeping guides from trying to explain too much. She also plans for safe transportation with seat belts for all youngsters, if travel is to be by car, and for safe routing if they will be walking. She usually walks a planned walking route herself to make sure it is easily passable and not too far. She guards against getting the children over-tired from too long a trip and tries to keep all outings under one hour from start to finish.

Ms. Reynolds thinks about the purpose of each field trip, trying to vary the purposes as well as the places. Some outings help children learn about processes, such as how houses are built or how bread is baked; others show behind-the-scenes activities, such as visiting a television or radio station, a restaurant, or grocery story; other trips help children explore the community geographically in relation to their school and homes. Sometimes she and the children take a trip just for the enjoyment of having an adventure, smelling growing things, and feeling the breeze (Figure 2.1).

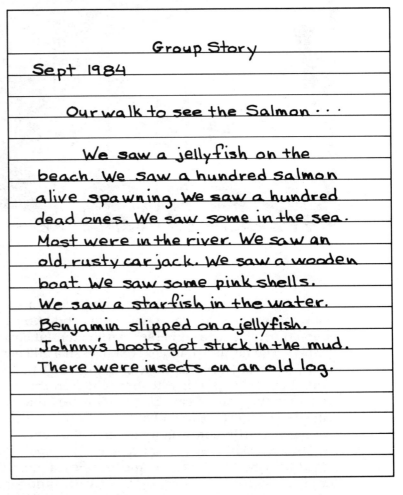

Group Story

Sept 1984

Our walk to see the Salmon · · ·

We saw a jellyfish on the beach. We saw a hundred salmon alive spawning. We saw a hundred dead ones. We saw some in the sea. Most were in the river. We saw an old, rusty car jack. We saw a wooden boat. We saw some pink shells. We saw a starfish in the water. Benjamin slipped on a jellyfish. Johnny's boots got stuck in the mud. There were insects on an old log.

Figure 2.1   A description of a class field trip dictated by a small group of students.

Ms. Reynolds prefers to have small groups go on most of the outings she plans rather than taking all twenty children at one time. With a group of five children and one adult, all children can get close enough to see and hear. Their interaction tends to be relaxed, and the quality of discussion that can occur on the spot is much greater with a small group than a large one. Sometimes all the children take turns visiting the same place on the same day; on other occasions the teacher or parents take a different group each day for a week. Because the children have taken certain trips many times, such as going to the store to get food for snack or to the library to exchange books, only a small group is usually interested. The children know that they will get another opportunity later if they are too busy painting or doing woodworking to go today.

This small group approach to field trips contrasts to another approach which Ms. Reynolds will never forget seeing during an outing to the zoo. She had her entire class at the zoo that day, but they were spread out in groups of five, with a parent volunteer in charge of each group. Each parent leader wore a construction paper flower, and each child wore a construction paper headband with his or her name on it. Every leader's flower was the same color as the headbands of the children assigned to her. Each adult could easily spot one of her charges in the crowd if a child wandered. Suddenly, down the middle of the broad path between animal cages marched a troop of children clutching a long rope and being herded by several adults. The children were not allowed to gather in clusters around animals that particularly inter-

ested them and certainly discussion of what they saw wasn't easy while walking single file. Adults spent their energy keeping children in line instead of talking with them. Ms. Reynolds and her students could only watch in amazement.

Choosing Locations for Outings

With many interesting places to visit, choosing a destination is a challenge. Ms. Reynolds takes her cues from children's interests as she observes their play and listens to their conversation. Some successful trips have included the shoe repair shop where Timmy got his shoe fixed, and where the children got to touch the tools and take some pieces of leather back to school to play shoe repair; the pizza parlor where they got to help put their own ingredients on a pizza and eat it; the animal shelter where they got to pet the animals; and the dentist's office where they sat in the examination chair, looked inside each other's mouths with the little mirror, and then received new toothbrushes.

Children do not necessarily have to travel to an experience; sometimes that experience can come to them. Many people are flattered when a teacher asks them to come to school to share something about themselves or the work they do. A carpenter might come and demonstrate his tools, maybe even spend time helping interested children in the woodworking center. A plumber or an electrician would be equally fascinating. Every year, Ms. Reynolds invites the mother of a new baby to bring the infant to school and let the children watch her bathe the baby in a plastic bathtub. This event always sparks bathing of dolls for several days. Artists, musicians, potters, and weavers could provide wonderful demonstrations for youngsters. Persons from other cultures could bring art work, clothing, or food samples to share with children. Many of the interesting persons who might come to your class would be the parents of your students.

Possibilities exist for mini-field trips within the school building. A visit to the principal's office, a visit to see what the school secretary does, a visit to the nurse's office, or a peek inside the custodian's domain all inform and interest youngsters. Children also enjoy seeing other classrooms and meeting other teachers. Of course children enjoy and benefit from frequent visits to the school library and from visiting the librarian.

Many classes which do not meet in schools meet instead in churches. These settings offer the teachers and students the possibility of meeting the minister, seeing his office, and getting him to show youngsters the chapel and sanctuary. Churches often include a kitchen which could be useful for cooking experiences and have a recreation hall useful for large muscle activities. Sunday school rooms which are unused by the kindergarten or preschool during the week also interest youngsters.

Every community and every part of the country has unique features and locations that contribute to the culture of that area. These can be the basis for fascinating field trips. For instance, children living in southeast Alaska should explore the harbors and fishing boats. They should be shown around a ferry, a hydrofoil, and a tourist cruise ship; they should get to examine a float plane and watch a helicoptor transport machinery to a logging camp. For these children no highways or railroads link communities, and their studies should reflect this reality. They do have knowledge of glaciers, icebergs, forests, beaches, eagles, and sea lions, however. And they have the rich cultural heritage of the Indians who first lived there and still thrive there.

Children living in Phoenix, Arizona would have a different set of relevant experiences. Instead of going to the woods to pick blueberries, they would visit the desert to examine the delicate cactus flowers in the spring, learning to avoid cactus needles. Instead of learning how to keep warm in winter, they would learn how to avoid overexposure in the summer. Instead of discovering the wonders of the beach at low tide, they would discover the difference between a dry riverbed and that same riverbed after a rainstorm. The animals, birds, and trees these children learn about differ from those in Alaska, but would certainly be no less fascinating. The world of Arizona children would include black widow spiders, rattlesnakes, and buzzing locusts, as well as orange blossoms and palm trees. The Indians native to that area would weave blankets and make intricately painted pots instead of totem poles. Both sets of experiences are equally valid for young children, and they should have them.

LEARNING TO READ THROUGH LITERATURE

When a child has the chance to hear
one good story after another,
day after day,
He is being taught to read . . .

(James Hymes, 1965)

Why teach children how to read unless we teach them to *want* to read? Unless they want to read, children won't do enough of it to ever become good at it. When adults read stories to young children, we introduce them to the magic of books and awaken their desire to read for themselves. When we share quality literature with youngsters, we give them a glimpse of the excitement, the drama, and the beauty that is contained in books. When we share our enthusiasm for a good story with children, we provide a model for them to imitate. As children imitate adults who read to them and interact with adults about stories, children gradually, naturally, and without pressure, become readers.

Research project after research project comes up with the same conclusion: Reading to children is a successful way to teach them to read. Reading specialist Delores Durkin's (1980) studies of children who read early found that being read to frequently was the one common factor. Language development specialist, Courtney Cazden, (1981) found reading to children to be a superior method of assisting their language acquisition. Researchers at the University of New Mexico recently determined that children learn ways of constructing meaning for print as adults interpret stories for them (Altwerger et al., 1985). Kindergarten specialists, Cohen and Rudolph, (1984) found that a combination of reading to children and follow-up activities such as creative dramatics or discussion related to the story were particularly helpful to reading achievement. Therefore, not surprisingly, Charlotte Huck (1979) says in her book on children's literature that teachers should feel a responsibility to read to their students every day. Professor Huck refers to all teachers, not just teachers of small children.

The research indicates that the earlier adults start to read to youngsters, the greater the benefits. As with many other developmental tasks, the early childhood years are of the greatest significance in exposure to literature. Even before babies can talk, they enjoy looking at books and being read to. They are able to understand some of what is read to them, just as they are able to understand some of what is said to them, months before they say their first word. Even before babies understand the content of stories, they enjoy the process of being read to: being held closely and hearing the soothing voice of a loving adult.

The intimacy of enjoying a story with a parent or a teacher adds to a child's pleasurable feelings about reading which make children want to read. Attitudes toward reading can begin in infancy and be enhanced

throughout childhood. As with so much of teaching, parents should be the first and foremost influence, with teachers coming to assist and extend what has begun.

Look at Betsy, who at six months of age is developing an interest in books and stories. Already Betsy wants to be included when someone reads a story in her busy household. She has ample opportunity since her oldest sister reads well and is willing to entertain the younger ones, her oldest brother enjoys sharing his new powers as a beginning reader, and her preschool brother and her toddler sister frequently request stories. Of course Betsy's mother and father also read to the children when they have a chance. When asked at what age youngsters should be introduced to books, Betsy's mother says that her theory about that is similar to her theory about when they should be introduced to solid food. Deborah says, "When they grab food off your plate and eat it, they're ready for real food." So, whenever her youngsters crawl over to hear a story, they are included.

Betsy's brothers and sisters enjoy books and have been exposed to them since they were babies. By the time he was two, her brother, Joe, had borrowed *The Little Fire Engine* (Lenski, *1946*) from the library so often that he got his own copy for his second birthday (Figure 2.2). After he outgrew his interest in hearing that same story over and over, a younger sibling came along to love the simple, satisfying plot and the drawings that correspond so well to the story. Before long Betsy took her turn. Just as 5-month-old Betsy cried for a piece of toast when her sister Amy had one, she already wanted to share a story

Figure 2.2   From: *The Little Fire Engine*. **Reprinted by permission from the Lois Lenski Covey Foundation.**

when someone read. By the time she could walk, Betsy was toddling around with a favorite book, handing it to someone to read to her.

When Betsy is old enough for preschool, her teacher, Ms. Reynolds, can tell that she has been read to frequently. Not all of the children in Ms. Reynolds's class exhibit Betsy's interest in books and story times. Ms. Reynolds doesn't force stories on these youngsters by insisting that everyone has to come to story time. Instead, she concentrates on making story time as inviting as possible, gradually luring children away from other pursuits to join the story group. As youngsters overhear the exciting plots and observe the interest of other children, they become willing to listen to stories. Until that time, Ms. Reynolds allows them to choose other quiet activities which won't interfere with the story.

Guidelines for Sharing a Story

Ms. Reynolds never shares a book with youngsters before she has become familiar with it herself. By reading a book to herself, she discovers whether or not it is of sufficient quality and whether it is appropriate for the age and interests of her preschoolers. She also wants to know the story well enough to share it effectively. She concentrates on developing proper expression and pacing as she reads, so that she can convey the book's full meaning and impact. She also wants to be able to paraphrase or skip any long descriptive passages which would lose her listeners' interest. Whenever possible, Ms. Reynolds reads a story over several times and practices it before she shares it with children. Children are enthralled by an exciting scene which Ms. Reynolds reads with breathless haste, they are captivated

General Guidelines For Sharing Stories with Children

- ☐ Telling a story is often better than reading it.
- ☐ Never share a story without being prepared.
- ☐ Never share a story just to fill time.

Arranging the Story Environment

- ☐ Sit on a low chair or on the floor.
- ☐ Share stories in small groups rather than large ones.
- ☐ Allow children to choose whether or not to listen to the story.

Effectively Sharing Stories

- ☐ Use a conversational tone of voice, speaking slowly and distinctly. Avoid excessive use of "and" or "er". Avoid a sing-song, uneven tone and a high pitched voice.
- ☐ Look directly at the children. Include all members of the group, not just those directly in front of you.
- ☐ Use timing effectively; vary the tempo. As action increases and things begin to happen, hurry the tempo. Before a moment of question, surprise, or awe, a pause can be most effective.
- ☐ Keep the story or listening period within the limits of the children's attention span. This may range from seven to twenty minutes for pre-school children and gradually increase.

by the suspenseful moment in which Ms. Reynolds pauses for effect, and they gain immeasurable meaning from the expressive way she reads direct quotes so as to bring the characters to life.

Often Ms. Reynolds will choose to tell the story in a book rather than read it. This approach allows her to maintain eye contact with youngsters for a more personal communication. She receives better feedback about what parts of the story most interest her listeners and what ideas she may need to explain. Using this technique, she can adapt a longer, more sophisticated story to the level of her students. Of course some books, such as Dr. Seuss stories, rely on the specific sounds and rhythm of the words for effectiveness and should not be paraphrased. Whether she is reading or telling a story, Ms. Reynolds keeps a conversational tone and maintains frequent eye contact with all listeners. She responds to whatever story she is reading with appropriate comments and questions, such as "Oh, what a lot to eat!" when she reads *The Very Hungry Caterpillar*, or "Do you think Little Toot is afraid?" Children gather around Ms. Reynolds as she shares litera-

ture with them. She usually sits on a low chair or the floor to enhance interaction and cozy togetherness. The children in Ms. Reynolds's preschool are learning a great deal about reading long before they are able to read on their own.

Preparing and Telling a Story

☐ Think of the story structure and patterns (e.g. cumulative tale, repetitions of threes, comparisons, etc.)
☐ Read the story slowly, forming a picture in your mind of each character and event.
☐ Close the book and think through the story in terms of the structure and patterns you have noted.
☐ Read the story again for language. The words fit themselves into the pictures, and the story takes form.
☐ Adopt a special voice when each character speaks.
☐ Plan a good beginning to gain the attention of the audience.

In big sister Amy's kindergarten class, Mrs. Hanna doesn't require attendance at story time by all children either. If she wants to instill a love of reading, won't forcing stories on children accomplish just the opposite? Mrs. Hanna relies on the intrinsic pleasure of a good book to bring her students together. She merely invites them to hear a story and begins as soon as a small group has gathered. She does not interrupt those who are still too engrossed in a previous activity or those who simply prefer one of the acceptable alternatives to story time. Mrs. Hanna knows these children will be able to overhear the story as they work puzzles or draw pictures. Often one or two will leave what they are doing and join the story group as the story gets exciting. Sometimes a child just isn't ready to be part of a large group and prefers to listen from the side. Some children find it difficult to sit still and listen without doing something else to occupy their hands. Mrs. Hanna's system provides alternatives to meet the varying needs and maturation levels of her kindergarteners.

Mrs. Hanna believes children whose past experiences did not provide for optimum language development can be helped by being read to. Her prescription for counteracting language deprivation is large and frequent doses of story time—on a one-to-one basis if possible since this allows each child to better view the pictures and compare the print to the oral reading. Most of all this allows important interaction about the story, perhaps expressions of amazement, sympathy, or outrage. The interaction can also be a way of relating a story to a child's personal background. The reader may ask Megan if she has ever seen a kangaroo when they discuss *Katy No Pockets.*

Instead of trying to condense several years of missing language enrichment into synthetic substitutions such as flash card drill, Mrs. Hanna attempts to provide that which was missing from the previous years. She enlists the aid of older students and parents to help provide the one-to-one attention needed by some youngsters; so we will see a fifth grader in a pillow-softened corner reading to a kindergartener who is leaning on the older child's arm to better see the pictures in the book.

First grade teacher Mrs. Thomas also believes in making time for reading to children. Because the educational system expects students to complete so many specific tasks, little time seems open for relaxing and escaping into a story together. But, Mrs. Thomas knows that unless she can balance the time spent on reading skills with that spent on reading pleasure, children will want to escape *from* reading instead of to it.

As part of making books and reading attractive, Mrs. Thomas never begins a story time with admonishments to "sit still and be quiet." Instead of demanding the children's attention, she grabs it with questions or comments to bring them into the mood of the story. No

one wants to miss a word, and everyone pays attention. At the first of the year, she limits her book selection to those that can be read in one sitting and won't tax either her reading endurance or the children's listening endurance. By the end of the school year, she is generally able to share a lengthy book with her class by reading a chapter or short selection daily. The children have matured intellectually and in their story sophistication so that they can hold the idea of the plot in their mind from day to day. Their interest and enjoyment in the unfolding story can be heard in their reminders to the teacher not to forget to read the story today.

Each one of these teachers is careful not to ruin a good story with moralizing about the message at the end, but they often plan a follow-up activity or discussion. Ms. Reynolds's students are challenged by the "game" of re-telling the story in sequence either from the pictures in the book or with appropriate felt characters on a felt board. At this age many youngsters also like to read the book from memory on their own, thereby gaining valuable insights as to what reading is all about.

Following the Story

☐ Following the story the children may have questions or comments. Take time for these, but do not force discussion by the use of questions. This procedure often detracts from the child's enjoyment of the story.
☐ If, during a story, a child interrupts to relate an incident, encourage him/her to keep it until the story is finished. Occasionally such a contribution is valuable and should be allowed, but many such interruptions can spoil the story.
☐ Do not moralize.
☐ Follow-up activity ideas:
   1. Re-tell the story in sequence
   2. Act out the climax
   3. Think critically: Do you agree?
                     What would you have done?
                     How do you feel about it?

Story Follow-Up Activities

Mrs. Hanna enjoys assisting children to dramatize sections of a story as a way to internalize the meaning. For instance, she follows up a reading of Steven Kellogg's *The Island of the Skog* with a suggestion that the children show her how the mice must have felt when they saw the monstrous creature lurching toward them on the beach. She encourages the youngsters to show emotion with their whole body as well as facial expressions. Then she asks what they might say when they felt that way. These creative dramatics experiences often reappear as children incorporate them into their dramatic play. So the Skog might come to visit the domestic scene in the play house the next day, and we might find the play house peopled by mice who prepare meals of chocolate waffles and coconut cherry cheese pie.

Since reading critically as well as reading for comprehension is a necessity in our society, Mrs. Thomas makes sure to incorporate critical reading for comprehension into story time. When she reads William Steig's *Doctor DeSoto*, she encourages discussion of whether the mouse dentist should have risked treating the fox's toothache and whether it was fair for him to glue the fox's teeth together at the end. *The Story of Ping* by Marjorie Flack presents a topic of personal interest to children as they discuss whether or not Ping should get a swat for being last over the bridge onto the wise-eyed boat. When conflicting opinions are solicited and respected, children learn that they can come to their own opinions about what they read rather than accepting whatever is in print. Through such interaction about stories, children can develop a variety of competencies in meaningful text construction before they can read anything on their own.

A teacher may use many activities relevant to a book as preparation for the story rather than as follow-up. Often a prior personal experience will give meaning to a story otherwise incomprehensible to young children. Playing outside in the snow and making "angels" gives meaning to Ezra Jack Keats's *The Snowy Day*, picking blueberries adds to a reading of Robert McCloskey's *Blueberries for Sal*, and children who are familiar with salmon, eagles, and beaches of western Canada and Southeast Alaska will have a better understanding of Betty Waterton's *A Salmon for Simon*. All of these stories would probably correspond with experiences of children from Juneau, Alaska but would not be as suitable for children from Phoenix, Arizona.

Ms. Reynolds's preschool class enjoyed the day when they used the blueberries they had picked for learning activities: Several children were involved in dying yarn in mashed blueberries, and all who were interested took turns making batches of blueberry muffins. Everyone ate the muffins for snack. Naturally *Blueberries for Sal* was the story of the day (Figure 2.3)

Selecting an Appropriate Story for Children

We have discussed why to read to children and how to read to them. Let's address the issue of what to read to them. All books are not created equal. When Betsy's mother goes into the grocery store or the toy store, she feels assaulted by the masses of poorly written and

Figure 2.3   From *Blueberries for Sal*, by Robert McCloskey. Copyright © 1948 by Robert McCloskey, renewed © by Robert McCloskey 1976. Reprinted by permission of Viking Penguin, Inc.

unimaginatively illustrated books on the shelves. Just as she is careful in selecting nutritious food, instead of junk food, she wants to select books which will fill her children's minds with curiosity and stimulate their thinking, instead of offering them books whose story lines and illustrations are based on Saturday morning cartoons.

Even book stores often have a disappointing selection of quality children's literature. Deborah reads the reviews of children's books in *Parents* magazine, and follows the Caldecott award winners as ways of keeping up to date on quality children's literature. She then places special orders at the bookstore when necessary. She also makes requests at the library and encourages ordering of books with good reputations.

Her children's teachers have similar problems locating current quality literature. They do find reviews in professional journals to be helpful. *Young Children,* the journal of the National Association for the Education of Young Children, and *Language Arts,* the journal of the National Council of Teachers of English, both have reliable book review sections. Mrs. Hanna finds the children's literature list in the back of the book *Before the Basics* (Bos, 1983) to be an excellent resource. Ms. Reynolds uses and recommends to parents *Getting Ready to Read* (Glazer, 1980) and Jim Trelease's *The Read-Aloud Handbook* (1982) for book suggestions according to children's ages. These teachers also have created their own collection of personal favorites and share them with youngsters year after year. When an adult personally loves a story, sharing it becomes special experience both for child and adult.

Teachers cannot possibly find an expert opinion on every book, nor should they. Instructors must develop their own criteria for what constitutes a good book and then form an opinion about which books are right for certain children and in which specific situations. One simple guide is to decide if you like a book yourself. Good children's literature isn't just interesting to children; it is timeless. Have you picked up a child's story book and found that you couldn't put it down until you finished it? That's definitely a good book.

A good book for any age is one which catches and holds the reader's interest. Suspense or tension of some sort is the classic way of hooking a reader into a story; a book without this has a poorly constructed plot. A good plot is important. For young children the plot should be simple, without subplots or flashbacks to confuse them. The action should be believable without being predictable, and the problems should not be too quickly overcome. Lenski's *The Little Fire Engine,* so beloved by Betsy's brother Joe, has a simple plot suitable for a young child but remains exciting from the beginning, when the fire alarm sounds, to the end, when everyone is safe and the fire is out.

Some books can exist without suspense or plot because they offer something else. The sounds and rhythm of language can be pleasurable

Criteria for Selecting an Appropriate Story for Young Children

An appropriate story contains:

1. A simple, well-developed plot, centered about a sequence of events, with action predominant. A slight surprise element makes the children wonder what will happen next and can add much to a story. e.g.: *Fireman Small*
2. A large amount of direct conversation. e.g. *Katy No Pockets*
3. Use of repetition, rhyme, and catch phrases that children memorize quickly and easily. e.g. Dr. Seuss books
4. Use of carefully chosen, colorful language.
5. Situations involving familiar happenings. The new, unusual, and different may be included, but there must be enough of the familiar with which children can identify. e.g. *Katy and The Big Snow*
6. A simple and satisfying climax.
7. One main character with whom children can easily identify, e.g. *Ping* Too many characters can be confusing.
8. A variety of ethnic, cultural, and racial backgrounds. Such stories should present realistic pictures, not ridiculous sterotypes of racial or ethnic groups.
9. Illustrations: Young children "read" pictures. Pictures need to accurately portray the content and mood of the story.

in themselves. Readers enjoy books like Dr. Seuss's *McElligot's Pool* or Emberley's *Drummer Hoff* and of course there is the fun of nursery rhymes for youngsters. Some books don't even require words to be fascinating. More and more beautifully detailed wordless picture books are appearing for children. These books are designed especially for children who are in the stage of reading the pictures. Spier's *Noah's Ark* and Ormerod's companion books, *Sunshine* and *Moonlight* offer delightful opportunities for children to create their own stories to accompany the pictures (Figure 2.4). Mercer Mayer's series of small, wordless, story books are also a wonderful examples of this book type.

Whether or not a story relies on words or plot, a main character in a story with whom children can identify is important. Children easily identify with Flack's little duck, Ping, as he tries to escape punishment. They can relate to the daily routines of the nameless little girl in Ormerod's books, and they can step into Peter's snowsuit and experience the wonder of *The Snowy Day* created by Keats.

Figure 2.4 From *Sunshine,* by Jan Ormerod. Copyright © 1981 by
Jan Ormerod. By permission of Lothrop, Lee & Shepard Books. A Division
of William Morrow & Company.

Direct conversation in a children's book can enhance its sense of
immediacy and action. In *Katy No-Pocket* the author adds drama by
presenting Katy's conversations with the mother crocodile, the mother
monkey, and the wise owl as Katy seeks a solution to her problem of
how to carry little Freddy.

Whether a plot should be about the familiar or the unusual depends
upon the age of the children for whom we are selecting the story. Very
young children like stories about their own lives and are limited in their
understanding to that which they have experienced. As children mature,
they gradually become interested in and are able to imagine that which
they have not experienced. Stories about daily routine become boring.
They then want adventure and fantasy.

Whether the book depicts the mundane or the exotic, the pictures
must accurately portray the story's action and mood. Children just
beginning to read words or not yet able to read them will pay very close
attention to the pictures. The detail in Steven Kellogg's and Peter
Spier's illustrations delights adults as well as children. The simplicity
and color in Ezra Jack Keats's and Gerald McDermott's illustrations

also attracts all ages. The whimsical elements in Mercer Mayer's and Maurice Sendak's art are widely irresistible. Different children's illustrator's have merit for different reasons. However, not all children's book illustrations are art. Teachers and parents need to protect children from too much overly "cute" art. That level surrounds us in the mass media, and we need to counteract its influence in order to help children develop taste and to provide worthy models for their own art efforts.

A final word in selecting books: Take note of the values represented in the stories and illustrations. Sexism, racism, and gratuitious violence need to be avoided. Hendrick, in her book *The Whole Child,* (1984) offers a guide called "ten quick ways to analyze children's books for racism and sexism" in the appendix. Other guides are available elsewhere. It is worthwhile to search for books which represent the values we wish to pass on to children.

SUGGESTED FOLLOW-UP ACTIVITIES

1. Observe children engaged in dramatic play. Note their use of props and other examples of symbolic representation. Note how the roles they play affect their vocabulary and otherwise impact their language.

2. Help a small group of children plan and present a puppet show. Assist them to focus on the language content of puppet interaction rather than on the physical interaction.

3. Observe preschool children's use of playground climbing apparatus. Contrast their activity with primary grade children's activity in a similar situation. Note differences in their physical strength and agility.

4. Watch as preschool children build with blocks. Note their processes and type of products they achieve. Arrange to watch older children building with blocks. Compare their levels of manipulative dexterity, symbolic representation, goal-oriented behavior, and quality of products.

5. Plan and implement an activity with a small group to enhance the experience base of young children. Follow guidelines provided in this chapter.

6. Find a current list of Caldecott Award books at your local library; examine as many of the books on the list as possible. Note the quality of illustrations which won the award and also analyze the stories for their appeal to children.

7. Using the guides in this chapter, select, prepare, and share a book or story with a group of youngsters. Ask a peer to observe and help you critique the experience.

DISCUSSION QUESTIONS

1. The principal walks into your class and observes block play, dramatic play, water play, various art and manipulative materials activities, all happening in a happy clamor. He interrupts your supervision of a cooking activity to ask why you aren't teaching reading according to the day's schedule. What is your response?

2. A parent is visiting your classroom. Before leaving, she expresses her concern that children aren't learning to sit still and be quiet in this setting. How can you deal with this concern?

REFERENCES AND SOURCES FOR FURTHER READING

Books

Arnheim, D.D., & Pestolesi, R.A. (1978). *Elementary physical education: A developmental approach.* St. Louis: C.V. Mosby.

Arnheim, D.D. & Sinclair, W.A. (1979). *The clumsy child* (2nd ed). St. Louis: C.V. Mosby.

Boegehold, B.D. (1984). *Getting ready to read.* New York: Ballantine Books.

Bos, B. (1983). *Before the basics.* Sacramento, CA.: Cal Central Press.

Carle, E. (1983). *The very hungry caterpillar.* New York: Philomel Books.

Cazden, C. (ed.). (1981). *Language in early childhood education.* Washington, DC: National Association for the Education of Young Children.

Cohen, D. & Rudolph, M. (1984). *Kindergarten and early schooling.* Englewood Cliffs, NJ: Prentice-Hall.

Curtis, S.R. (1982). *The joy of movement in early childhood.* New York: Teacher's College Press.

Durkin, D. (1980). *Teaching young children to read.* Boston: Allyn and Bacon, Inc.

Emberley, B. (1968). *Drummer hoff.* Illustrated by Ed Emberley. Englewood Cliffs, NJ: Prentice-Hall.

Foreman, G. & Kuschner, D. (1984). *The child's construction of knowledge: Piaget for teaching children.* Washington, DC: National Association for the Education of Young Children.

Flack, M. (1933). *The story about ping.* Illustrated by Kurt Wiese. New York: Viking Press.

Flinchum, B.M. (1975). *Motor development in early childhood.* St. Louis: C.V. Mosby Co.

Geisel, T.S. (Dr. Seuss). (1947). *McElligot's pool.* New York: Random House.

Gerber, M. (1979). *A manual for parents and professionals.* Los Angeles: Resources for Infant Educators.

Glazer, S.M. (1980). *Getting ready to read: Creating readers from birth through six.* Englewood Cliffs, NJ.: Prentice-Hall.

Gramatky, H. (1939). *Little toot*. New York: Putnam.

Hendrick, J. (1984). *The whole child*. St. Louis: Times Mirror/Mosby.

Hendricks, G., & Hendricks, K. (1983). *The moving center: Exploring movement activities for the classroom*. Englewood Cliffs, NJ: Prentice-Hall.

Hirsch, E. (1974). *The block book*. Washington DC: National Association for the Education of Young Children.

Huck, C. (1979). *Children's literature in the elementary school*. New York: Holt, Rinehart and Winston.

Hymes, J.L. (1981). *Teaching the child under six*. Columbus, OH: Charles E. Merrill.

Keats, E.J. (1962). *The snowy day*. New York: Viking Press.

Kellog, S. (1973). *The island of the skog*. New York: Dial Press.

Lee, D., & Allen R.V. (1963). *Learning to read through experience*. Englewood Cliffs, NJ: Prentice-Hall.

Lee, D., & Rubin, J. (1979). *Children and language*. Belmont, CA: Wadsworth Publishing.

Lenski, L. (1946). *The little fire engine*. New York: Henry Z. Walck, Inc.

McCloskey, R. (1948). *Blueberries for Sal*. New York: Viking Press.

Monaghan, A.C. (1974). Children's contacts: Some preliminary findings. Cited in Cazden, C.B. *Paradoxes of language structure*. In K. Connolly and J. Bruner (Eds.), *The growth of competence*. New York: Academic Press.

Omerod, J. (1981). *Sunshine*. New York: Lothrop, Lee and Shepard Books.

Omerod, J. (1982). *Moonlight*. New York: Lothrop, Lee and Shepard Books.

Pangrazi, R.P., & Dauer, V.P. (1981). *Movement in early childhood and primary education*. Minneapolis: Burgess.

Payne, E. *Katy no-pocket*. (1944) Illustrated by H.A. Rey. Boston: Houghton-Mifflin Company.

Piaget, J. (1962). *Plays, dreams, and imitation*. New York: W.W. Norton.

Piaget, J. (1973). *To understand is to invent*. New York: Viking.

Piers, M., & Landau, G.M. (1980). *The gift of play*. New York: Walker and Co.

Segal, M., & Adcock, D. (1981). *Just pretending—ways to help children grow through imaginative play*. Englewood Cliffs, NJ: Prentice-Hall.

Spier, P. (1977). *Noah's ark*. Garden City, New York: Doubleday and Company, Inc.

Steig, W. (1982). *Doctor De Soto*. New York: Farrar, Straus and Giroux.

Stewig, J.W. (1982). *Teaching language arts in early childhood*. New York: Holt, Rhinehart and Winston.

Teale, W.H. (1984). Reading to young children: Its significance for literacy development. In H. Goelman, A. Oberg and F. Smith, (Eds.), *Awakening to literacy*. Exeter, NH: Heinemann Inc.

Trelease, J. (1982). *The read-aloud handbook*. New York: Penguin Books.

Waterton, B. (1978). *A salmon for Simon*. Illustrated by Ann Blades. Hartford, CT: Connecticut Printers, Inc.

Periodicals

Allen, B. (1982, Winter). Take a five senses walk. *Day Care and Early Education,* pp. 14–17.

Altwerger, B., Diehl-Faxon, J., & Dockstader-Anderson, K. (1985). Read-aloud events as meaning construction. *Language Arts, 62* (5), 476–484.

Christie, J.F. (1982, May). Sociodramatic play training. *Young Children, 37* (4), 25–32.

Donmeyer, R. (1981, Spring). The politics of play ideological and organizational constraints on the inclusion of play experiences in the school curriculum. *Journal of Research and Development in Education, 14* (3), 11–18.

Dukes, L. (1982, Spring). Dramatic play + symbolic props = reading. *Day Care and Early Education, 10* (3), pp. 11–12.

Essa, E.L. (1981, Winter). An outdoor play area designed for learning. *Day Care and Early Education, 9* (2), pp. 37–42.

Feeney, S., & Magarick, M. (1984, November). Choosing good toys for young children. *Young Children, 40* (1), pp. 20–25.

Fein, G. (1979). Play and the acquisition of symbols. *Current Topics in Early Childhood Education,* pp. 195–225.

Geller, L.G. (1983, February). Children's rhymes and literacy learning: Making connections. *Language Arts, 60,* pp. 184–193.

Giordano, G. (1984, Spring). Play learning. *Day Care and Early Education, 11* (3), pp. 17–21.

Goldfield, B. (1984, Winter). The fine art of reading aloud. *Beginnings,* pp. 27–29.

Honig, A.S. (1982, November). Language environments for young children. *Young Children, 38* (1), pp. 56–67.

Hymes, J.L. (1965). Being taught to read. *Grade Teacher, 82,* 88–92.

Kent, R. (1984, Spring). Schoolgrounds: Have you looked at them lately? *Day Care and Early Education, 11* (3), pp. 12–16.

Kamii, C. & Randazzo, M. (1985, February). Social interaction and invented spelling. *Language Arts, 62,* pp. 124–133.

Lamme, L.L., & Denny, P.L. (1981, Fall). A writing curriculum for preschoolers. *Day Care and Early Education, 9* (1), pp. 12–15.

Leipzig, J. (1982, Fall). Field trips for children under three. *Day Care and Early Education, 10* (1), pp. 6–8.

Martinez, M. (1983, February). Exploring young children's comprehension through story time talk. *Language Arts, 60,* pp. 202–209.

Merenda, R.C., Bloom, J. & D'Iorio, A.J. (1984, Spring). Visual presentation to parents. *Day Care and Early Education, 11* (3), pp. 9–11.

Nilsen, A.P. (1983, February). Children's multiple uses of oral language play. *Language Arts, 60,* pp. 194–201.

Packer, A, Lamme, L.L., & Roberts, D. (1984, Winter). All the ways to talk: The world of adult-child conversations. *Beginnings,* pp. 24–26.

Provenzo, E., & Brett, A. (1984, Spring). Creative block play. *Day Care and Early Education, 11* (3), pp. 6–8.

Roser, N., & Martinez, M. (1985). Roles adults play in preschoolers' response to literature. *Language Arts, 62* (5), 485–490.

Steele, C. (1981, Spring). Play variables as related to cognitive constructs in three to six-year-olds. *Journal of Research and Development in Education, 14,* (3), 58–72.

Tipps, S. (1981, Spring). Play and the brain-relationships and reciprocity. *Journal of Research and Development in Education, 14* (3), 19–29.

Tubbs, J. (1984, Winter). Children's conversations: Why are they important? Talking with and through puppets. *Beginnings,* pp. 36–37.

Turner, A., & Bradbard, M.R. (1981, Winter). The representational play of lower-class preschool children. *Day Care and Early Education, 9* (2), pp. 23–26.

Wolfgang, C., & Sanders, T. (1981, Spring). Defending young children's play as the ladder to literacy. *Theory Into Practice, 20* (2), 116–120.

3

A Natural Introduction to Written Language

Reading and writing experiences at school should permit children to build upon their already existing knowledge of oral and written language.
(International Reading Association, 1986)

T alking, writing, and reading are all part of the same communication process. Let's think about the sequence of learning involved. Traditionally, schools have taught children to read and then have taught them skills to write. But when teachers observe children learning on their own, we see a different sequence in their approach to literacy. We notice as did Rudolph and Cohen (1984) that "comprehension precedes speech; speech precedes writing; and writing is grasped before reading" (p. 57). Adults expect children to talk before they read, but they may not have noticed that children are interested in writing before they can read.

When children write, they are able to use a trial and error approach to making sense of written language. They construct a set of rules for written language while they practice writing, much as they construct a set of rules for oral language as they practice speaking. When adults allow children to use this trial and error approach, the children build firm understandings of the significant concepts and then are able to transfer these understandings to a variety of related situations. As discussed previously, the exploration and discovery approach to learning is the only effective method for children in the preoperational stage of intellectual development.

When well-meaning adults try to keep children from "wasting time" by making mistakes, they deprive children of significant learning experiences. Telling children the principles involved not only truely wastes the child's time; this method also may deprive the child of the chance to formulate basic concepts. Understanding may be replaced by rote memory of a few facts. A child cannot easily transfer specific facts to other situations and will have to learn more facts by rote. This

approach has the additional danger of discouraging thought through suggesting to children that they cannot figure out things on their own, but must rely on an authority.

When we consider beginning writing an initial experimentation with the written word, our expectations for young students change. Instead of expecting children to form letters correctly and spell words according to custom, we can appreciate each small step toward standard written expression. We can rejoice with a young child over approximations of intent in writing, just as we do with a toddler who makes an imprecise attempt to say a new word.

Writing as Social Interaction

We watched Betsy as she learned to communicate orally through the help of her nurturing family. Now let's watch Betsy again. Her oldest brother and sister are sitting at the kitchen table doing homework, and three-year-old Betsy climbs onto a chair, demanding paper and pencil too. She has been doing this for about a year now, and the marks she makes on the paper have changed. At first she would make a few large marks at random, just to try out the effect of the pencil on the paper. Soon she began to make her marks more purposefully; frequently they would consist of a circle with face-like markings. This symbolic representation of a person was a step toward other written symbolic representation. Betsy expressed that symbolism when she pointed to her picture and said, ''Mama.''

Today Betsy appears engrossed in making squiggle lines across her page. Her lines start on the left side of the paper and proceed fairly straight across to the right side, just like the writing of her sister and brother. She has now made an initial distinction between drawing and writing, which involves both the linear characteristic and repetitious nature of writing (Figure 3.1). Nearby her mother is washing dishes and comes over to comment on how hard everyone is working. Betsy tells her proudly that she is writing.

Betsy is learning about writing the same way she learned about talking: She imitates others, gets a response to her efforts, and continues to refine her understanding with continued practice. In this sense, her scribbles are to writing what her babbling was to talking. Her family doesn't criticize her errors either in speech or in writing, so she does not feel discouraged from continuing to practice both. As she practices both talking and writing, she also develops important reading concepts—such as the purposes of language, the nature of written language, and a store of vocabulary words. Perhaps the most important progress she is making toward reading right now, however, is her eagerness for learning more and her confidence in her ability to master the task.

Just as Betsy knew that oral language was more than making sounds, she knows that written language is more than making marks. Betsy understands that both have the intent of communication. She knows this from observing how her parents and siblings use writing. She hears her brother Joe read the book report he has written and her

Figure 3.1   An example of the linear, repetitious writing phase.

sister Mandy read parts of her social studies report on Alaska. She hears her mother read a letter written by her aunt. She sees her dad write a note reminding Joe to do his jobs after school. We see Betsy's family unconsciously socializing her into the world of literacy. They don't do these things purposely to teach; reading and writing are just part of their life.

Betsy shows her mother what she wrote and asks what it says. What a problem! Should Betsy's mom admit the marks don't say anything, or should she make up something? She decides to turn the question around and ask Betsy what the marks say. Her approach works, and Betsy "reads" her writing, "Dear Aunt Marjie, come to see me." Since this has now been identified as a letter, Betsy's mother respectfully puts it in an envelope, addresses it and sends it to its intended audience. When a return letter arrives, Betsy will discover the power of written language to communicate over distance.

Preschool Writing

Two mornings a week, Betsy goes to preschool where Ms. Reynolds provides further experiences with written language. At preschool Betsy sees her name in writing; this important experience is just one of a wide variety of literacy events in preschool. Betsy's name appears on the cubby where she puts her coat when she arrives; she wears a nametag so parent aides know her name; and her name is written on her paintings.

Betsy loves to paint and works at the easel almost every time she comes to school. She is still experimenting with the way the paint drips down the page and what happens when she paints one color over another. But Ms. Reynolds sees that Betsy is beginning to move from exploring this medium to using it for a purpose. One day Betsy says that her painting is a dog. While Betsy watches, Ms. Reynolds writes the word *dog* on a piece of paper and, with Betsy's permission, attaches it as a caption to the painting. Betsy can read this caption. So can her father when he comes to pick her up, and so can the rest of her family when she takes her painting home. Betsy's art work is too immature to look like anything real, but when she decides it represents something, she greatly enjoys having captions or labels for it. Making a symbol for a dog with paint is a step toward writing and so is knowing that the letters her teacher wrote say *dog* (Figure 3.2).

Sometimes Ms. Reynolds will write down Betsy's thoughts about other things. For instance, Betsy was excited about the gerbil when it arrived in class, and Ms. Reynolds wrote down what Betsy wanted to remember to tell her sisters and brothers about it. For now, Ms. Reynolds remains content to let Betsy initiate these dictated stories,

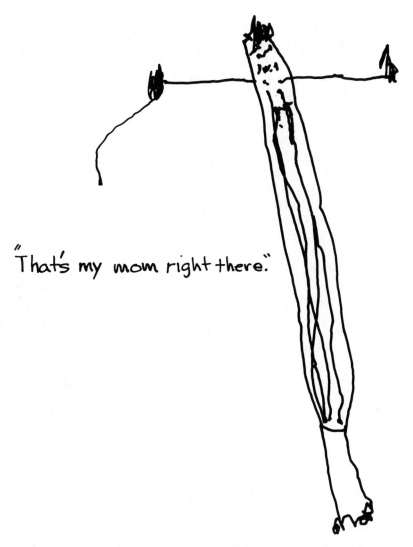

"That's my mom right there."

Figure 3.2 An example of a child's art where an adult wrote the child's label.

but Ms. Reynolds will encourage them more often as Betsy matures in her print awareness and interest.

With her four-year-old class, Ms. Reynolds spends more time calling children's attention to words and what the words say. Although she reads aloud every day to both classes, Ms. Reynolds often points out significant words in what she reads to the older group. She frequently runs her hand along words as she reads them to a child, in order to emphasize that the written part tells the story, rather than the pictures. As children encounter signs and labels, she calls attention to them—a stop sign during a walk, the *float* and *sink* signs in a science experiment, or the labels on empty cereal boxes in the play store. This teacher knows that children's first reading and writing focuses on these types of contextualized print.

Ms. Reynolds makes sure children see her writing and using that form of communication as she continues the process of socializing youngsters into a literate world. When Justin proudly announced that he had succeeded in putting together a certain difficult puzzle, Ms. Reynolds congratulated him and wrote a note to his parents telling them about his achievement. Justin watched as she wrote and listened as she read the note back to him. When he carried the note home and heard his mother read it, he had a greater sense of what writing was about. Ms. Reynolds encourages children to express themselves in writing for a variety of purposes. When Tanya brought her favorite doll to school and didn't want anyone to touch it, Ms. Reynolds wrote for her, "please do not touch Tanya's doll." This notice was taped onto the doll, which Tanya then placed in the specially designated "precious place" where all unsharable possessions are kept.

In addition to providing opportunities for children to experience print in a variety of circumstances, Ms. Reynolds encourages independent writing by both three-and four-year olds. They have access to blank paper, marking pens, crayons, and pencils. Ms. Reynolds understands the importance of children freely exploring written language to unlock its mysteries. She enjoys watching children "play around" with print in the same way they explore with clay or blocks. These preschoolers are free to squeeze and smash clay, to stack and scatter blocks, and to scribble and scratch with writing utensils (Figure 3. 3). The preschool parent helpers are used to the idea of process being important whether or not there is any product. Parents are therefore comfortable with the lack of "correct" writing in the writing center.

The wide range of writing levels she sees demonstrated in children's paper and pencil work fascinates Ms. Reynolds. Their understanding of writing forms ranges from random scribbles and drawing, to linear markings, to letter-like forms, to actual letters. Many children write their own names with some accuracy, but most tend to turn the letters around randomly. Some children confidently experiment with letters and letter-like forms, while others limit themselves to tracing or copying correct forms, and still others apparently have no interest at all in writing yet.

What does preschoolers' writing say? Some children don't care about the answer to this question; others will decide after they are through that their scribbles look like something specific. Some will ask an adult what their writing says, and some know exactly what they want it to say. Kelly has created a combination of scribbles, drawings,

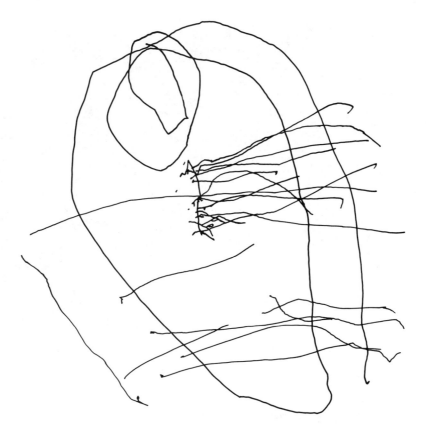

Figure 3.3　　**An example of the scribble stage of writing.**

and letter forms which she explains orally in elaborate detail. By
listening carefully, Mrs. Reynolds discovers that Kelly has a well-
developed story in mind, but simply lacks the technical skills to put it
into readable form. Mrs. Reynolds is delighted with Kelly's writing
progress. Kelly knows what writing is for, she understands that symbols are used to communicate ideas, and she has the ability to express
herself.

Tanya's writing has no plot but is limited to marks which she has
designated symbols for people and for things important to her. Tanya
is at the stage where she considers print to represent things, rather
than language. Mrs. Reynolds isn't worried since she knows this phase
to be a natural one. She is worried about Justin. His paper has only
perfectly spelled words on it since he will only copy words from around
the room. He lacks the confidence to try writing on his own. Always he
anxiously asks, "Is this right?" Mrs. Reynolds wonders if his parents'
efforts to teach him the alphabet and sounds at home cause Justin's

concern about correctness. All she knows for sure is that Justin's concern is getting in the way of his ability to explore and learn about written language.

Kindergarten Writing

Betsy's sister, Amy, just started kindergarten and has discovered that spaces appear between segments of writing and that specific kinds of marks make certain letters. Amy has noticed that some writing is made from combinations of straight lines, some from curved lines, and some from both (Figure 3.4). She has been exploring these observations during the past year, moving from making long rows of circles to creating more letter-like forms

Amy also enjoys copying actual letters and words from cereal boxes, books, and signs. She doesn't always copy letters accurately or in any specific sequence because she doesn't yet know the rules governing written language. Like most five-year olds, Amy isn't aware that the sequence of letters determines which word they represent. Nor does she realize yet that when she faces a *b* in a different direction, it becomes a *d*; or that when she makes the stem on an *n* longer, it becomes an *h*; or that when she makes the stem on a *b* go down instead of up, it becomes a *p*. Making a letter upside down or backwards doesn't seem significant to her, since she has learned that other things in her world don't change identity when she tips them over or views them from a different angle.

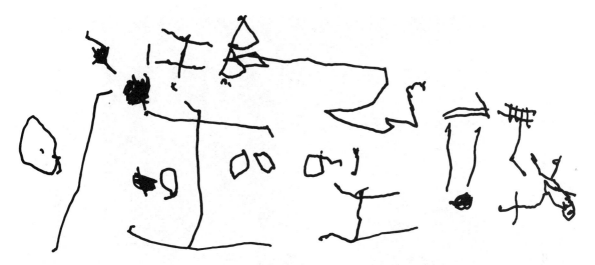

Figure 3.4   A young child's writing combining straight and curved lines.

Amy has learned the alphabet song at home, but she has not related that rhyme to the fact that writers use a limited set of letters in a variety of sequences to create a variety of meanings. She has much learn, but she is making progress. Amy isn't discouraged when she discovers that she has to revise some initial hypotheses.

At school, Mrs. Hanna encourages Amy to continue her explorations. She provides unlimited quantities of scrap paper and writing utensils. Used computer paper, ends of newsprint rolls, and backs of old memos are excellent sources of paper. Additionally, Mrs. Hanna has given each child a "journal"—a small, empty booklet with a sturdy contact paper cover bearing his or her name. Mrs. Hanna encourages the youngsters to write in these journals, even those children for whom writing is drawing or scribbling. What or how they write doesn't matter. What does matter is that they spend energy exploring writing.

Unlined paper seems best for most of Mrs. Hanna's students. They are so busy trying to make letter forms that the additional challenge of staying within lines discourages them. Most of the children prefer to use the water base marking pens with distinct lines and bright colors. Mrs. Hanna also provides pencils and crayons. The crayons are regular size rather than the fat kind often recommended for small hands, since Mrs. Hanna finds that those are actually harder for youngsters to hold than the smaller ones. She says the most important ingredient in a successful writing center seems to be her frequent presence. "Where I am physically is what children see me valuing," she explains.

Amy frequently chooses to work in the writing center. There she alternates between copying words she knows from around the room and creating new ways of putting her own ideas into print. She particularly likes to write her own name and the names of her friends. She has become skilled at making the letters in her own name and has noticed that these same letters are also in some other names. Often as she writes, she uses random assortments of letters bearing no apparent relationship to the sounds of words in the message she may "read" from her paper. Her work and that of her classmates is not just playing around prior to really learning to write; the children's exploration stages of writing are essential elements of learning to write.

Some of her classmates have not made as many discoveries about writing as Amy; some have progressed much further than she. Jeff's writing doesn't look much like letters yet, and his difficulty with copying existing print keeps him from wanting to practice. Mrs. Hanna doesn't pressure him to work at a task which he finds frustrating due to his immature coordination. Instead, she encourages him to pursue a variety of other activities which will increase that coordination. He likes to create designs with rubber bands on the geoboards, and Mrs.

Hanna suggests that he copy those designs onto forms which duplicate the pattern of the blank geoboard. By drawing lines between the dots on the paper which represent the nails on the geoboard (Figures 3.5), Jeff can practice eye-hand coordination as well as experience symbolic representation.

Christy is maturationally able to write, but past experiences have made her so concerned about spelling that she won't explore with print. When Mrs. Hanna excourages journal writing, Christy begs her teacher to tell her how to spell the words she wants to write. Mrs. Hanna's

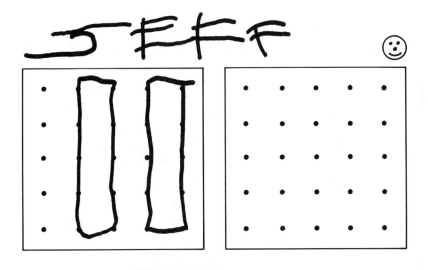

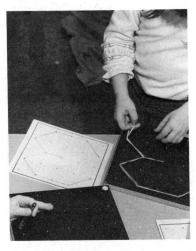

Figure 3.5 A child's drawing of his geoboard design (top) and children playing with geoboards (bottom).

sympathy for Christy's fear of failure makes her want to give in, but her concern that Christy become truly literate, not just a copier of words, makes her hesitate. Mrs. Hanna tries to show she accepts mistakes during various school activities. She calls attention to herown errors such as misplacing a book or miscounting the number of materials. She publicly admires children's writing with invented spelling. Mrs. Hanna tells all the children to spell however seems right to them, not to worry about spelling for now. She explains to youngsters that they don't have to spell right when they are learning. Gradually Christy relaxes and tries to write on her own. Mrs. Hanna feels relieved.

Writing Stages

	Characteristics
1. *Marks*	Random scribbles with no differentiation between drawing and writing.
2. *Differentiation*	Linear, uniform in size, repetitious symbolic. Looks like writing.
3. *Letter-like Forms*	Looks somewhat like letters. No more than two letters alike next to each other. Imitating process, having no understanding of details.
4. *Letter and Word forms*	Imprecise forms which adults may not easily recognize. Child explores sound/symbol relationship through invented spelling. Letter name stage of spelling comes first: letter name is used as sound, (ex: *hrh* for *church*). Single letters may represent whole words; frequently no spaces between words. Child may skip endings or use nonsense symbols when tired.
5. *Standard Spelling*	Child compares his spelling with that in books and that done by adults. Self-correction to match models results in more standard spelling.

Maria has played with print long enough to discover that a relationship exists between sounds and letters. She writes stories in which most of the major sounds are represented by a letter which has a name similar to that sound. She is in what Temple (1982) calls the *letter naming phase of writing*—a fascinating time when children spell words their own way to create intricate stories which only they or an expert in early spelling can read. For instance the word *China* would probably be spelled with an *H* to represent the *ch* sound, since the *ch* sound is heard when we say the letter name *H*. As children begin this stage, adults find their writing difficult to read since children typically represent a word or each syllable with only one or two letters—usually the beginning sound and another prominent one (Figure 3.6). Sometimes too, youngsters will represent the initial sound with an appropriate letter and fill out the rest of the word with a random assortment of letters making it long enough to look like a word (Temple et al., 1982). Many children believe that a word for something or someone big must be long and a word for something small should be short (Ferreiro and Teberosky, 1982).

Larry has mastered the distinguishing characteristics of letters but has only a vague awareness of a symbol-sound relationship. He has figured out that writing uses a few characters over and over again, and he may have noticed that only ten basic shapes are used to make these fifty-two letter forms which represent the twenty-six letters. His writing conforms to standard writing as it is a series of letters with not more than two alike adjacent to one another. As we view his work, it looks so much like adult writing that we might think it says something. How-

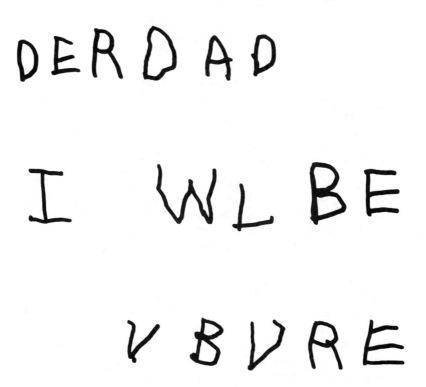

Figure 3.6　　An example of writing where the word *the* is represented by only one letter, *v*. ("Dear Dad, I will be [in] the bathroom.)

ever, the groups of letters do not make words. Larry's written work is reminiscent of Betsy's talking at the stage when she could string together random speech sounds using actual language intonations, and we would be fooled into listening carefully, trying to pick out words that weren't there. Larry's concept of the relationship between letters and sounds hasn't reached the point where he knows that each sound is to be represented by a letter. Sometimes he represents a word with one letter; sometimes he represents syllables with one letter. He must continue working before he can select appropriate letters for the sounds he hears, and then work some more before he can master standard spelling conventions plus the many exceptions to the rules.

Maria, Amy, and Larry are all at a point where they can profit from further examination of written words. Mrs. Hanna knows that children find the concept of individual words difficult. To help them, Mrs. Hanna copies a sentence from a book a child knows well or from a child's dictation onto tagboard strips. Today she uses sentences from Bill Martin Jr.'s *Brown Bear* book (1970) which these three children know well. The entire story has been displayed for a while on a wall chart, with color-coded picture clues to help children read the story. Additionally, each child has had an opportunity to illustrate his own book with a different segment of the story copied onto each page. Together Mrs. Hanna and the three children read a sentence written on a strip. Then they take turns cutting individual words off an identical strip. As they cut off each word, the children read the remaining part of the sentence to emphasize the absence of that word. After she gets them started on this activity, Mrs. Hanna works with another group of children, leaving Amy, Maria, and Larry to reconstruct the sentences by matching them with them intact identical strips. Amy puts cut-apart words directly on top of the matching words, but Maria prefers the increased challenge of lining up the words beside the matching sentence. Larry takes a set of words over to the classroom computer, finds the letters on the keyboard, and copies the sentence onto the monitor.

Mrs. Hanna knows that all these children are making their own best progress. She plans specific activities to assist them to discover and develop concepts for which they are ready. The activities always emphasize the children's own experiences and discoveries since Mrs. Hanna believes this approach is the only effective way for her students to learn. In her planning, Mrs. Hanna remembers that learning to write must begin with a child understanding the nature of writing, progress to a child having knowledge of the distinguishing features of writing, and finally result in a child having a more and more refined ability to match those features to the accepted way of writing the message he wishes to convey. This whole-to-part sequence conforms to the pattern of how children learn to speak correctly, gradually figuring out gram-

mar rules for themselves as they compare their own speech to that of adults.

We can observe this sequence of understanding the whole and then its parts in children's spontaneous learning. Children first perceive the gross aspects and gradually refine their understandings. For example, the toddler first labels all wheeled vehicles *car* and later refines the categories to include trucks, buses, and vans. In order to preserve this natural sequence for children, Mrs. Hanna avoids trying to teach them about letter sounds before their learning has reached that point. Even then, she knows better than to teach by telling. Instead, she provides experiences and activities through which children can discover letter-sound relationships and the many exceptions to those relationships.

First Grade Writing

Mrs. Thomas believes children should continue these types of writing and print awareness experiences in first grade. She continues to provide materials and opportunity for free exploration with writing; she continues to take dictation from children; she continues the practice of showing children her own use of writing; and of course, she continues to read to them. Mrs. Thomas extends these activities as the children's understandings of writing and symbolic representation become more sophisticated.

During first grade most of Mrs. Thomas's students will become writers. Although their ability to write according to standard conventions will vary greatly, all children in Mrs. Thomas's class come to consider themselves authors (Figure 3.7). They all write and all are encouraged to read what they have written to their classmates. Their

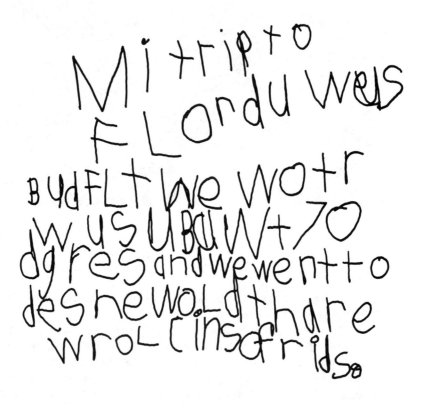

Figure 3.7   A child's story about her vacation. ("My trip to Florida was beautiful. We [went to the] water. [It] was about 70 degrees, and we went to Disney World. There were lines of rides.")

Figure 3.8   Invented spelling using a fairy tale format.
To be read from bottom to top. (Once upon a time. There
lived a wolf. Who loved [to] eat little girls.)

desire to have others read their writing becomes a major impetus to learn more about spelling and punctuation.

The content of what children write in this classroom is amazing. Even children who rely on pictures and use few words have wonderful stories to tell. Mrs. Thomas sees a direct relationship between the literature she shares with her students and the type of writing they do (Figure 3.8). From their knowledge of fairy tales, these children have a useful model of story structure, and many of their stories start with *Wuzupnatm.*

From other stories they gain favorite characters to write about, such as Curious George. From still others they learn how to use direct dialogue or a narrative form. Television also serves as an inspiration for children's writing. Mrs. Thomas allows children to write about whatever interests them, even if it is a Saturday morning cartoon character or plot.

Children seem to inspire one another in their writing. We can observe this as Heidi and Becky discuss their writing, sharing ideas and viewpoints. Mrs. Thomas is confident their writing will be better for the interaction. Sometimes the interaction itself is the content of writing, as when someone started a "love note" fad. From this event Mrs. Thomas got the idea of encouraging note writing between children. At Christmas time, she hung up construction paper Christmas stockings for each child. She suggested students might have fun putting notes in a friend's stocking. She says, "They went wild with writing."

Many of her students are trying to match the sounds of their language with the letters to write it. Some children are just beginning to explore this concept, like Larry in the kindergarten class. Many are working at the letter-naming level, like Maria in the kindergarten class. Some have made the discovery that the names of letters and their sounds aren't always the same. Whatever their level, Mrs. Thomas values and encourages their attempts without criticism of the product. She has found that writing in her own journal during daily journal writing time not only provides a model of adults-as-writers, but also keeps children from asking her how to spell words. She can more easily encourage students to construct their own spelling if she shows she is too busy writing to spell for them.

These children are working on the immense complexity of the sound-symbol relationships in the English language. They will have to grapple with the fact of silent letters as markers as in *light* and *bite*, the use of different letters and combinations for the same sound as in *just*, and *giant*, the use of the same letter for different sounds as in *cat* and *city*, and a wide variety of confusions over the irregularity of our language spelling (Figure 3.9).

Although some spellings defy categorization and have to be memorized, most of the English sound-symbol system follows certain principles which children can discover intuitively as they read and write. Since most adults have an intuitive rather than a conscious knowledge of the system, they find explaining the system difficult. If adults are inhibited from attempting such explanations, their hesitancy is for the best, since such explanations may confuse children and deprive them of the ability to figure out spellings for themselves and truly learn what they need to know.

Tyler is grappling with this confusion in a systematic way. He carefully says each word several times as he listens for the sounds to write down. When he writes that he wants to *jriv* a car, Mrs. Thomas compliments him on hearing the sounds in the word *drive*. If the child asks, she may acknowledge that the word isn't really spelled that way, but she will admire Tyler's spelling as a "good" way to spell. Mrs. Thomas frees children to write and explore writing by not insisting that they spell words correctly at this point. She makes a distinction between

Jessica   5-3-8

               I Want too go Ewt too Plaey. Ewt side   And

Plae All Day.

Jessica 5-8-85

Figure 3.9   A child's experimentation with spelling irregularities.

the "right" way to spell and a "good" way to spell. When Tyler uses his best knowledge of sounds and the letters that represent them to spell a word, his efforts constitute a good way to spell. His teacher congratulates him for his efforts, and she focuses his attention on the message of the writing rather than the spelling. This is exactly how adults encourage children to learn oral language; adults respond to the content of what children say rather than the errors they may make in saying it. If youngsters had their babytalk and incomplete or ungrammatical sentences corrected every time they spoke, they probably wouldn't talk very often—or make much progress in speech.

This teacher knows that invented spelling does not represent mistakes which she should merely tolerate or ignore for fear of discouraging a child's efforts. Invented spelling serves as an important stage in the process of deciphering the sound-symbol system of written language. Mrs. Thomas explains to parents and administrators that this active exploration of the system will enable children to construct a personally meaningful and useful set of encoding/decoding rules. She explains that this is the best way for youngsters to learn phonics and other word recognition skills (Willert and Kamii, 1985).

Children do make progress in standard spelling through their observation of print, through discussions with peers about how to spell, and through Mrs. Thomas's assistance (Figure 3.10). Children who write tend to naturally compare their spellings of words with spellings in books and elsewhere, gradually revising their own spelling until it conforms to what they see. In this classroom they make faster progress because their teacher encourages them to collaborate on spelling while they write; several children who are writing at the same table will discuss and compare ideas about how to spell any word in question. The process of explaining their own rationale for spelling a certain way, coupled with the process of considering and accepting or refuting a classmate's differing ideas, greatly enhances children's understand-

```
                           MY  TRIP


Neal  Johnson        5-7-85



I  lik  to  go  on  a  trip  and  it  is  fun  I  rod  a  erplan  it  is  fun  to

ride  it  .  I  frup  win  I  was  slepen.  I  wit  to  chrch  teh  end.
```

Figure 3.10   An example of transitional (invented to standard) spelling. (I like to go on a trip and it is fun. I rode a airplane. It is fun to ride it. I threw up when I was sleeping. I went to church. The end.)

ings about spelling (Kamii and Randazzo, 1985). Additionally, Mrs. Thomas assists her students in focusing on the correct spellings of words which are important to them individually and used frequently in their own writing or dictation. She helps each child create a "word bank" into which they deposit cards with the correct spellings of certain words. She helps children make file boxes for their word banks from milk cartons. Alphabetical dividers made for such boxes help children organize their words by beginning letter. Only words which a child can read belong in that child's word bank.

Suppose Mrs. Thomas wrote the correct spelling of *drive* for Tyler, and he filed it in his word bank under *D*. This wouldn't do him much good unless he already knew that the word started with a *D* rather than a *J*. However, beginning sounds are the easiest for children to hear, and this system does work for most words, allowing children to look up correct spellings for frequently used words. Children tend to want to spell words correctly so they quickly learn standard spellings for words they often write. For a time, they will use some spelling principles incorrectly (Figure 3.11), much as they overregularized grammar rules when learning to speak. However, they will sort these out with practice.

In addition to learning the twenty-six letters and the forty-four sounds represented by those letters, children must learn the mechanics of writing. Mrs. Thomas often notes with amazement how perfectly some of her students can write in mirror images. Mirror image writing would be difficult for her to do, but if a first grader accidentally starts on the right hand side of the paper, that child may easily write everything exactly backwards. So Mrs. Thomas carefully points out where on the page writing and print begins, and she points out the return to the left side after coming to the end on the right. Most of her first graders have internalized this guideline, but sometimes she finds a child who will come to the end of the page and write down the side. Most of her first graders also are now able to deal with the concept of negative space between words, but she must still remind a few and help others with activities similar to the cut-apart sentence exercise which Mrs. Hanna did with Amy, Maria, and Larry. Some children initially use periods as markers between words. Mrs. Thomas must help her

```
I like submrense becuse I think they are neat.

I like korvets becuse I think ther awesome.

They are exulint.
```

Figure 3.11   **Invented spelling sample.**

students deal with punctuation too, but for now most of them aren't ready to do more than just notice it.

Mrs. Thomas believes that children will learn phonics principles much more effectively through writing to express their ideas than through drill on isolated sounds. They will learn spelling, handwriting, and even punctuation as they strive to make their writing understandable to others. Like Mrs. Hanna, Mrs. Thomas attempts to make learning in her classroom follow the natural pattern of learning. Therefore, she too assists children in understanding the whole before the parts of a concept. The biggest and most important academic idea that she wants her students to learn is that writing and reading can be useful communication tools and satisfying activities. Even more important to her is that each child learn to believe in his or her own ability to be successful with these skills.

Mrs. Thomas has to defend these beliefs most vigorously when teaching children whose homes didn't provide all that Betsy's and Amy's home did. Children who lack basic understandings about print due to insufficient background experiences are often given intensive doses of information to be learned by rote. Some educators, in their eagerness to help those youngsters catch up, seem to hope that knowledge can somehow be "injected" as a time saving tactic. Yet, when teachers use this short-cut approach, they doubly deprive the young-

sters who previously missed out on important literacy socialization experiences. These youngsters missed out at home, and then they miss out again at school when they are not allowed the time and experiences to internalize understandings about written language. Ironically, those children who least need free time to explore print, those who already understand it, are more likely to be allowed the freedom to continue their explorations. Those who most need that opportunity are too often kept busy with remedial drill (Dyson, 1984). Mrs. Thomas continues to work at counteracting this practice. She strives to allow each child the necessary experiences for building firm foundations of understanding.

LEARNING TO READ THROUGH DICTATION

Even before children can independently write anything readable, they can have the satisfaction of seeing their ideas written down. Any child that can talk can dictate thoughts for someone else to transcribe. When we take dictation for children, we assist growth in all areas of the language arts: We encourage oral language, we model written language, and we provide material to develop reading enjoyment and skill. Now we will examine how parents and teachers should take dictation, and why both the process and the product are important for helping a child learn to read.

The Dictation Process in a Kindergarten

In preparation for a language experience writing session, Mrs. Hanna has assisted the children in her kindergarten class to make initial choices among several learning activities available today. With the other students constructively involved in their chosen activities, Mrs. Hanna feels free to concentrate on a group of five children seated at a table with her. She first gets them talking about a topic which interests them: what each will dress up as for Halloween.

Zachary is planning to be a space man, Jennifer describes how her mother is making a princess costume, and Billy explains how he is going to make himself look like a monster. After encouraging a spirited discussion by asking leading questions, Mrs. Hanna gives each child a piece of paper. She suggests that they either cut out and paste on a picture of what they want to be or draw a picture. In addition to providing marking pens and crayons, Mrs. Hanna gets out a stack of pages torn from magazines with pictures showing possible costume options. She wants to give each child the choice between drawing or choosing a realistic picture since few can draw anything recognizable. She carefully organizes the activity so she won't set the children up for failure.

Dictation Procedure

1. Encourage discussion to formulate ideas first.
2. Write exactly what the child says.
   Accept run-on sentences.
   Accept ungrammatical sentences.
   Do correct for mispronunciations.
3. Make sure the child can see you write.
   Be sure your hand is not in the child's way.
   Be sure the paper is in front of the child.
4. Write legibly and form letters consistently.
5. Read dictation back to child when finished.
   Run your hand under words as you read.
6. Encourage child to take the completed transcript to another adult to read.

Mrs. Hanna tries to help children plan space on their page to accommodate both writing and an illustration. Today, she suggests folding the paper and using the upper portion for the picture while saving the lower portion for the writing. Zachary quickly finds a picture of a space man to paste on his paper; now he is ready to tell his teacher what to write below the picture. Mrs. Hanna moves her chair beside Zachary. Since she is right handed, she makes sure to sit on his right so that her hand won't be in the way of his seeing what she is writing. She leaves the paper in front of the child and reaches over in front of him to do the writing so that he can see exactly how she holds the pencil, how she forms the letters, and where on the page she begins writing. As she makes these preparations, she asks Zachary what he wants to say about his Halloween costume. He responds, "I'm a space-man, and I got a rocket." Mrs. Hanna writes his exact words as he watches with interest.

Mrs. Hanna says the words as she writes them. As she is ready to write *spaceman*, Zachary proudly volunteers the information that it starts with an *s*. Mrs. Hanna makes a mental note of Zachary's progress but doesn't stop the dictation since her main purpose is to get Zachary's ideas written down. She wants to focus on the meaning of the words rather than the specifics of how to write them for now. However, she carefully forms each letter in a consistent manner since she knows that kindergarteners are still sorting out which variations in letter forms are significant differences.

As a final step, Zachary hears his whole sentence read to him. He nods his head, yes, that is what he said. Now he looks over and admires Billy's scary monster drawn in bold green and black scribbles. Zachary and two other children waiting their turn to dictate watch as Mrs.

Hanna moves beside Billy and writes down what he says about his Halloween costume. When Jennifer has her turn, Zachary notices that she and Billy both have the word *I* on their page, just as he does. He is excited because he can read this word.

Mrs. Hanna posts the five Halloween costume papers completed today on a bulletin board for everyone to read. By the end of the week, the entire class has papers hanging there. The children enjoy reading names and pictures, reading from their own papers to each other, and discovering words that are the same. On Friday, Mrs. Hanna takes the papers down and lets children take them home to read with their families; but first she makes copies of them to keep at school for instructional purposes. She assembles these into a book by stapling a construction paper cover on the front and back and reinforcing the stapled side with library tape to help the book withstand many readings. Then she writes the title, "Our Halloween Costumes." She places this book in the library nook so children may read it over and over.

The Halloween book is a group book which resulted from teacher planned dictation sessions. This is just one type of dictation process. Mrs. Hanna regularly involves her students with many other types of language experience processes. The Halloween costume book sparked several Halloween, scary stories, some which children dictated and some which they wrote independently. Mrs. Hanna tries to involve each child in dictation at least three times a week, if not daily.

Sometimes Mrs. Hanna experiences difficulty finding enough time to complete all dictations herself and gets help from parent volunteers and older children she has trained to take dictation. As much as she values long and involved stories, Mrs. Hanna cannot give each child unlimited attention; volunteer assistants are especially helpful for finishing long dictation processes when the teacher's attention is called elsewhere. If the topic allows, Mrs. Hanna may ask a child to limit dictation to one or two main points (Figure 3.12). This helps children practice organizing ideas as well as helping their stories conform to the time available.

Dictation in a Preschool

Ms. Reynolds also places great value on dictation as part of the print-rich environment in her preschool program. As we walk into her classroom, we see her engrossed in conversation with Tanya in the art area. Apparently Tanya has spent a great deal of energy creating a collage this morning and wants Ms. Reynolds to make a sign describing it. Ms. Reynolds writes on a piece of tagboard as Tanya tells her about the different items she has glued onto her collage. As Ms. Reynolds writes, Tanya watches, stopping her narrative occasionally to allow the writing to catch up. Although the end result is a giant run-on sentence with minor grammatical errors, Tanya grins proudly when she hears her words read back from the paper.

After Ms. Reynolds moves on to assist other children, Tanya reads the sign from memory several times to herself. Then she goes to get her friend, Justin, so she can read it to him. Still intrigued with the written form of her own speech, she gets several color crayons and traces over the letter forms which Ms. Reynolds wrote. Colorful wavy lines now cover the original writing. The dictation is difficult to read, but Tanya thinks it's beautiful.

While Tanya makes her sign colorful, Ms. Reynolds responds to a request to get the bunny out of his cage. She stays with the youngsters who are petting him and responds to questions and comments about the rabbit. As the discussion focuses on proper ways to treat the classroom pet, she suggests that the children make a sign by the cage about how to treat bunnies. The four youngsters seem enthusiastic, so Ms. Reynolds quickly gets a portable easel with chart paper already on

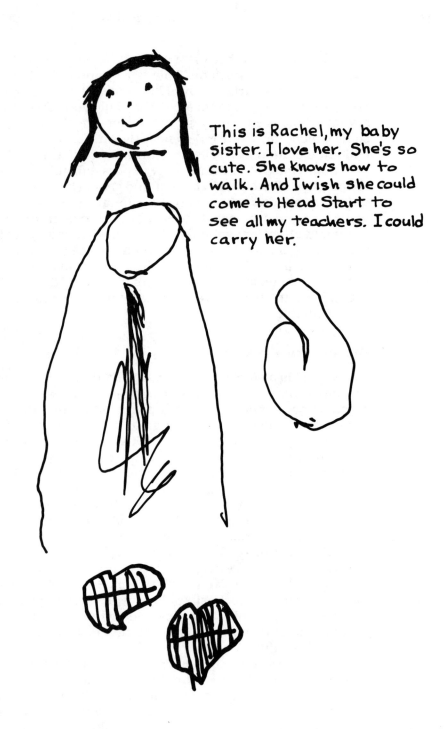

This is Rachel, my baby sister. I love her. She's so cute. She knows how to walk. And I wish she could come to Head Start to see all my teachers. I could carry her.

Figure 3.12   An example of a child's dictation.

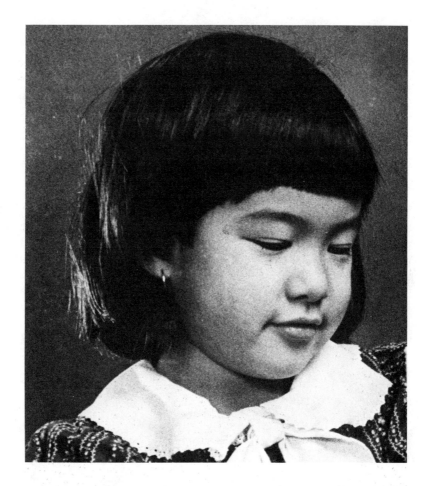

it. She writes with a marking pen instead of a pencil so that the writing will be visible to the group.

Each child contributes a rule of personal importance. Kelly says, "Don't touch his nose." Betsy says, "Don't squeeze him." Timmy adds, "Just feed him lettuce." Caleb warns, "He might poop on you." All of these are written down just as stated by the children. Then they all read them together as Ms. Reynolds moves her hand under each line of print. The children and Ms. Reynolds carefully hang the new sign on the wall beside the rabbit cage, and all the authors importantly point it out to other children in the class.

When Ms. Reynolds composes her monthly newsletter for parents, she quotes these and several other compositions in describing class activities. She credits the authors, who then experience a wider audience and a different printed form of their thoughts. Although neither the individual collage description or the small group rabbit rules were preplanned as language experience lessons, Ms. Reynolds stays receptive to opportunities for children to translate their experiences into oral and then written language. A classroom environment which encourages this type of activity results in frequent spontaneous requests by children for adults to take their dictation (Figure 3.13).

The four-year olds as a group are more interested in art project captions and story dictation than the three-year olds. Some children dictate lengthy descriptions or stories which Ms. Reynolds makes into small books with construction paper covers for the reading corner. Ms. Reynolds also places books and stories of children's drawings and written attempts done without adult assistance in the class library. Children who have authored a book in the reading corner enjoy inviting friends over and reading their book to them. Generally the reading consists of a remembered version of the dictation or writing, but some children recognize a few specific words in their stories. Whether they are reading from memory or from letter cues, they are experiencing that their ideas can be put into writing and can be read. As children see books dictated by other children, they often discover that some of the

It's a dragon.
I did a dragon.
All by myself.
Actually, it's a horse.

Figure 3.13   A child's spontaneous drawing and dictation about what he drew.

same words are in their own and their friend's book. Sometimes they can then read words from someone else's book.

When writing with four-year olds, Ms. Reynolds often mentions details such as the shape of a letter, the fact that a word starts like a child's name, or where on the page she begins writing. Although she points out the spaces left between words, four-year olds find the idea of negative space an abstract concept, difficult to grasp. Ms. Reynolds doesn't expect children to master any of these concepts yet; she merely helps them begin to take notice. She knows that she cannot speed conceptual learning; it has to come from experiences which assist children in the development of hypotheses—hypotheses which will be challenged, discarded, and replaced through further experience. Writing with adult assistance helps children who cannot yet write something readable to see themselves as writers, causes them to notice more, and, therefore, helps them learn more about how writing is done (Smith, 1983).

First Grade Language Experience Writing

Mrs. Thomas's first graders explore still other versions of language experience lessons. Mrs. Thomas knows that meaningful content is essential to language arts skill development. Therefore, she manages to integrate social studies, science, art, and music as well as literature into her morning schedule of language arts lessons. Several youngsters are working on their contributions to a class book on the subject, "Our Community." Each has selected a picture of a personally important or beautiful place around the town from an assortment of chamber of commerce brochures and picture postcards. This activity culminates in a social studies unit about the community. The children have taken field trips to points of interest, met the mayor and the police chief, and discussed local highlights with the chamber of commerce director. Children have enjoyed oral language and dramatic play opportunities which will assist them in deriving personal meaning from these experiences. Now as they dictate their thoughts for the class book, Mrs. Thomas hopes that the children will show a greater awareness and understanding of the subject.

Tyler has chosen a picture of the nearby ski area and, as he plans what he wants to say about it, he draws a picture of himself on the page next to where he pasted the picture. Although Tyler often writes for himself with invented spelling, today he requests teacher help and prefers to dictate his message. Mrs. Thomas notices how dictation experiences and invented spelling practice work together to help children understand written language. Some children choose to dictate their book contributions and others prefer to write their own. Both types of writing constantly occur in her classroom.

Contributions to the book range from simple statements about the picture—"This is my park," to sophisticated, environmentally aware analyses—"I like this town because it has lots of parks and places where people can be in nature." Some children have so much to say that the teacher must write on the back of the page. Mrs. Thomas must prompt others to respond even with a sentence fragment to a question of what they like about their town. At the end of the lesson, however, each child will have shared authorship in the class book and feel competent with this approach.

Meanwhile, David has signed up for an individual conference with Mrs. Thomas. As soon as she gets a free minute, Mrs. Thomas goes to see what he wants to discuss. David wants help with a long story he has been writing. Having written two pages using invented spelling, he is growing weary of the effort involved in sounding out each word, figuring out which letters might correspond to those sounds, and then forming all those letters. Still eager to finish getting his ideas down on paper, David asks to dictate the rest to Mrs. Thomas. David's level of sound-symbol understanding guides Mrs. Thomas as she requests David's involvement in spelling the words. However, as always, Mrs. Thomas's main purpose in taking dictation is to get the communication onto paper. This being David's intent too, he feels delighted with the finished product. Mrs. Thomas helps him make a cover for his book with the title and author printed boldly onto the wallpaper sample he has selected for the covering. After David has practiced reading his story aloud, Mrs. Thomas arranges for him to go to the kindergarten and read it to children there. David feels proud of his work.

Both teacher-initiated and child-initiated writing and dictation are vital elements of this first grade program. They provide process as well as content for beginning reading (Figure 3.14).

SPECIFIC READING SKILLS LEARNED

Have you been thinking about what these children are learning through the various writing activities and language experience lessons previously described? Just as we cannot link any of the procedures to one specific grade level, we cannot link any of the reading and writing skills to one grade level. As when children learn to talk or to write, they progress from the whole to the part as they learn to read. They address the entire scope of language arts at all times, with each child delving into more detail as that individual better understands the total concepts involved. The children described earlier were working at their own level to learn sight words, phonics, word analysis, context clue use, and the mechanics of writing and reading. At the same time they were improving their ability to give and receive oral communication, to gain satisfaction from literature, to understand the purpose of written language, and to become aware of the interrelationships among these activities.

Most importantly, they were becoming truly literate: a process in which reading involves *interacting* with the thoughts someone else has expressed in writing, in which writing is perceived as recording one's own thoughts, and in which thinking is basic. In the classrooms described, the teachers do not define reading as saying words, no matter how accurately or with how much expression. These teachers are so committed to the concept of reading as an active rather than a passive process that they are not satisfied with readers who merely repeat facts from what they read and attain good literal comprehension scores. These teachers encourage the critical thinking and reading

Papa went and got some halibut from his friends. We ate it. When we were done we put the tail and head on our compost. This bear smelled it and papa threw things at it but he wouldn't go away. The neighbor came and gave Larry a rifle and he shot the bear right between the eyes. The neighbor went home and the bear was dead.

Figure 3.14 An example of a child-initiated dictation.

between the lines that results from interaction with print. They want children to question and to criticize, to exclaim and to cry; they want children to be *involved* with reading.

However, teachers usually have a responsibility to keep track of what children have learned and what they yet need to learn according to given lists and charts. Though the teacher may accept the concept of a natural and gradual refinement of the language skills which the child discovers to be important and useful, she still feels pressure for account-ability, to be able to document exactly what the child is learning and when and how the child learns. Although we know that these bits and pieces do not add up to literacy, we must live in the imperfect, real world. Therefore, let's analyze the writing and dictation process and follow-up activities in terms of specific skill learning.

Sight Words

Those instantly recognizable words, that no longer require effort from a child, stand out as important for beginning reading. They provide youngsters success in their reading efforts, and they provide a starting point for learning phonics and word analysis skills. Children learn most words through repeated exposure to them while reading various materials. Did you notice in the previous descriptions of dictation how children would recognize frequently used words and delight in pointing them out? These dictations provide an excellent way for children to develop a beginning sight word vocabulary. Signs, labels, name tags, and other print in the environment will add to it. As children become aware of and interested in print, they automatically begin to learn some of the words around them which have personal meaning.

When children's own words about something important to them are written down, they can read those words. This reading may be memorized reading at first, but through matching print with memorized words, children come to recognize how those words look. Zachary spontaneously pointed out the word *I* in his and his friends' sentences, but for children who do not do this naturally, Mrs. Hanna calls their attention to identical words. Sometimes she will take dictation with a carbon and give the carbon copy to the child later for an activity such as finding all the words that say *and*. She much prefers that children who require skill building activities do them with materials which provide a context for the child, rather than with workbook drill. Mrs. Hanna and Mrs. Thomas strongly oppose having children learn isolated words. They insist that words have no meaning without context rele-vant to the child's experience, and that reading must involve getting meaning from written words.

Children's own compositions serve as perfect beginning reading materials since they meet the criteria which basal readers constantly strive for unsuccessfully: compatibility with the language of the child and relevance to the experience of the child. Children's own dictation and writing is their language and it is their experience. Children most easily read and take pleasure in reading what they have dictated.

Mrs. Thomas frequently compares her experiences teaching with basal readers to teaching with children's compositions and child-selected reading. She thinks of one reading lesson when several of the children in the group had been involved in dramatic play about deep sea diving just before reading time. They came to the group still in costume and still in animated discussion. She had to spend a great deal of energy to get even minimal attention for a story in the reader about a chameleon and the letter carrier who helps a boy find him. Few of her students had ever seen a chameleon, and in their experience letter carriers didn't walk around a neighborhood carrying a bag on their shoulders. Most importantly, chameleons weren't on their minds at the moment: diving was.

Now Mrs. Thomas doesn't waste energy fighting children's interests; she uses these interests as teaching vehicles. Children can learn the same skills from most reading materials, but they learn better when they are interested. She would now encourage further discussion about diving among those interested and suggest a trip to the library to look up information. She could probably also inspire them to write or dictate stories about diving procedures or make-believe diving adventures. The children involved could then read their stories to classmates and possibly to other classes. Perhaps a book about diving would result. Certainly, a more valuable learning experience would result.

Once children can read their own compositions, they can read parts of other written materials. They begin reading their peers' writings and commercially published books. Their sight word vocabulary is now extensive, and to the children's dismay, many of the words look so much alike that they cause confusion. All those words that start with *wh: what, where, when, why,* and *who*; and those other ones that start with *th: then, there, they, those,* and *them* can slow reading progress. The children have learned these words in a meaningful context, but now they need to develop rapid, rote memory to distinguish between them. Mrs. Thomas is willing for children to work with isolated words for drill under these circumstances. She has created a type of bingo game for practicing quick identification of these words. A fifth grader comes to the first grade classroom several times a week to play this type of game with the first graders who are having difficulty with those abstract *wh* and *th* words.

Some teachers feel more comfortable if they compare their students' sight word vocabulary against a scientifically developed list of frequently used words. Mrs. Thomas wouldn't ask any child to read from a word list since lists of words have no meaning, but her own records do compare each child's reading and understanding vocabulary of words in context with the school district grade level list. She doesn't do this by limiting children's reading to vocabulary-controlled and graded reading books. She knows that appropriate reading materials must have personal meaning and interest for the reader.

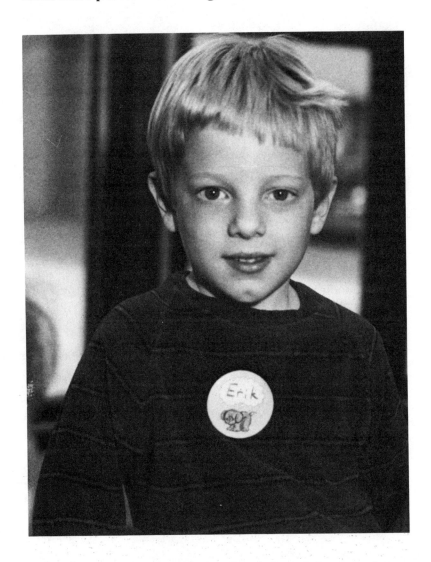

One isolated word does have meaning and children learn it by itself. That word is the child's name and is generally the first sight word a child learns. Most children also quickly learn to read the names of other children in their classroom if name labels are used frequently for attendance, chore assignments, and identification of work and possessions. This learning of names provides a store of knowledge for comparisons with new words encountered. For instance, when Larry dictates a story about his beach trip, he can be helped to notice that *shell* begins like his friend Shawn's name. This contributes both to recognizing a new sight word and to an understanding of the nature of sound-symbol relationships, better known as phonics.

Phonics

Mrs. Thomas doesn't take part in any arguments over whether or not to teach phonics. She thinks it is silly to suggest that children will learn to read by learning the sounds of the letters, but she thinks it is just as silly to suggest not helping them acquire this useful tool. Mrs. Thomas has a clear idea of the role of phonics in learning to read: definitely a supporting role and not the lead. Mrs. Hanna agrees and explains to concerned parents that children learn phonics from reading and writing, not reading and writing from phonics. This approach supports the whole-to-part philosophy of learning that Ms. Reynolds describes to parents who worry that their preschool children aren't getting specific academic background.

All three of these teachers help their students learn about phonics. They provide help at the appropriate level for each child, and they use the mode of assisting personal discovery—always within the context of meaningful words and sentences. For many of Ms. Reynolds' preschoolers, phonics awareness remains at the stage of discovering that print, not pictures, tell the stories in the books she reads to them. Other children have discovered the print and show their interest through repeated questions of, "What does it say?"

Although Ms. Reynolds thinks she would be wasting preschooler's precious time by drilling on letters and sounds, she always responds to children's questions about letters. She believes that information in response to questions insures that the child is ready for the information and also insures that the information will have some personal meaning to that child. She is careful not to tell more then the child wants to know.

Ms. Reynolds understands that children need help to develop the concept of separate words before they can hope to decipher phonics principles. Since no spaces exist between spoken words, children tend to lump together phrases such as "Once-upon-a-time" and consider them as words. When they find out their understanding isn't correct, they often over-correct and think that each distinct sound in a word makes up a separate word. Having these confusions, children experience difficulty in matching oral and written versions of language (Clay, 1975). Until this confusion clears up, children cannot progress in discovering sound-symbol relationships. Ms. Reynolds carefully says each word as she writes it during dictation, and she leaves distinct spaces between words. Later, when she and the child read back what was written, she runs her hand along under each word as they read it. Through these kinds of experiences, repeated over and over, children gradually formulate the basic concepts upon which to base understandings of phonics and other word recognition tools.

When she takes dictation from her preschoolers, (Figure 3.15) Ms. Reynolds also may comment about the letters she writes, such as, "This word starts with the same letter as your name." With the occasional child who shows readiness through interest, she will follow the dictation process with a game of finding words in the dictated piece that start with other letters that the youngster knows. Many preschoolers are not able to distinguish between the letters, have only a general idea of acceptable letter forms, and have just a vague understanding that letters represent language. Ms. Reynolds knows that with continued

"I live at my house."

Figure 3.15   A preschooler's picture and short dictation.

exposure to reading and writing situations, these children will refine those understandings and become literate. She doesn't try to rush them past their discovery of foundational concepts and into specifics of letter names and sounds. She certainly doesn't use phonics work sheets or flash cards. She wants them to build on firm foundations for a lifetime of rewarding reading.

Mrs. Hanna also tries not to move too quickly into specifics since many kindergarteners are still building their personal foundations of understanding about written language. Most have learned the names of the letters and can recognize them in both capital and lower case form because they have watched television shows having that emphasis. Mrs. Hanna is grateful that parents no longer think they must teach their children only capital letters. What problems that idea caused: she would write a child's name in lower case except for the first letter, and the child would protest, "That's not my name!" Now that most parents realize children need exposure to the most common forms of letters for recognizing them in books and magazines, few children arrive in kindergarten knowing only capitals.

Although most of her students have learned letter names, few have progressed beyond letter names as sounds. Since many letter sounds are the same or similar to their names, this is a good start. When she takes dictation, Mrs. Hanna often asks children to contribute the starting letter of words which begin with one of these easier sounds. Since children's comments during dictation are not restricted to answering the teacher's questions, Mrs. Hanna learns about children's perceptions of letters and sounds from their comments. She learns even more from analyzing their invented spelling strategies. Such information guides her in planning follow-up activities appropriate for each youngster.

Letters which sound like their names:
B, P, F, V, M, N, T, D, S, K, J, L, R

Amy demonstrates that she is moving beyond letter names as sounds by saying, "I know what that word starts with! It starts with *Y*!" as Mrs. Hanna prepares to write what Amy is telling her about what she did *yesterday.* Now her teacher knows to involve Amy in discussions about letters which do not make their name sound, but which are nevertheless regular enough in the sounds they represent to be fairly easily learned. Amy progressed to this point through continued exposure to correct spelling in books and on signs, rather than through direct instruction in these letter sounds. When she discovers for herself that the conventions of her language indicate a certain symbol for a certain sound, she truly knows the rule. If she hadn't spontaneously discovered the principle, Mrs. Hanna eventually would have begun calling it to her attention casually during dictation until she did discover it. Mrs. Hanna knows that the best way of teaching phonics is through repeated experience with written forms of language meaningful to the child. She knows that isolating the sounds from words and meaning in workbook or flashcard drill is counterproductive for most kindergarteners (Willert and Kamii, 1985).

Apparently some children thrive on worksheet phonics drill. Doesn't this refute the theory that such teaching procedures are inappropriate? Actually, the fact that some children are able to make sense of those pieces of information about the sound-symbol system testifies to the effectiveness of the natural learning approach, not the workbook approach. Those who succeed with the phonics drill are those who have experienced reading and writing as part of their daily environment; they have learned on their own through exploration and discovery the basic premises of our written language. For those children, the specific information about letters and sounds has attained a meaningful context (Dyson, 1984). Probably, given a continued print rich environment and continued literacy socialization, these youngsters would have conducted their own exploration of the world of literacy and discovered the phonics principles independently. Piaget's work repeatedly tells us that knowledge children construct for themselves is that which they truly know.

As Mrs. Hanna encourages her class to discover print for themselves, most of her kindergarteners progress to the point of recognizing the regular consonant sounds at least in the beginning and ends of words; some students recognize the more prominent sounds in the middle of words too. The long vowel sounds are easy since they follow that wonderful rule of having the same name and sound. Short vowel sounds are another matter, however. Mrs. Hanna thinks confusing kindergarteners with this mass of irregularity and indistict sounds is cruel. Since vowels in unaccented syllables all have basically the same *schwa* sound, knowing the vowel that appears in which word is really a matter of memory through familiarity rather than of learning rules. Mrs. Hanna prefers to allow children to take their time with this frustrating aspect of phonics and considers it inappropriate for the kindergarten curriculum.

Even most of Mrs. Thomas's first graders aren't ready for short vowel sounds. Since children use many other word recognition skills besides phonics, Mrs. Thomas doesn't find it necessary for her students to know every sound in a word in order to be successful readers. Yet, she assists her students in extending their understandings of phonics principles and of other word formation principles. She too works on

My Kitty

His name is Smokey. He jumps and climbs
trees. He catches mice, so we don't have
them in our house. He sleeps with me, too!

Figure 3.16   A child's illustrated dictation.

helping children develop these understandings through discovery. Such discoveries usually result from repeated reading and writing experiences, but may be assisted by informal comments during dictation and by games and discussion during follow-up activities.

Children's dictated and independent writing appears everywhere in her classroom (Figure 3.16). The library corner has many colorfully bound books authored by individual students and by the group. After these books have been available in the classroom for awhile, Mrs. Thomas glues a library card pocket onto the back cover and writes the book title and author on a check-out card provided by the librarian. The book is then ready to be checked out and taken home to read and share with family members. Before writing is bound into books, it is often displayed on a bulletin board since material authored by friends makes popular reading.

Youngsters wrote many of these books on their own with invented spelling. Mrs. Thomas particularly encourages this approach to discovering phonics rules and admires the ways children have figured out how to represent word sounds with letters. If children do want to make a book to share with others and express a desire to meet standard writing norms, Mrs. Thomas helps them with editing to make the material more easily readable. She helps children make corrections due to their own desire to communicate effectively, but she never merely marks the errors on their papers. Mrs. Thomas is aware of the discouraging effect such feedback has on budding writers.

Phonics and Word Analysis Activities

Sometimes Mrs. Thomas makes charts from group dictation or charts of excerpts from stories by one or several children. Sometimes children make charts of recipes they have used for a cooking activity, poems they have written, or special words. Right now a chart of Halloween words children might wish to use in their writing appears on the wall. The words *bat, witch, ghost, jack-o-lantern,* and *cat* are written beside identifying illustrations. Several charts hang at a child's eye level on which children may write words they have used which start with a certain letter. We see an *H* chart and a *W* chart and are told that different letters are used each week. Tyler and Eric are finding words that they know on the *H* chart, and Heidi has been inspired to see how many different words she can make that rhyme with *bat* and *cat*. When Heidi has discovered eight more letters that create *at* words, Mrs. Thomas makes a rhyming word wheel (Figure 3.17) which lists the beginning letters Heidi discovered. Heidi enjoys sharing her rhyming game with others in the class. She and Becky decide to work together to find other words that can be similarly changed.

The next time we visit Mrs. Thomas's room, we find that Heidi and Becky have continued their interest in rhyming words. Having composed a rhyming poem, they are copying it onto heavy paper to display for the group. They have apparently internalized the word analysis concept of word matrices. Mrs. Thomas encourages another word analysis reading skill by beginning another chart. This chart displays compound words that children have recently dictated, written, or discovered in their reading. She encourages children to add to the chart as they discover more words that are made by putting together two shorter words. In a card pocket below the chart are tagboard strips on which youngsters can write the separate words which make up their compound word. Taking these words strips out and putting them together like a puzzle is an attractive activity to many of the first graders.

Configuration Clues

Good readers rely on a variety of clues for identifying words as they read. We generally teach phonics and word analysis clues but sometimes overlook word configuration clues. Mrs. Thomas knows that the general shape of a word, possibly coupled with the initial letter, is often sufficient information to the reader engrossed in the meaning of the

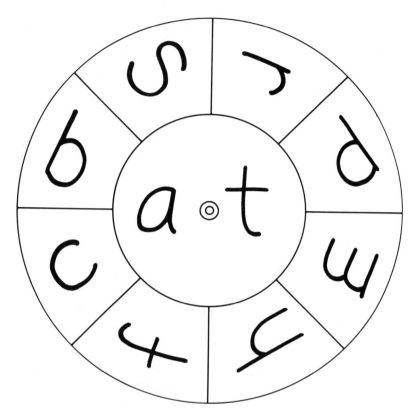

Figure 3.17   Rhyming wheel illustration.

material. Although this shortcut to sightword identification is generally intuitive, Mrs. Thomas helps children notice the general shape of words as she writes and reads with children. She comments on such things as the two tall giraffe neck letters in the word *giraffe*, she points out that the double *oo's* in *look* remind her of eyes looking at her, and she mentions when a word is very long or very short. Once children begin noticing the shape of words, they continue to store up this useful information on their own.

Context Clues

None of these word recognition clues is useful without the use of *context clues—the single most used reading clue*. Since this reading skill relates directly to the meaning of what is read and therefore reflects the true purpose of reading, all three of the teachers previously described are enthusiastic about helping children learn to use it. The teachers find that the experience of being an author helps children realize that other authors also record their own experiences and ideas. When children make the major discovery that "reading is talk written down," (Lee and Allen, 1963) they subsequently expect to find meaning in what they read. This guides children to think about what word would make sense in the story when they get stuck on a word.

Remember the description of a good reader in Chapter 1: the description of Mandy reading her book without knowing all the words. Because she knows most of the words, the ones she does recognize give her sufficient clues to make a reasonable guess at those she doesn't know. If her guess is wrong enough to affect the sense of what she is reading, she goes back and tries again. Then she might use her phonics knowledge. She could always go to the dictionary, but how much fun would reading be if she had to spend much time with that kind of interruption? After Mandy has encountered a word several times, she will have a good idea of its meaning, whether or not she knows the correct pronunciation. Like most of us, Mandy's reading vocabulary

exceeds her speaking vocabulary. Just as our oral vocabulary increases through hearing words used in context, we increase our reading vocabulary through seeing words used in context. Looking up words in dictionaries gives us definitions, but does little for our ability to use words appropriately. Think about reading words you don't recognize yourself in order to verify the value of context clues.

Even before children are reading, they can become familiar with the idea of finding a missing word in a sentence. Context clue games make useful transition time fillers. Mrs. Hanna often plays guessing games with her kindergarteners while they wait in line for the bus. She incorporates context clues into the games with sentences which have a missing word to be filled in. "We are going_____now," she says. "We will ride on the_____bus." Where there are several possible correct answers, she at first accepts all of them. Later, as children develop proficiency with other word recognition skills, she will encourage combining them with guesses at what makes sense. She will give clues such as, "It starts with *H*," or "It rhymes with *fellow*."

Ms. Reynolds often uses story time for teaching context clues by stopping to allow the children to fill in a word. Her preschoolers especially enjoy chiming in on rhyming words in stories or poems. Mrs. Thomas demonstrates the value she places on context clues when her first graders read aloud to her. When a child stops on a word, Mrs. Thomas first asks, "What word would make sense?" rather than, "What are the sounds of the letters?" If the child's guess is close in meaning, but incorrect, Mrs. Thomas continues the flow of the story by telling the child the word rather than stopping to sound it out. However, she often does mention a distinguishing characteristic of the word such as the beginning consonant as she tells the child the word. She might say, "Yes, it means *mail* but it starts with an *L* and is *letter*." Mrs. Thomas is guided by the individual child's needs in what kind of feedback she gives each student. A child confident and excited about reading can profit from more correction than a child who hesitates about the process. For an insecure reader, Mrs. Thomas simply supplies the missing word in order to allow the reading to continue and the child to gain satisfaction.

Reading Mechanics

Use of these various word recognition skills assumes some basic knowledge of the conventions of print. Adults often tend to think of reading from left to right and putting spaces between words as self-evident. Of course these conventions are not self-evident, and children must learn about the commonly accepted format of written language. Ms. Reynolds believes that youngsters learn the forms of written language the same way they learn the accepted forms of spoken language—with adultmodels playing a strong role. As she writes children's thoughts for them, she calls to their attention what side of the page she begins writing on. She also involves them in deciding what to do when she reaches the other side of the page. She helps them notice when she leaves spaces, when she uses capital letters, and when she uses periods or question marks or exclamation points. She makes sure that youngsters can see how she holds the pencil and how she moves her hand to form various letters. Naturally, she doesn't expect them to master this knowledge in preschool, but she is making sure that they begin the process of collecting data on the subject through their observations.

When Mrs. Hanna takes dictation from her kindergarteners, she also provides an example of how writing is done. Her students are still working on internalizing the concepts and need repeated exposure to models and opportunities to practice imitating the process. Although they have mastered the basic idea of the linear quality of print and know that it is supposed to start on a certain side, they still sometimes start on the wrong side and begin to write backwards. Mrs. Hanna knows that children must practice these concepts in order for them to become second nature.

The books made from the children's dictation and writing provide the youngsters an opportunity for learning about books. When Zachary helps Mrs. Hanna put together the Halloween costume book, he finds that knowing which side is the front is important. When he and the other youngsters read this book, their respect for it helps them remember about proper page turning. Such experiences help children use commercially produced books too.

In first grade, Mrs. Thomas continues and extends the process of children learning about reading and writing mechanics through discovery. Her example as she writes continues to be an important model to youngsters, and they strive to imitate her. She often uses ruled paper when she writes for children, although the children themselves are free to choose either lined or unlined paper for their own writing. She wrote Tyler's entry in the book about his community on half-ruled paper, which left half the page for the pictures. This paper has dotted lines to indicate the proper height of shorter letters and solid lines to indicate both the base line and the upper limit of taller letters. Mrs. Thomas finds that many first graders can profit from observing how she forms letters in relation to these lines. Many are interested in trying to make their own writing conform to the lines, while others are still striving to master the letter forms themselves and cannot cope with the additional challenge of staying within lines.

Accountability

We teachers need a system for keeping track of each child's progress through so many different concepts and skills. Mrs. Thomas uses the skills list which accompanies the basal readers her school has adopted. Although she doesn't teach reading in the way that the reading series teacher's guide recommends, she finds the evaluation guide useful. By using this guide, Mrs. Thomas simplifies her accountability to the principal. She accepts the goals, or ends, specified by the basal program, but not the means to those ends.

She confides, however, that she adds a number of goals for her young readers to those listed in the basal readers. Mrs. Thomas considers attitudes about reading to be at least as important as reading skills, since a child who does not like to read will not read enough to truly learn any reading skills well. Conversely, she does not overlook the importance of reading skills, since skill deficiencies can cause children problems which will make them dislike reading. Besides adding reading attitudes to her evaluation guide, she also added several writing skill, concept, and attitude measures. She considers reading and writing development inseparable.

Mrs. Hanna participated in a district-wide kindergarten curriculum project which developed appropriate expectations for kindergarten achievement. This teacher-developed guide provides useful criteria for

---

Description of a Developmentally **Appropriate** *Kindergarten Reading Program*

1. Young children learn through experiences that provide for all of the developmental needs—physical, socio-emotional, as well as intellectual.
2. Young children learn through self-selected activities while participating in a variety of centers which are interesting and meaningful to them. (Learning Centers include: socio-dramatic, block, science, math, manipulatives, listening, reading, writing, art, music, and construction.)
3. Young children are encouraged to talk about their experiences with other children and adults in the classroom.
4. Young children are involved in a variety of psychomotor experiences including, music, rhythms, movement, large and small motor manipulatives and outdoor activity.
5. Young children are provided with many opportunities to interact in meaningful print contexts: listening to stories, participating in shared book experiences, making language experience stories and books, developing key word vocabularies, reading classroom labels, and using print in the various learning centers.

Description of a Developmentally **Inappropriate** *Kindergarten Reading Program*

1. Formal kindergarten reading programs usually focus upon whole group instruction in visual-motor and phonics lessons with commercially prepared workbooks and ditto sheets.
2. Formal kindergarten reading programs usually include reading instruction in a basal reading series. This process frequently involves the learning of *rules* with emphasis upon the *form* rather than the *meaning* of written language.
3. A formal kindergarten reading program often requires children to sit for inappropriately long blocks of time in teacher directed activities with over emphasis upon table work and fine motor skills.
4. A formal kindergarten reading program focuses upon isolated skill oriented experiences which include repetition and memorization.

Source: Developmentally Appropriate Kindergarten Reading Programs: A Position Statement by J.K. Black and M. Puckett, 1984, Denton, Tx: Texas Association of the Education of Young Children. Copyright 1985 by Texas Association for the Education of Young Children.

keeping track of children's growth in reading and writing. These criteria appear as evaluation tools on report cards too.

Ms. Reynolds has no school board or principal to satisfy, but she does have a parent board which develops preschool policy and which hired her for their co-operative preschool. The board hired Ms. Reynolds for her professional expertise, however, and respects her judgement about appropriate goals for preschool education. She feels a serious responsibility to help parents understand her goals and why she chose them. Ms. Reynolds wrote the school's curriculum plan, required for state certification, with the cooperation of the parent board. The plan provides a general description of skills and concepts that children work on in the preschool. From this guide, Ms. Reynolds developed a checklist which helps her keep track of each child's accomplishments. Parents find this checklist helpful in understanding their own child's growth.

Due to individual differences, some youngsters are barely aware of print both in preschool and first grade, and other youngsters are able to read well both in preschool and first grade. The teachers who have been described find that the free exploration of writing and the language experience approach to literacy are so flexible that they can accommodate any level of ability through modifications in what is essentially the same activity. The individual child's own progress deter-

mines what he can gain through a specific lesson, and the teacher needn't set apart groups of children as fast or slow. The learning process we have been observing does not segregate the more verbal children from the less verbal ones, separating those who most need verbal stimulation from their peers who can best provide it. Instead, all children are experiencing their oral language in print and all are exploring print at their own level. Therefore, all are gaining feelings of success and pride.

Helping children to understand how reading and writing are used for communication and pleasure along with helping them to feel proud of their success at mastering this form of language are the goals of all three teachers. They keep track of the specific skills and knowledge children attain, but they keep clearly in mind the larger goal of helping children become literate adults.

SUGGESTED FOLLOW-UP ACTIVITIES

1. Provide blank paper and writing materials to preschool or kindergarten children and encourage them to write. Observe their various perceptions of the writing process.
2. Ask to borrow (or copy) samples of children's writing and compare these papers with children's writing samples collected by others. As a group activity put in sequence the samples of children's writing according to stages described in this chapter.
3. Encourage a child or a small group of children to tell about an experience or make up a story for you to write down. Follow dictation procedures described in the chapter. What did you learn about the child or children in this activity? What did you learn about yourself and the dictation process?

DISCUSSION QUESTIONS

1. A fellow teacher questions your kindergarten journal writing program, saying, "They don't even know their letters and sounds yet. How can they write?" What is your response?
2. A parent complains because her child is bringing home creative writing papers with misspelled words. How do you explain the approach to writing you are using?

REFERENCES AND RESOURCES FOR FURTHER READING

Books

Baghban, M. (1984). *Our daughter learns to read and write.* Newark, DE: International Reading Assoc.

Boegehold, B. D. (1984). *Getting ready to read.* New York: Ballantine Books.

Chomsky, C. (1979). Approaching reading through invented spelling. *Paper Presented at the Conference on Theory and Practice of Early Reading.*, Hillsdale, NJ: Erlbaum.

Clay, M.M. (1975). *What did I write?* Auckland, New Zealand: Heinemann Educational Books.

Cochran-Smith, M. (1984) *The making of a reader.* Norwood, NJ: Ablex.

Dyson, A.H. (1983). *Understanding the how's and why's of writing: The development of children's concepts of writing in primary classrooms* (Vol. 1, the kindergarten data). Urbana; IL: National Council of Teachers of English Research Foundation.

Ferreiro, E., & Teberosky, A. (1982). *Literacy before schooling.* Exeter, NH: Heinemann Educational Books.

Glazer, S. M. (1980). *Getting ready to read.* Englewood Cliffs, NJ: Prentice-Hall.

Graves, D.H. (1983). *Writing: Teachers and children at work.* Exeter, NH: Heinemann Educational Books.

Lee, D., & Allen, R.V. (1963). *Learning to read through experience.* Englewood Cliffs, NJ: Prentice-Hall.

Lee, D., & Rubin, J. (1979). *Children and language.* Belmont, CA: Wadsworth Publishing.

Martin, B. Jr. (1983). *Brown bear, brown bear what do you see?* New York: Holt, Rinehart and Winston.

Pearson, P.D. (1984). *Handbook of reading research.* New York: Longman.

Pflaum, S. (1978). *The development of language and reading in young children.* (1978). Columbus, OH: Charles E. Merrill.

Rey, H.A. (1941). *Curious George.* Boston: Houghton Mifflin.

Rudolph, M., & Cohen, D. (1984). *Kindergarten and early schooling.* Englewood Cliffs, NJ: Prentice-Hall.

Schickedanz, J.A. (1986). *More than the ABC's: The early stages of reading and writing.* Washington, DC: National Association for the Education of Young Children.

Smith, F. *Understanding reading.* (1982). New York: Holt, Rinehart and Winston.

Temple, C.A., Nathan, R. G., & Burris, N.A. (1982). *The beginnings of writing.* Boston: Allyn and Bacon.

Tucker, N. (1982). *The child and the book: A psychological and literary exploration.* New York: Cambridge University Press.

Vacca, R. (1981). *Content area reading.* Boston: Little, Brown.

Vygotsky, L.A. (1978). *Mind in society: The development of higher psychological processes.* (M. Cole et al., Trans. & Ed.). Cambridge, MA: Harvard University Press.

Periodicals

Applebee, A.N., & Langer, J.A. (1983, February). Instructional scaffolding: Reading and writing as natural language activities. *Language Arts, 60,* 168-175.

Atkins, C. (1984, November). Writing: Doing something constructive. *Young Children, 40* (1), 3-14.

Brandt, A. (1982, March). Writing readiness. *Psychology Today,* pp. 55-59.

Busch, R.E., Jr. (1984, July). A red marble! Guidelines for speaking to children. *Young Children, 39* (5), 64-66.

Catroppa, B.D. (1982, October). Working with writing is like working with clay. *Language Arts, 59,* 687-695.

Cazden, C.B. (1980, May). What we don't know about the language arts. *Phi Delta Kappan, 61,* 595-597.

Chafel, J. (1982, May/June). Making literacy a natural happening. *Childhood Education, 58* (5), 300-304.

Chomsky, C. (1981). Write first, read later. *Childhood Education, 47* (6), 296-299.

Chomsky, C. (1976, March). After decoding what? *Language Arts, 53,* 289-294.

Darrell, N. (1983, December). Concept of word and phoneme awareness in the beginning reader. *Research in the Teaching of English,* pp. 359-373.

Dyson, A.H. (1982, October). Teachers and young children: Missed connections in teaching/learning to write. *Language Arts, 59,* 674-680.

Dyson, A.H. (1982, November/December). Reading, writing, and language: Young children solving the written language puzzle. *Language Arts, 59,* 829-839.

Dyson, A.H. (1982, Fall). The emergence of visible language: Interrelationships between drawing and early writing. *Visible Language,* pp. 360-381.

Dyson, A.H. (1984, December). N spell my grandmama. *The Reading Teacher, 38* (3), 262-271.

Dyson, A.H. (1985). Puzzles, paints, and pencils. Writing emerges. *Educational Horizons, 64* (1), 13-16.

Early Childhood and Literacy Development Committee of the International Reading Association. (1986). *A policy statement concerning literacy and pre-first grade.* Newark, DE: International Reading Association.

Freeman, Y., & Whitesell, L.R. (1985). What preschoolers already know about print. *Educational Horizons, 64* (1), 22-24.

Feeley, J.T. (1984, Spring). Print and reading: What do preschoolers know? *Day Care and Early Education, 11* (3), 26-28.

Fields, M.V. & Hillstead, D.V. (1986, May). Reading begins with scribbling. *Principal, 65* (5), 24-27.

Goodman, K., & Goodman, Y.M. (1983, May). Reading and writing relationships: Pragmatic functions. *Language Arts, 60,* 590-599.

Goodman, Y.M. (1980). The roots of literacy. In M.P. Douglas (Ed.), *Claremont Reading Conference Forty-Fourth Yearbook.* Claremont, CA: Claremont Graduate School Center for Developmental Studies.

Goodman, Y.M. (1985). Developing writing in a literate society. *Educational Horizons, 64* (1), 17-21.

Kamii, C., & Randazzo, M. (1985, February). Social interaction and invented spelling. *Language Arts, 62,* 124-133.

Kamii, C. (1985, September). Leading primary education toward excellence—beyond worksheets and drill. *Young Children, 40* (6), 3-11.

Kirkland, E.R. (1978, February). A Piagetian interpretation of beginning reading instruction. *The Reading Teacher, 31* (5), 497-503.

Lamme, L.L., & Denny, P.L. (1981, Fall) A writing curriculum for preschoolers. *Day Care and Early Education, 9* (1), 12-15.

Lavine, L. (1977). Differentiation of letterlike forms in prereading children. *Developmental Psychology,* pp. 89-94.

Markham, L.R. (1984, May). De dog and de cat: Assisting speakers of black English as they begin to write. *Young Children, 39* (4), 15-25.

Newkirk, T. (1984, April). Archimedes' Dream. *Language Arts, 61,* 341-350.

Newman, J.M. (1983, October). On becoming a writer: Child and teacher. *Language Arts, 60,* 860-869.

Piazza, C., & Tomlinson, C.M. (1985, February). A concert of writers. *Language Arts, 62,* 150-158.

Richgels, D. (1982, Fall). The language experience approach: A transition from oral to written language. *Reading Horizons,* pp. 47-53.

Schickedanz, J. (1981, November). Hey this book's not working right! *Young Children, 37* (1), 18-27.

Seefeldt, C. (1984, May). Tomorrow's kindergarten: Pleasure or pressure? *Principal, 64* (5), 12-15.

Seefeldt, C. (1984, July). What's in a name. *Young Children, 39* (5), 24–53.

Smith, F. (1976, March). Learning to read by reading. *Language Arts, 53,* 297-299.

Smith, F. (1983, May). Reading like a writer. *Language Arts, 60,* 558-567.

Smith, J.A., & Gray, J.M. (1983, November). Learning about reading, writing and fish with the help of the word processor. *Australian Journal of Reading,* pp. 186-192.

Solsken, J.W. (1985, September). Authors of their own learning. *Language Arts, 62,* 491-499.

Stine, S. (1980). Beginning reading—naturally! In M.P. Douglas (Ed.), *Claremont Reading Conference Forty-Fourth Yearbook.* Claremont, CA: Claremont Graduate School Center for Developmental Studies.

Sulzby, E., & Teale, W. (1985). Writing development in early childhood. *Educational Horizons, 64,* (1), 8-12.

Tate, A. (1983, June). Myth and reality of reading readiness. *Australian Journal of Reading,* 57-65.

Thomas, K.F. (1985, September). Early reading as a social interaction process. *Language Arts, 62,* 469-475.

Van Dongen. D. (1984, September). Children's meaningful encounter with print. *Insights into Education,* pp. 1-8.

Vukelich, C. (1984, January). Early writing development and teaching strategies. *Young Children, 39* (2), 3-10.

Willert, M.K., & Kamii, C. (1985, May). Reading in kindergarten: Direct vs. indirect teaching. *Young Children, 40* (4), 3-9.

Wittrock, M.C. (1983, May). Writing and the teaching of reading. *Language Arts, 60,* 600-606.

Wood, M. (1982, October). Invented spelling. *Language Arts, 59,* 707-717.

4

Extending Reading and Writing Skills

Having watched children get started as readers and writers, let's follow this approach to literacy through the primary grades. As a teacher, if you believe that children learn that which is relevant to their own experiences and interests, you will continue emphasizing those experiences and interests in classroom activities at any grade level. If you believe that children learn in an active rather than a passive mode, you will continue the exploration and discovery approach to learning beyond first grade. If you believe that children learn best when they believe in themselves as learners and experience joy in the learning process, you will nurture successes rather than point out failures for second and third graders, as well as for younger students.

Chapter 3 described how children become literate through their experiences with language and print. Chapter 2 described how children also become literate through experiences in general: sensory experiences, large muscle experiences, play experiences, and experiences of being read to. None of these should stop just because a child can now read independently. Being talked to, listened to, and read to continue to be important for a budding reader and writer. Having opportunities to climb and jump, build block towers, and dam up mud puddles continue to provide insights, understandings, and enthusiasms for writing, and talking, and reading.

Chapter 3 described how children learn to read through their own writing and through dictating ideas for others to write. This chapter will describe how children learn to read better through additional writing experiences and learn to write better through additional reading experiences. Which shall we start with, reading or writing? The chicken or the egg? Each is essential to the other.

WRITING IN THE PRIMARY GRADES

> When children are makers of reading, they gain a sense of ownership over their reading. As we've seen again and again, owners are different from tenants.
>
> (Lucy Calkins, 1983)

Beginning writers are not proficient writers, but they can most quickly become proficient by doing more writing. If you waited until your students could spell correctly, could write legibly, and used proper punctuation, a long time would pass before they could become writers. By waiting until they became proficient, they would waste valuable time when they could be gaining the benefits of actually writing: understanding the purposes and procedures of communication through print. They would also waste the best opportunities to learn more about spelling and punctuation and to practice handwriting. Probably, the biggest waste would be the lost enthusiasm and confidence of writers freed to put their ideas on paper without fear of criticism for errors.

An Environment for Writing

An environment conducive to writing means an accepting one. In this environment, the teacher understands that first drafts by nature are messy and contain mechanical errors. The teacher understands some writing is for personal purposes and needn't be corrected. The class schedule includes time for thinking about a writing topic and getting inspired before having to come up with a product. In fact, the process of writing is valued even more than the products.

Remember Betsy's big brothers and sisters? Remember Joey? His second grade teacher, Mr. Larson, knows how to encourage kids to write. Mr. Larson is willing to fight through 100-word, run-on sentences with no punctuation and little recognizable spelling to find out what a child is trying to say. He then responds to the message in the writing rather than to the mistakes. He may comment that he can tell from Joey's story about fishing with his Dad that Joey felt scared when they almost capsized in some rapids on the river.

What about the twenty-five misspelled words and the twenty missing periods? Are we going to raise a generation of writers whose writing no one can read? No one wants that, of course, but neither do we want people who can pass spelling and punctuation tests but don't write.

How do we get the best of both worlds? We rely on Joey's own desire to communicate through his writing. When he is enthusiastic about his ability to express his feelings and share his experiences through writing, he will want to make sure others can read what he has written. At this point, after Mr. Larson has responded to the meaning and purpose of the writing, he helps Joey edit and proofread his story in preparation for sharing it with others.

Mr. Larson makes his classroom even more safe for young writers by letting them see him write, make mistakes, get frustrated, and have to revise and, perhaps, throw away writing attempts. Sometimes a visitor can walk into his room, and see everyone busily writing, including the teacher. Sometimes writing time can get noisy and look like conversation time: That's part of the editing process, when you need feedback from someone else to find out if he said what he meant to say. Mr. Larson will often read something he has written to the class or one or two students to get their ideas. He finds student in-put especially helpful when he tries to describe class activities for the parent newsletter. Mr. Larson's writing isn't limited to newsletters, however. He composes funny rhymes about students and class activities which all the class enjoys, and he writes stories to entertain his own three little boys.

A Process for Writing

Next year in third grade, Joey hopes to be in Mrs. Williams's room since she was his big sister Mandy's favorite teacher. If he gets his wish, he will continue to be immersed in writing activities. Mrs. Williams has been involved in writing project classes and is excited about the results of the techniques she has learned there.

While visiting her classroom, we observe youngsters in all five phases of the writing process (Figure 4.1). Many students are working on phase one, the *prewrite experience.* Aaron and Ruben are discussing soccer prior to writing about their involvement on a soccer team. (Their actual experience playing soccer also served as an important part of the prewriting experience for this topic.) They review events of the last game, make notes about interesting plays, and brainstorm together, recalling events to include in a story. They make a list of special words needed for this story: referee, goalie, forward, halfback, and score.

Michelle works on phase two, the *fast write,* which will result in her first draft. If she were writing in her personal journal or doing some other writing which she didn't plan to share with anyone, and had no desire to polish, this could be her last draft. Sometimes the writing experience is valuable just for getting ideas or feelings on paper; spelling, punctuation, and style become unimportant. Today Michelle writes a letter to the editor for the local newspaper. Her letter requests better enforcement of the leash law for dogs; she is upset about this because a dog chased her cat up a tree yesterday (Figure 4.2).

In this case, Michelle wants to write as correctly as possible, clearly stating her case. So, she moves into phase three—*sharing a draft and requesting peer response.* First, she reads the letter to her friend, Courtney, to find out if she has clearly stated her message. Together the girls plan some changes that they think strengthen the argument in favor of better canine control. Michelle then revises the letter and plans to read it to a group for further feedback tomorrow.

When Michelle meets with a small group the next day to read her letter draft, the others in the group are also in phase three of their writing. Each child takes turns sharing a draft and requesting peer response. They have practiced the procedure with Mrs. Williams and now can meet without her. Their comments emphasize the positive, and we hear statements such as, "I liked the part about how glad your cat was to get down from the tree." or "You really made me feel how scared your kitty was." Other comments help focus on clarifications needed such as, "I don't understand how the law will protect your cat."

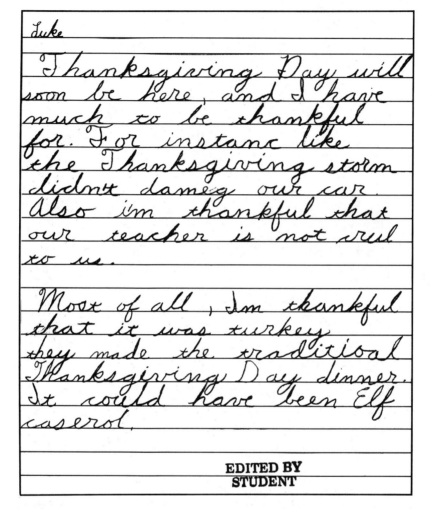

Luke

Thanksgiving Day will soon be here, and I have much to be thankful for. For instanc like the Thanksgiving storm didn't dameg our car. Also i'm thankful that our teacher is not crul to us.

Most of all, Im thankful that it was turkey they made the traditioal Thanksgiving Day dinner. It could have been Elf caserol.

EDITED BY
STUDENT

Figure 4.1   A student writing sample which another child has edited.

Michelle makes further changes in her letter following this session and feels satisfied that it makes her point. She doesn't plan to ask for any further feedback on content, although when she wrote a fairly long play recently, she went through the feedback and revision process several times before she felt satisfied with her final product. Now she is ready for phase four, *polishing*. This is the time for worrying about checking details such as spelling, grammar, punctuation, paragraphing, and handwriting. Mrs. Williams helps with the proofreading, involving Michelle in the process through comments such as, "Do any of the words look funny to you?" Mrs. Williams wants her students to learn spelling as a visual image of how a word looks as well as an intuitive,

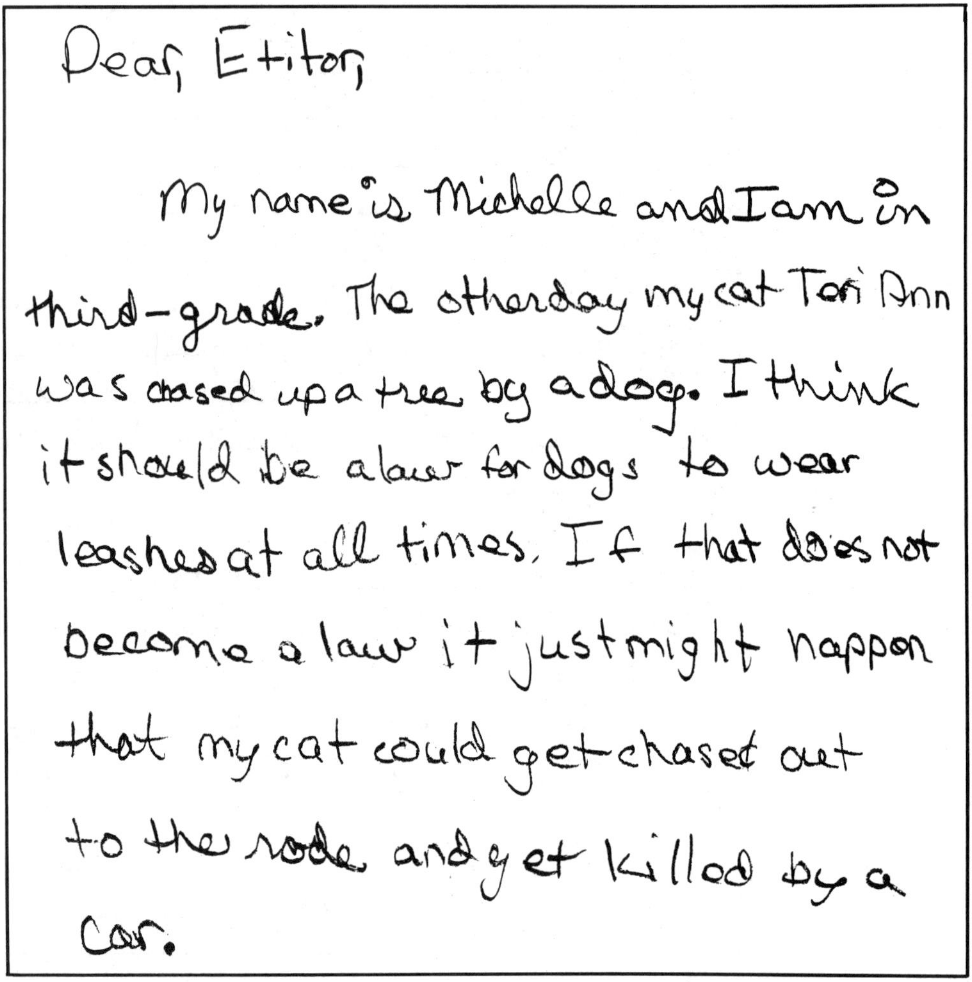

Dear Etitor,

My name is Michelle and I am in third-grade. The otherday my cat Tori Ann was chased up a tree by a dog. I think it should be a law for dogs to wear leashes at all times. If that does not become a law it just might happen that my cat could get chased out to the rode and get killed by a car.

Figure 4.2   Michelle's letter to the editor.

kinesthetic knowledge of which letter to write next. She never uses oral spelling drill or even written practices of writing words over and over. She knows that neither of these approaches will carry over to the actual use of spelling in writing.

The amount of punctuation proofreading varies with different students. Michelle is fairly sophisticated in her understanding of punctuation, but other students may only be ready for some basics. Mrs. Williams encourages all students to read their work aloud to determine where punctuation marks might be needed to direct the reader. Long pauses may require periods; small pauses may require commas. The inflection and tone of voice will indicate questions marks and exclamation marks. Mrs. Williams usually does not introduce how to use semicolons to third graders. When children learn punctuation and paragraphing as part of making their writing more clear to others, they truly understand punctuation concepts and are able to use them in future writing.

Only now, for the final copy, do neatness and handwriting count. Michelle carefully rewrites her letter making it ready for the fifth and final phase, *publishing*. In this case, the letter will be published in the community newspaper. Other types of publishing include making copies of a story or poem for the class or school library, sending a factual report of information requested by younger students to their classroom, putting on a play or puppet show, or simply sending a letter to an intended audience.

Mrs. Williams encourages students to use the classroom computer for word processing if their written work is lengthy. Using word processing makes the revision and polishing processes much easier, since the entire paper doesn't need to be rewritten each time a child makes a change. Of course having used the computer, the final product looks professional, with a perfectly typed copy.

Making the Process Work

Are you impressed at how independently Mrs. Williams's students function while using the five-step process? The children's independence didn't happen overnight or by accident; it happened following their teacher's careful preparation and hard work. Of course, this process isn't equally successful for all students. Some still don't like to write, some are afraid to fast write and ignore spelling uncertainties, and some remain too insecure to take constructive peer criticism. Mrs. Williams adapts the situation to each student, but she continues to strive for some basic understandings. She most enjoys the small group sessions where she helps children learn how to give positive feedback to their classmates about their writing. She feels pleased with the progress her third graders have made in their ability to tell one another what they think their writing is saying. Many children have also progressed in learning to point out the strong parts of a plot, character development, or argument.

Shawn has little interest in writing, but he has many other interests. He likes jokes, so when he tells a joke for sharing time, Mrs. Williams writes it down and suggests that he might want to write others down to make a joke book. Because each item is a short and manageable writing segment, Shawn feels more comfortable with this task

If they put me in the zoo
what could I do?
I could be a Elafint
or a Sercas trainer
or maby a little scinyor.
I would fly and jump.
Or maby ride on a hump.
And sing with the Birds
And eat erbs
And crackl! crackl! snackl! snackl!
If they put me in the zoo
wat could I do?

Figure 4.3   Poem by Summer Koester, August, 1985.

than writing a story. Besides he has fun writing his jokes. Similarly, a
little girl enjoyed writing the short, humorous poem in Figure 4.3.

Short writing often serves as the best starting place. Mr. Larson's
class is having fun with bumper sticker messages. The students look
for them when they go riding with their families and when they ride on
the school bus. They try to remember their favorites to write on the
supply of "bumper sticker paper" Mr. Larson keeps on hand. Making
up messages of their own, they have revealed some of the unique
aspects of second grade humor. Mr. Larson and Mrs. Williams know
that what children write is not as important as the fact that they are
writing.

Mrs. Williams encourages her students to analyze magazine and
television commercials and to write their own. She knows television
commercials grab children's interest with their catchy jingles and fast
pace. Commercials offer children a high interest topic for writing. She
helps youngsters think about the persuasive techniques used in advertising, and asks such questions as, "Will you really have as good a time
as they show people having if you drink that brand of pop?" Mrs.
Williams's students respond by making up their own advertising skits
and rhymes with outrageous claims for fictitious products.

Helping students establish their purposes for writing is essential.
When children have a message and an audience in mind, they want to
write. Neither of these teachers assigns writing topics or even insists
that all children write at a given time. The teachers know that desire to
write must come from the child's own interest. They have found that
allowing children not to write when they don't feel like it does much
more for attitudes about writing than insisting that every child write

every day. Of course, their goal remains to have children writing on a daily basis.

Guidelines for Teaching Writing

1. *Children strive to write so that others understand their meaning.* Arrange opportunities for feedback to help children revise their writing so that others understand it.
2. *Children use their natural language when they begin to write their thoughts.* Accept all of children's writings until they are confident that they can write. Then, gradually introduce polishing for more effective communication and standard language usage.
3. *Children continue to discover how language works when they write frequently and for various purposes.* Provide opportunities for children to use their writing to explore alternative ways of expressing thoughts.
4. *Children write more often, and more effectively, if they are aware of progress and success in writing.* Focus on specific areas of progress in responding to a child's writing; encourage this same focus in feedback from peers.

To help children establish purposes for writing, these teachers provide a stimulating environment where much happens to write about. Animals in the class, field trips, visitors to the class, science experiments, and new books continuously provide exciting subjects. Books and poetry shared with students have the dual effect of providing ideas for content and for form. Youngsters may try to write in the style of a much-enjoyed author such as Judith Viorst or start writing poems similar to the humorous ones by Shel Silverstein.

If children can identify broad ideas of possible audiences for their writing, they may see a variety of writing possibilities. Mr. Larson helps children distinguish private and personal writing from public writing. He encourages his students to keep private, daily journals. He doesn't correct any of the journal entries and only reads them at the invitation of their owners. This arrangement provides a non-threatening writing situation which stimulates a free-flow of ideas. Students often generate ideas for other writing while working on their journals. Some of these ideas are also for a private audience such as a letter to a friend; other ideas include a public audience such as a poem for the class newspaper.

Mrs. Williams further expands the students' ideas of a writing audience. Students learn that not only are they as individuals an audience for their own private writing and that classmates are an audience for public writing, but also that a *specific* or *known audience* differs from the *general* or *unknown audience*. Mrs. Williams spends time asking children to think about who will read their writing and what those people will know and not know about the subject. She tries to get students to consider viewpoints other than their own, but she knows not all third graders are mature enough to be able to do that.

Mrs. Williams and Mr. Larson both prize a child's unique style of writing. The youngsters may not be sophisticated enough to discuss the concepts of voice and style, but they do respond to their teachers' appreciation and acceptance of their personal ways of expressing themselves.

By reading and discussing works by various authors with different styles, students begin to appreciate differences in writing. When children get a chance to meet the author of a book they have enjoyed, their ideas of a personality behind writing grow. Jean Rogers came to Mrs. Williams's class and told about writing her book, *The Secret Moose* (Greenwillow Books, 1984). She made a big impression when she explained how she decided what to write and about throwing away her first efforts. Knowing that writing isn't easy even for a published author, but that it is rewarding to them and worth the effort, is an important concept for the children to hear.

Mrs. Williams and Mr. Larson not only communicate their beliefs about writing to their students, they also communicate them to their students' parents. The teachers explain the goals of their writing program, and invite parents in to observe the children in class. They explain about peer editing and use of the "student edited" stamp. The teachers want to help parents become involved in what their children are learning and they try to enlist the parents' help. Certainly, parents continue to influence their children's attitudes and motivations.

READING IN THE PRIMARY GRADES

Reading has become less like romping about in one's backyard and more like those stifled, pained visits to a grandparent's house.

(Lucy Calkins, 1983)

A purpose for reading is just as important as a purpose for writing. When we help children discover different purposes in reading, we help them focus on meaning. Identifying purposes for reading also works toward the all important goal of helping kids want to read.

Today Katy reads a library book about the adventures of a girl her own age. Since she loves a good story, her purpose is just to enjoy reading and to find out what happens. Lying on the rug in the classroom library nook, she is engrossed in her story. Ruben's purpose in reading today is to find information about comets. He has gone to the school library and checked out several reference books that listed comets in the index. The librarian helped him find an edition of *Odyssey* magazine that had an article on comets. Now Ruben has spread these materials on a table and is looking up the information in each. These two children are experiencing different but equally valid purposes for their reading. In each case the purpose is the child's own purpose: something that child wants to do.

An Environment for Reading

An environment conducive to reading provides much freedom. Students have the freedom to choose what to read, to decide when and where to read, and even not to read what they've started. Why are these student freedoms important? Let's face it, we never *want* to do what we *have* to do. Adults have to free kids from *having* to read, so they can *want* to read, so they *will* read. Surely we agree that children can never become proficient readers unless they read more than what is required in school. The child who sneaks a book and a flashlight into bed at night will be truly literate.

The second and third grade classrooms we are observing provide choices for what to read and offer options within the room of where to read. Additionally, children have some choice of when to read. Mrs. Williams does not use reading a book as a "filler" after other work is done. She thinks this practice makes a value statement that reading is less important than the work to be done first. Instead, she arranges

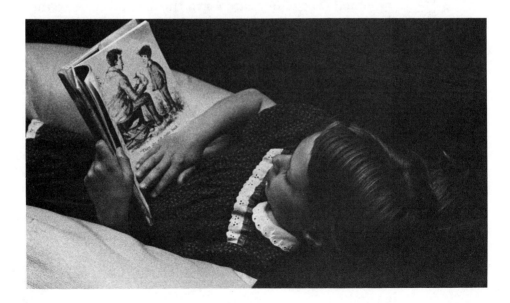

time for reading a story in the class schedule, but students get some choice in the sequence of their day's activities. Obviously, Mrs. Williams feels comfortable with not having everyone doing the same thing at the same time.

Mr. Larson's has filled his room with books. He doesn't confine books to the class library area because he wants his students to think of books all the time. He makes sure books about gerbils are by the gerbil cage; he displays books about rockets and planets beside the solar system chart Rubin brought to share; and he puts all kinds of books along the chalk boards. Mr. Larson has noticed that children respond more to books when they can see the front with the picture on it than when books are shelved so that only the bindings show.

Mrs. Williams's classroom has reminders about books and their contents on posters and charts hung around the room. She encourages her students to make posters, book jackets, costumes, and displays as book reports to let other children know about especially good books. She also copies poetry she thinks they might enjoy onto wall charts for their casual reading.

Both classrooms have specially designated library areas where most of the class books are kept. Both Mr. Larson and Mrs. Williams have made their class libraries inviting and pleasant places. Old rugs, cushions, and beanbag chairs provide cozy places for reading and browsing through books. The teachers feature books by displaying them on top of the book shelves where children can easily find them. The teachers frequently exchange the books that children have tired of or which they didn't care for in the first place. Also the teachers select books on topics that interest individual children. Decorated book boxes containing a variety of books and interesting materials on a specific topic create special attractions in Mrs. Williams's room.

Sometimes these teachers experience difficulty finding interesting books that second and third graders can read. Most of the quality children's literature that we have advocated reading to youngsters is too difficult for beginning readers to read independently. Mr. Larson and Mrs. Williams are always on the look-out for good but easy trade books. Mrs. Williams has a huge personal library of children's books that she has collected over the years. She says bookstores are her downfall. She enjoys owning books and encourages her students to experience the pleasure of also owning books. She finds school book clubs a good way for children to buy books at reasonable prices; and the free books for teachers who participate help build the classroom library. The RIF (Reading Is Fundamental) book distribution program is another source of book ownership for youngsters. Mr. Larson has been impressed at how much his students value those books they are given to keep.

Easy to Read Booklist for Grades 1, 2, and 3

☐ Andersen, C.W., *Billy and Blaze* First of a series about Billy and his many adventures with his horse, Blaze.

☐ Baker, Betty, *Little Runner of the Long House* Little Runner begs to be allowed to don a mask with the older boys and take part in the New Year's festivities, but his mother knows he's really after maple sugar.

☐ Bang, Molly, *Wiley and the Hairy Man* Wiley must outwit the hairy swamp monster three times before he will leave him alone.

☐ Benchley, Nathaniel, *The Strange Disappearance of Arthur Cluck and a Ghost Named Fred* Easy-to-read mysteries.

☐ Bonsall, Crosby, *And I Mean It, Stanley* A little girl builds a masterpiece from discarded junk, pretending that she doesn't know her friend, Stanley is hiding behind the fence.

☐ Brandenberg, Franz, *What Can You Make of It?* Mouse children recycle junk to create a circus.

☐ Gackenback, Dick, *Hattie Be Quiet, Hattie Be Good* Hattie is trying to please her mother by visiting a sick friend. Then she crawls into bed with her so she can have some ice cream too.

☐ Hoban, Lillian, *Arthur's Honey Bear* Arthur is parting with all the toys he has outgrown. But what about his beloved Honey Bear, that his father gave him when he had the chicken pox?

☐ Hoff, Sydney, *Grizzwold* Grizzwold, a bear so big "three rabbits can sit in one of his footprints," tries to find a place where he can live happily ever after.

☐ Hoff, Sydney, *Walpole* Walpole, the biggest and strongest of the walruses, doesn't want to lead the herd; he just wants to take care of the baby walruses.

☐ Hurd, Edith, *No Funny Business* Carl, the cat, finds a way to get *out* of mischief.

☐ Gage, Wilson, *Mrs. Gaddy and the Ghost* Mrs. Gaddy is stuck with a ghost who doesn't want to leave her farm.

☐ Johnston, Tony, *Night Noises and Other Mole and Troll Stories* Gentle stories about two friends; one concerns Mole's wishes which Troll promises to fulfill.

☐ Lobel, Arnold, *Mouse Soup* A clever mouse talks his way out of becoming the key ingredient in a weasel's soup.

☐ Lobel, Arthur, *Owl at Home* Owl trembles at two strange bumps at the food of his bed and shares his recipe for tearwater tea.

☐ Minarik, Else, *Little Bear* Little Bear is cold in his snowsuit until he takes it off. One of a series illustrated by Maurice Sendak.

☐ Margolis, Richard, *Wish Again, Big Bear* Big Bear encounters a fish who offers him three wishes in exchange for freedom.

☐ Marshall, Edward, *Troll Country* After reading a book about trolls, Elsie Fay takes a walk in "troll country" to meet a troll herself.

☐ Parish, Peggy, *Amelia Bedelia and the Baby* Amelia Bedelia is hired by unsuspecting parents as a babysitter.

☐ Peter, Jonathon, *Jokes and Riddles* Easy-to-read jokes and riddles.

☐ Ricciuti, Edward, *Catch a Whale by the Tail*   A true science book about whales.

☐ Schick, Eleanor, *Neighborhood Knight*   David lives in an apartment house, but in his heart, he's a valiant knight in a castle.

☐ Sharmat, Marjorie, *Mooch the Messy*   Mooch the mouse is a messy housekeeper. When his father arrives for a visit, a housecleaning is in order, but Mooch longs for his happy disorder.

☐ Van Woerkom, Dorothy, *Harry and Shellburt*   Harry the hare wants to show Shellburt the tortoise that the famous race was only a fluke and he can beat Shellburt anytime.

☐ Wiseman, Bernard, *Morris Has a Cold*   Morris has a cold and Bear tries to cure him.

Compiled by: Donna Pierce, Director of Libraries, Juneau, Alaska. Used with permission.

Some of the books children want to read can even be found in the grocery store. They may not be the quality literature discussed previously, but short books printed on inexpensive paper, sticker books, and comic books provide a source of reading entertainment and are acceptable as one type of reading. Young children's magazines such as *Cricket* or *Scholastic Magazine* and magazines for older children such as *World* and *Odyssey* also provide interesting reading material. Some children find magazines and newspapers aimed at adults interesting, especially if these periodicals include pictures with captions. Catalogues and other advertising material may also appeal to youngsters: The Christmas "Wish Book" is always a favorite in December.

Many youngsters are fascinated by reference books,—encyclopedias or information books on topics such as the sea, space, or animal life. Aaron brought a book to school to share called *ABC's of Nature: A Family Answer Book* (Reader's Digest, 1985). Even though the vocabulary was advanced, the many pictures and the short entries made the book accessible to third graders. The Golden Book Encyclopedias have entries written at a level most primary grade children can understand. Joey admires Jacques Cousteau and wants to be an oceanographer when he grows up. He reads all he can about undersea life and is especially interested in whales and dolphins. He has checked out library books about the sea and sea creatures and also has purchased paperback copies of books on those topics through Scholastic Book Services. Joey has learned so much in his interest area that Mr. Larson calls him "Whale Man." Joey beams with pride at this title.

Whatever the source or topic of reading material, the criteria for selection must be relevant to the intended reader. Ideally, what children read should be relevant to their experiences, their interests, and their reading ability. Since a class of twenty-five students will surely have twenty-five different sets of experiences, interests, and abilities, the teacher will have to provide a wide variety of reading materials. Trying to keep up with such diversity keeps Mr. Larson on the alert for his students' changing interests and for reading materials to match. Frequently he consults the school librarian for ideas and help.

Children are almost always interested in stories, books, and poems written by their classmates. Once they are capable of more sophisticated writing, the student-authored materials serve as an even more important part of the class library. Joey has written a fact book about dolphins and is working on one about whales. He is also making a scale drawing of a humpback whale for the school hallway. His reading told him how long to make the drawing, but not how wide. He was stumped for awhile until he decided to write to a whale research scientist whose picture he had seen in the newspaper with a beached humpback.

Michelle has written some entertaining stories about the antics of kittens, based on her own cat's adventures. Ruben's report about comets can be made into a book and is sure to be of general interest. Shawn's joke book, which he adds to continually, is frequently read by his classmates.

We haven't yet said anything about textbooks. Actually, to spend so much money on twenty-five copies of the same book instead of buying twenty-five different books seems a shame. However, if your school has already bought textbooks, they shouldn't be wasted. Good material does appear in them, and they are written for a specific grade level. Textbooks for science and social studies can be wonderful reference books for topics of special interest. Children do need to be cautioned not to rely on just one source for information, so you would want just one or two copies of several different texts in each subject.

Similarly, we feel children should not rely on one reading text. In those texts that don't sacrifice meaning for controlled vocabulary the stories can be interesting. The teacher's manual may have some great ideas for activities related to some stories too. But having each child read each story in sequence and simultaneously seems inappropriate, and to expect all youngsters in a given group to be interested in the same story at the same time seems unreasonable. If we apply the tests of relevance and freedom, textbooks must be just another choice of reading material.

Mrs. Williams has available in her class library a few copies of the various level books from several reading series. She has shelved these among the trade books, and children may freely choose one for any story that attracts them. No child is required to read any book from beginning to end; rather, youngsters select only stories which interest them. Mrs. Williams remembers getting in trouble when she was a child in a reading group: She was always reading the more interesting stories at the back of the book when she was supposed to be following along

Guidelines for Helping Children Learn to Read

1. *Children work hard at reading whatever is important to them.*
2. *Children learn to read by reading.* At first they may understand the thought and express it in somewhat different words. As they continue reading, gradually they become more accurate. As they experience the process and talk about it, it becomes clearer to them.
3. *Children learn to read intuitively.* Since learning to read is largely intuitive, as most learning is at this age, explanations, directions, and direct teaching may do more to confuse than to help. After children have established successful reading processes, they can discuss ways to gain greater depth and evaluative ability.
4. *Reading involves understanding written thoughts.* To find out how well children read, ask them to tell you about what they have read. Ask follow-up questions in terms of the purpose for which they were reading.
5. *Children need to develop self-confidence as readers.* When children select their own reading materials and can talk about what they have read, they experience success. When helping children who have difficulty, emphasize how much they were able to understand on their own.
6. *Each child's development and experience with reading is unique.* Since no two children learn at the same rate, listening and responding to them individually and in small groups is more useful than group instruction.
7. *When children read effectively, they understand the meaning but may or may not report it in the exact words of the print.* As long as they do not seriously distort meaning, teachers should make no issue of it. If there is distortion, teachers should allow time for children to self-correct. If children do not question the meaning of the distorted sentence, teachers should then raise the question of meaning.
8. *Children learn to read most effectively when what they read is important to them.* When children choose their own reading material, it is automatically more important to them than what might be assigned, and they want to find out what it says. They concentrate on getting the meaning.

with the round-robin reading of the story of the day. She finds the round-robin reading as boring now as she did then and never uses that approach.

The Teacher's Role

If the teacher doesn't have reading groups, doesn't assign required stories, and doesn't listen to children taking turns reading from an assigned story, what does the teacher do? Certainly not correct workbooks! Neither Mr. Larson nor Mrs. Williams believes in workbooks. They see little carry-over to actual reading or writing from the isolated drill provided in workbooks. Mrs. Williams does see one carry-over: a negative attitude toward reading. She says, "If you must use workbooks, just don't call it reading." She often gets children in her class whose past school experience leads them to equate reading with workbooks.

What *can* you do to help children become readers? We have already described the important role of the teacher in setting the physical and emotional environment conducive to reading. Work on the physical environment involves time before and after school for selecting, sorting, and displaying reading materials. At the beginning of the school year, teachers arrange a library area so that children perceive it as semi-secluded and comfortable. Maintaining this positive emotional environment, fostering freedom to choose what, when, and where to read becomes a teacher's on-going job. However, neither developing the physical nor emotional setting for reading gives you something to do during reading time.

If you aren't tied down to meeting with each of three reading groups, you are free for spontaneous interaction with individuals. You can circulate while children work, asking a question here, making a suggestion there. You can spend time guiding children in working independently. For instance, you can help them get materials without disturbing others. You can help children learn to find books of interest and help them learn to select books of appropriate difficulty. Mr. Larson shows Sue the *Rule of Thumb* way to choose a book (Veatch, 1968). He has her find a book, open it to the middle, and start to read. Every time she finds a word she can't read, she puts down one finger. If she uses up all the fingers on one hand before she finishes the page, and has to put down her thumb too, the book is declared hard reading. Of course she can try it anyway if she thinks it looks worth the effort. Freedom of choice means freedom to choose books above and below personal reading level.

If kids aren't tied to workbook pages, they are free to try creative writing, make displays or puppet shows about their reading, write letters, write journals, make newspapers, and write and read some more. They will also have time to create art projects and to participate in drama and music activities in response to what they read. At first you will need to provide guidance so they can learn the limits about where they can work, how noisy they can be, and what materials they can use. But gradually you will be needed less and less to teach independence as your students actually become independent learners. But, after you've developed independent learners, what do you do?

TEACHER - PUPIL CONFERENCES

Having turned your classroom into a center where children can work independently, now you have time to really get involved in the learning process. You have more time for meeting with your students individually in conference sessions. Ms. Reynolds and Mrs. Hanna start this process on an informal basis in preschool and kindergarten just by stopping to talk with individual children about what they are working on. Mrs. Thomas begins scheduling planned formal conference sessions with her first graders as they individually arrive at the "Aha, I can read!" stage. In second and third grade, all children should be able to profit from regular one-on-one sessions to discuss their reading and writing with the teacher.

Mr. Larson has a special conference table set out of the line of traffic in order to be secluded, but still provide him a view of everything in the classroom. He posts a sign-up sheet there so children can easily schedule themselves for an appointment as they feel the need or desire for one. If a child goes for a week without signing up for a conference, Mr. Larson seeks out that child and spends time casually discussing his or her reading and writing. Mr. Larson tries to make the discussion

non-threatening and supportive to encourage the child to request a conference. Some children seem to sign up all the time. Do they want the additional attention, or are they too dependent on teacher direction or praise? With these youngsters, Mr. Larson tries to figure out the cause of constant requests and then deal with that cause. Generally, he urges his students to try to work a day without teacher direction between conferences.

Conferences may last for only a minute or two or be as long as fifteen minutes. Usually, they last from five to ten minutes, and Mr. Larson is able to meet with about ten children daily. Are you shocked that he doesn't try to hear each child read each day? Mr. Larson has found that giving his undivided attention a few times a week to each child is far more valuable than meeting daily with that child in a group. Of course he circulates among the whole class between conferences and interacts with students incidentally during those times too.

Mr. Larson keeps his files and records for conferences in the conference area so that he can pull out an old sample of a child's writing for comparison to today's work. Children can see their progress when they have these comparisons. Mrs. Williams keeps her records of conferences in a notebook with a section for each child, just as Mrs. Thomas does. She records children's feelings about writing and reading as well as their skill. She likes for students to see what she is writing down about their progress, so she takes notes during the conference sessions. On occasion, she adds notes after a spontaneous interaction outside the conference session when she didn't have her notebook handy.

Content

Sometimes a child has writing to discuss, sometimes reading, and sometimes both at once. Whichever literary endeavor the teacher and student discuss, the teacher tries to always provide specific, positive feedback. Mrs. Williams cautions that positive feedback must be specific rather than general. With general praise, we run the risk of making children dependent on outside approval rather than helping them learn to rely on their own judgment. Mr. Larson has a reputation for boosting the self-esteem of kids who especially need it, and he is a master at positive feedback. He firmly believes that his purpose during conferences is to be supportive, constructive, and specific as he helps students set their next steps in progress toward their goals. He always notes the progress a child has made rather than the errors. He never tries to improve writing with a red pencil or to improve reading with lists of words missed. Instead of talking about errors, he discusses what needs to be learned by saying, "Now I think you are ready for . . . ."

When several children appear ready for a similar concept, Mr. Larson has them form a study group. The teacher can work with several children at once for efficiency, and the children have the benefit of working with peers. Mrs. Williams and Mr. Larson have many small group activities to help students learn the major concepts of their grade level. However, children do not need special help to learn most of the reading and writing skills. Children discover most skills in the process of reading and writing and do not need explanations.

People of all ages learn many things implicitly and effectively use that knowledge without ever verbalizing it to themselves or to others. In fact, our well-intentioned explanations can be a hindrance rather than a help, with explanations in someone else's terms resulting in confusion. Mrs. Williams thinks about explanations of how to get her car back under control when it skids on ice in the winter. She intuitively does the right thing, but explanations totally confuse her, and she has to ignore them in order to brake safely.

Children usually sign up for a conference with a specific purpose—requesting help, to find more information on a topic, wanting feedback on writing, or sharing a story that was particularly enjoyable. The teacher values the child's purpose and uses it as a starting place to extend the youngster's knowledge and understanding. For instance, when Ruben was trying to find information about comets, Mrs. Williams helped him become more proficient in using the table of contents and the index in books. She also felt that moment was a good time to send him to the school librarian who helped Ruben learn how to find things at the library. When information or skills are important to a child, he will learn them.

As children become more proficient and confident in using written language, their purposes change. Now that Michelle can write most words she uses, without laboriously matching the sounds of language to the letters, she is more free to concentrate on the meaning and form of what she writes. She no longer has to think about each word as she writes it, so she thinks about how to communicate more effectively. Mrs. Williams's responses to Michelle during conferences help her to think through the content and the way her thoughts are structured. Developing syntax, style, and the choice of words to express her thoughts comes next. Mrs. Williams doesn't spend time with details such as spelling until after Michelle has finished the important process of getting her ideas on paper (Figure 4.4).

Conferences have helped Joey become good at finding materials about dolphins and whales. Mr. Larson showed him how to scan a book to see what types of information it contains, then to skim a section if it looks useful, and finally to read in depth only those items he wants to know about. Mrs. Williams spends time helping her students achieve this type of reading flexibility too. Unless children become adept at

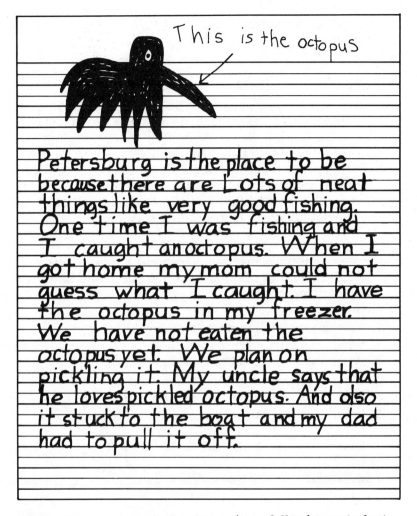

This is the octopus

Petersburg is the place to be because there are Lots of neat things like very good fishing. One time I was fishing and I caught an octopus. When I got home my mom could not guess what I caught. I have the octopus in my freezer. We have not eaten the octopus yet. We plan on pickling it. My uncle says that he loves pickled octopus. And also it stuck to the boat and my dad had to pull it off.

Figure 4.4 A student essay written following a student-teacher conference.

getting out of books exactly what they want, their reading will not meet their purposes and it will be less rewarding.

Mrs. Williams always tries to help children identify their purpose in reading or writing and be aware if one is missing. When Katy brought a book to a conference that she couldn't discuss with any understanding, Mrs. Williams' questions led to the conclusion that the particular book was not meaningful to her. Katy had no related experience to bring to the story, so it was inappropriate for her. Mrs. Williams encouraged Katy to put the book aside and choose something else. Similarly, when Shawn became bogged down while beginning to write something,

Mrs. Williams encouraged him to file that paper away and write on another topic.

Process

Conference sessions generally are a mix of listening to children, talking with them, and listening to them read aloud what they have been reading or writing. Mr. Larson often checks reading comprehension by requesting students to tell him about the most interesting (or funny or exciting) part. He also asks questions to encourage critical reading and reading between the lines. Mr. Larson's questions are the same type of questions you might find in a teacher's manual, but they are aimed at an individual child's own reading selection.

The following list of questions are some Mr. Larson finds useful during conferences he holds with his students about their reading.

1. How do you feel about what you are reading?
2. What interesting things did you find out from reading this?
3. What was exciting (or funny) about this story?
4. What are the main points in the story (or article)?
5. What kind of people are the characters?
6. Do they seem like real people that you might meet or have for friends?
7. How do you think the author felt about the people and the situation?

Mr. Larson tries first to get the student to initiate the discussion or volunteer information. He uses the questions only to probe for something not brought up. Also he stays alert for insights about how a child is managing the reading process. He knows that many children can tell him what bothers them when they read.

Mr. Larson encourages youngsters to come prepared to read a favorite section aloud to him. He doesn't want to ask anyone to read orally without having a chance to prepare first, since oral reading requires more skills than silent reading. This oral reading gives him clues about word identification strategies that children are using. Mr. Larson takes notes about miscues as the child reads, jotting down the type of mistakes made rather than how many. He wants to know whether words substituted make sense in context or whether they are simply similar in appearance. He got worried when Ron read *tree* for *three*, since it made no sense. But when Katy read *pond* for *lake*, Mr. Larson didn't worry at all. If the sentence and story make sense with the substitution, the reader is reading for meaning, and that is what the reading process is all about. But, if Ron says a word that makes no sense and doesn't correct himself, Mr. Larson suspects Ron is only reading letters.

Successes, as well as errors, in reading provide information about children's reading strategies. When Aaron read the word *reptile* in a book about alligators, Mrs. Williams asked him how he figured out that word and made note of his response. When children need help figuring out a word, both Mr. Larson and Mrs. Williams encourage them to use the strategy of making a guess based on what would make sense, and then to use phonics clues to check their guess. This approach keeps the meaning of the reading, rather than the sounds of letters, in the forefront. These teachers never encourage vocalizing individual letters in an effort to put sounds together. They know the worthlessness of that approach.

So, we see Mr. Larson and Mrs. Williams using conferencing to provide guidance when needed, to determine skill levels, to plan temporary skills grouping, to encourage continued progress, to provide feedback to children, and to enjoy their reading and writing with them. Next, we will see how they also use conferences for evaluation. Does it sound like the teacher has plenty to do? If you as a teacher still have time on your hands, one of the best ways of teaching is to read something or write something yourself. Let the kids see you writing and tell them about it. Also, don't forget to read aloud to your students daily; they're *never* too old for this activity. The relaxed time enjoying a book together can do much to enhance a love of reading. Children also often want to read a book to themselves after having it read aloud by the teacher. A story time can also provide interesting topics for group discussions and explorations. Besides, stories increase vocabulary and general language and listening skills in third grade as much as in kindergarten.

EVALUATION AND DIAGNOSIS

You do need some systematic way of checking how well your teaching procedures are working with each child. To assist your students with their next step in learning and also to provide accountability for your teaching efforts, you must have this information. This doesn't mean that you have to put aside your goals for your students and give unrelated tests in order to come up with a numerical score for someone's charts. When Mrs. Williams wants this specific information about the progress of each of her students, she relies on descriptive comments

about individual children rather than number or letter comparisons of children's progress.

Mr. Larson also wants to make sure he knows details of what children have learned so that he won't waste his time and theirs presenting what a student already knows. He makes a concerted effort to focus on successes rather than weaknesses during his evaluation and diagnosis. He finds this approach encourages children to tackle needed learning with more confidence. This approach also provides him with information about what each child sees as important to learn and about the learning procedures which might be most effective for each child. In spite of the specificity of narrative descriptions of children's progress, Mr. Larson admits and accepts that he can never know exactly where each child is in every area. This position can be acceptable when children, rather than the teacher, direct their own learning.

Your goals and purposes for teaching can continue to be your guide as you plan evaluation procedures. In fact, evaluation separate from educational goals would seem impossible. Impatient with many evaluation materials, Mrs. Williams thinks they confuse the ends with the means. She sees many detailed check lists of a multitude of sub-skills, but she sees nothing to determine the really important outcomes of education.

Determined not to get side-tracked by concerns about how many phonics rules children know, she has a clear idea of the following *literacy goals* for her students:

- ☐ To enjoy reading and writing
- ☐ To frequently choose to read and write
- ☐ To read with increasing depth of meaning
- ☐ To express thoughts with increasing fluency, accuracy, and adequacy in writing

These long-range goals are generally accepted by all educators, but in practice they often get lost in the crunch of daily concerns such as correct spelling or neat penmanship.

Teacher Observation

Observation of children's actions serves as the backbone of evaluation for most teachers. Observation provides the intuitive response to a child's needs and determines whether the teacher can accept test results as valid or ignore them as inaccurate. This test data can never equal intimate knowledge of a child's strengths, motivations, and personality.

Mr. Larson acknowledges that his perceptions can sometimes be too subjective, as they are affected by personal feelings and extraneous pressures. Because of this, he keeps an anecdotal file of his specific observations. This card file contains a section for each student. Mr. Larson records children's behaviors and his own comments here as often as he considers necessary. If Mr. Larson is concerned about a child, he might make a concerted effort to record daily behavior over a period to discover patterns or test his perceptions. For instance, he was worrying about Sue recently because she seemed to be constantly asking for help and was unable to work independently. When he kept a tally record of her requests, he discovered that the number was decreasing. He then felt reassured.

Notes about how children spend their reading time and their time for choosing material also provide Mr. Larson with helpful information. He keeps track of which children quickly begin reading and which ones seem continually distracted with other things. He notices if a child idly thumbs through books with no apparent purpose in selecting or reading anything. He also considers reading behaviors outside of class to be significant. He wants to know if his students check books out at the school or local library and if they are reading at home. All this information guides Mr. Larson in selecting the most appropriate strategy to encourage and assist each child's literacy development. He knows that he cannot force a child to want to read or write, but he must figure out how to help each child find personal meaning and satisfaction in those activities.

Mrs. Williams also observes her students during silent reading. She can find out what they have been reading during conferences, but she also gets clues about their progress from knowing how they are reading. She watches and makes note of the following:

Silent Reading Observation Guide

1. Is the child engrossed in the reading?
2. Is the child distracted? If so, by what?
3. How long does the child stay involved?
4. Is involvement time increasing or decreasing?
5. Does the child move his lips as he reads silently?
6. Does the child ask for assistance?
7. From whom is assistance asked?
8. Does the child only ask for help with words or does the child also ask about ideas expressed?
9. Are the words that the child can't read difficult to understand in context?
10. Does the child occasionally laugh or otherwise respond while reading silently?
11. How rapidly does the child turn pages?
    So slowly as to indicate subvocalizing?
    So rapidly as to indicate skimming?
    So irregularly as to imply carefully reading selected portions?

Information gained from these observations guides Mrs. Williams as she plans activities for her students.

Although less useful than the ability to read silently, oral reading ability is also important. Mr. Larson finds that listening to his students read aloud gives him useful information about their reading progress. He is careful to give them a chance to become familiar with the words and ideas in any material before attempting to read it aloud. While a child reads, Mr. Larson listens for intonation; he notes whether the flow of language sounds similar to natural talking and whether the intonation reflects the meaning of what is read. He also notices pronunciation so that he can help with any mispronounced words after the child is finished reading. Obviously, he doesn't interrupt a reader to correct mispronunciations.

If pronunciation problems stem from dialect or language differences, Mr. Larson ignores them unless the child requests help. Only after a child expresses a desire to develop standard dialect in oral or written language, does Mr. Larson consider correction appropriate. When the child requests help, teacher assistance is much more effective during preparation of oral reading than as criticism afterwards. Mr. Larson shares Mrs. Hanna's conviction that children perceive criticism of their language as a personal rejection. He also agrees with her that to keep talking and writing is in the child's best interest, whether the speech or writing is standard English or not.

Having kids write is one of Mr. Larson's primary goals. When he observes children writing, he has an additional set of specific goals in mind. He looks for children to increasingly:

Writing Goals

1. Find satisfaction in writing.
2. See a variety of purposes for writing.
3. Communicate thoughts, feelings, and information.
4. Expand their use of varied sentence patterns and their vocabulary.
5. Take into account their audience.
6. Expand the audience for their writing.
7. Develop their own style.
8. Build plot and characters into story writing.
9. Develop an ability to express themselves poetically.

Mr. Larson is convinced that if children can attain the first two goals, they will be successful in attaining the others. When a child shows little progress in goals three through nine, he takes a hard look at the child's progress toward goals one and two.

Comparing children's writing over time provides much useful information about their progress. Mr. Larson helps his students set up files for keeping representative samples of their writing. Looking back over earlier writing efforts helps children get a strong sense of accomplishment and progress. Mr. Larson evaluates writing progress on the basis of writing accomplishment, not on any artificial verbalizing of rules and procedures for writing.

Teacher-Made Tests

Other ways of gathering data help teachers supplement their observations. Mrs. Williams sometimes makes her own tests in order to focus

on what she considers important. A teacher-made test which she considers useful, a *cloze test,* is created by taking a reading selection and deleting words every so often. The teacher substitutes blanks which the child must fill in either orally or in writing. Any word that makes sense in the context of the selection and sounds like normal language is an acceptable answer.

When Mrs. Williams devises cloze tests, she can tailor them to individual students' levels of ability and reading interests. In fact, a teacher can even use a cloze test with children who cannot yet read by making it an oral test of their ability to use context clues. Ms. Reynolds sometimes uses the cloze technique as a game during storytime in preschool. She will read and then stop, giving children the chance to supply the missing word. When Mrs. Williams creates a paper-and-pencil cloze test, she uses a selection of at least 250 words, leaving a blank for every fifth word. The blanks are all the same length with enough room for students to write a suitable word. She gives each child as much time as needed so no one feels pressured.

When a child has finished a cloze test, Mrs. Williams has more information than just the number of words the child missed. By analyzing the choice of words, she can determine what reading strategies the child is using and what others the child needs. This process is rather similar to the *miscue analysis* procedure described by Yetta Goodman and Carolyn Burke (1972) in *A Reading Inventory.* They describe how to analyze mistakes children make on reading an unfamiliar passage for the first time. Teachers can categorize mistakes according to whether the word substituted looked or sounded like the original, whether the substitution made sense in the selection, and whether changes made sense grammatically. Although formal miscue analysis requires specialized training, Mrs. Williams finds that observing children's reading to determine what skills they do or do not use is a useful diagnostic process.

Mrs. Williams has also discovered a computer program which can assist students in using context clues or configuration clues. *M-ss-ng L-nks* (Sunburst, 1984), created by Carol Chomsky and Judah Schwartz, provides passages from many children's literature classics. The program allows youngsters to decide what level of challenge they prefer; they can choose from trying to read with just the vowels in words left out, with every other letter omitted, with only the first letter of each word left in, or—the ultimate challenge—with only blanks for all the letters. Children also can decide how many chances they will get before the computer fills in a blank for them. Mrs. Williams finds this program unique in providing skill practice within meaningful contexts. She also likes its focus on the skills that efficient readers use most. This process helps free children from ponderous attention to each letter.

Mr. Larson occasionally creates informal reading inventories to help him focus on the reading comprehension skills of his students. He picks three different reading materials at increasingly difficult concept levels and marks selections of two or three pages at the beginning of each. Matching a set of readings to an individual child's abilities, interests, and background seems easier to Mr. Larson when he compiles his own set of readings instead of using standardized informal reading inventories. Today will be Ron's turn, and Mr. Larson has geared the reading material to what he thinks Ron will find easy, challenging, and difficult. After Ron has had a chance to silently read the first selection, Mr. Larson asks questions which will tell him whether Ron is using higher-level thinking skills such as organizing ideas, evaluating critically, making inferences, or applying ideas to other situations.

After experiencing success at one level, Ron is able to face more difficult challenges. Mr. Larson tells him the next reading selections are pretty hard; he just wants to see if Ron can do them. This preparation keeps Ron from feeling like a failure if he isn't successful with all the material. When Ron's responses indicate that he hasn't understood all that he has read, Mr. Larson asks Ron to read aloud to him so that he can identify the cause of the problem. This type of testing procedure gives Mr. Larson more valuable information than any standardized tests, but sometimes, he must use standardized measures.

Standardized Tests

That most testmakers perceive reading as naming words appears obvious to Mr. Larson. He knows that in actual reading, long selections provide the natural redundancy necessary for best use of context clues and for greatest communication of meaning. Yet, most tests use short paragraphs exclusively and do not test reading as we use it in real life.

Mr. Larson knows that children who score best on these tests may be those who use the strategy of reading the questions first and skim for the answer, rather than reading the entire selection. He has seen children who are excellent readers score very low on such tests. Therefore, he questions the validity of these tests and uses them as only one of several pieces of evidence about a child's progress. He also questions the reliability of these tests, knowing that if a child took the same test on another day his score would certainly not be the same. For Juan and Thien, these tests are simply not fair. The tests' cultural bias keeps youngsters from different backgrounds from doing well.

Mr. Larson finds standardized tests especially dehumanizing because they condense all information to a few numerical scores with which to compare children. These scores don't give any information about why a child made a certain error or what kind of help would correct that error. Mr. Larson dislikes the whole idea of comparing children against one another; instead, he looks at the progress each individual makes.

Criteria for Evaluation

Mrs. Williams and Mr. Larson agree that evaluation must meet the following criteria in order to be effective:

1. *Evaluations must be continuous.* Following the accomplishment of each activity, and sometimes during an activity, learners ask themselves, "How am I doing?" Teachers should

consistently look for each child's accomplishments and successes, no matter how small, and share them with the child.

2. *Evaluation must include each child's self-evaluation.* The individual learner knows better than anyone else if a task is simple or confusing; he knows if he has accomplished the task. If teachers don't take advantage of this source of information, children may learn to discount their own evaluations and feelings.

3. *Evaluation must be related to long-term goals.* Immediate accuracy such as reading the correct word or correctly spelling a word cannot overshadow the important goals of helping a child love to read and find satisfaction in writing.

4. *Progress is shown by accomplishments in the real world.* Out of school reading and writing is probably more important than that done in school. Unless children read and write on their own initiative, they are not destined to be literate. Too often school learning does not relate to life-long skills, but only to contrived school situations.

5. *Evaluation is the basis of planning for future learning.* Feedback from evaluation should be used by both teacher and learner as they mutually determine the next steps in the learning process.

Record Keeping

Teachers need a simple means of keeping records to make sure this task does not get put off during a busy day. We have mentioned Mrs. Williams's and Mrs. Thomas's notebooks in which they keep records. These have the advantage of being portable; the teachers can take them to a conference anywhere in the room or take them home at night to plan. The notebooks record all language arts activities and progress for each child. Each child has a section in the looseleaf notebook, marked by his or her name on a notebook divider. Notes about children's progress can be kept on regular notebook paper for convenience. Using one thick notebook, Mrs. Williams manages to keep a whole year's worth of notes about her students.

Each time she has a conference with a child, she makes notes in her book. She dates each entry and records what the child has been reading and writing, what was discussed at the conference, and what plans the child made for his next reading and writing activities. Two narrow columns are marked at the edge of the page. Here Mrs. Williams records skills mastered and skills to work on next. This information about each child is also recorded on a master sheet in the front of the notebook. Here, Mrs. Williams keeps track of which children are working on the same skills so they may profit from working together.

Children have a responsibility to keep records as part of their self-directed learning and as part of their role in self-evaluation. For example, the cumulative files of sample writings clearly show children how far they have come since the beginning of the school year. Mr. Larson provides a bottom cabinet drawer with a folder for each child to file writing samples. The top file drawer contains his notes from conferences which are also in individual file folders. Children have access to their own files, but not to those of anyone else.

Journal writing, with dated entries, are themselves records of children's progress. Youngsters can also use their journals to note relevant information, such as the name of a book just finished or a reaction to a book. Children can also use their journals to record other reading and writing related activities, such as reading a story to a kindergarten child, making up a skit and sharing it with the class, completing a mural project about a book, or writing a poem for Mother's birthday. Records kept by both student and teacher are an important guide during teacher-pupil conferences.

As a guide to self-evaluation of writing, Mr. Larson has developed a set of questions for children to ask themselves. His students can read these questions from a chart in the conference area.

Guide to Self-Evaluation of Writing

☐ Am I writing more now than I was before?
☐ Do I like most of what I write?
☐ What have I written besides stories?
☐ Can other people understand what I write?

If a child is not keeping records or carrying out assumed responsibilities, Mr. Larson gets worried. He suspects a lack of personal commitment on the part of the student, which may result from the child considering record keeping as another teacher-assigned task. If this occurs, Mr. Larson backs off and attempts to find out what the child thinks is important.

Learning Problems

Sometimes a child just doesn't seem to progress. Mr. Larson works hard to determine the cause of the problem before he tries to remedy it. First, he considers if it is a school-based problem or a home-based one. Discussions with parents often lead to mutual efforts on behalf of the child. If a situation outside of school is causing learning problems, families can be helped to find counseling and other resources.

If the problem lies with the school situation, then Mr. Larson considers it his job to try and correct it. He has seen some youngsters who had trouble reading because they had a mistaken idea of what reading was. Their previous experience led them to believe it was naming words rather than a thinking process. In these cases, Mr. Larson provided experiences to counteract this previous learning. He has found that going back to taking dictation from a child sometimes helps a youngster make that missing connection between print and meaning.

Sometimes a child has not learned procedures for self-help. In this case, a youngster may become discouraged and stop whenever he encounters an unknown word, not knowing what to do next. If this seems to be the problem, Mr. Larson focuses on helping the student learn to ask questions like, ''What word would make sense here?'' and ''What word that starts with that letter would make sense?'' Mr. Larson also says not to worry about a word if the story makes sense without knowing what it is. Finally, he reminds the child that there are twenty-five other youngsters in the class who can help him, if he asks.

At other times a child may have a motivation problem. Perhaps a child may have been trying to read material that was of no personal interest. Another youngster may not believe that any reading is worth doing. And still another may be totally turned off by any kind of school work. If a teacher just needs to help a child find something more interesting to read, the problem is simple. But, if the problem stems from a negative attitude toward reading or school in general, then the problem is serious. Mr. Larson has spent time and energy trying to determine why a certain student had negative feelings about learning. He needs to know if these feelings reflect past failures with learning, home attitudes, or emotional problems with authority. Until he has this information, Mr. Larson may have a hard time helping a child.

Mr. Larson tries to keep kids ''turned on'' to learning. He tries to involve them in activities that they have selected, and he attempts to maintain teacher-student relationships which keep kids open to his suggestions. He knows that when children like their teacher and think their teacher likes them, they are influenced by the teacher's enthusiasm and suggestions. He also thinks that encouraging self-direction and personal responsibility for learning keeps kids involved and interested in school.

Mr. Larson doesn't put kids with reading problems in a group where they aren't expected to do much. He believes this action will just confirm that they will never do anything. He also doesn't like to send children out of the room for special reading help. This procedure marks

the student as different and adds to his self-esteem problems that accompany school failure.

Mr. Larson hesitates to endorse typical remedial procedures, especially those with an emphasis on drill over isolated letters, sounds, or words. He fears that this type of instruction will make learning meaningless and more difficult. On the other hand, he has known some excellent remedial reading teachers who used other approaches and who worked with reading problems within the regular classroom. He has learned much about the roots of reading problems and ways of dealing with them from these specialists.

Mr. Larson welcomes the help of these specialists in his classroom. Sometimes he and the specialists can together discover a gap in understanding and remedy it with such special attention. Any extra help can ease the burden of trying to provide for each child's interests, level of knowledge, and style of learning.

Of course, he must help parents understand and deal with their children's learning problems. Periodically, parents ask if their child is *dyslexic.* Then, Mr. Larson explains that the term, dyslexia, has no meaning other than "does not read." When Tom's parents were convinced that Tom was dyslexic because he sometimes wrote letters backwards, Mr. Larson explained that children just becoming familiar with print are often unaware of the importance of which way a letter faces. He assured them that most reversal problems disappear by themselves after more experience with print. Naturally, Mr. Larson knows that some children do have physical impairments to learning. These youngsters must be accepted as they are and helped to achieve whatever their potential may be.

Evaluation of Your Program and Yourself

Whatever your students' strengths and weaknesses, you will want to continuously evaluate your ongoing program. The end of the school year calls for an in-depth look at what really happened to the children in your care—what they accomplished on their way to becoming responsible, contributing citizens.

You will want to analyze your efforts in helping them move toward confidence in their own thinking, in their ability to identify a problem, and in their approaches to solving it. How much more responsibility are they taking for their own actions, for their own learning, for initiating useful suggestions and activities, for providing needed assistance to others? Other relevant questions include how much more clearly and effectively can they talk to others, write for useful purposes, and write for their own satisfaction? How far have they progressed towards becoming lifelong readers?

Input may include comments from parents, any school personnel, and the children themselves. The answer to these questions will vary with each individual. A teacher needs to consider each issue for each child to get a complete picture.

For yourself, other questions arise: How much more able am I to listen to children, to what they really mean? How much more confidence have I developed in children's abilities to learn, to think, to be self-directive, and to be responsible? How much more often do I raise challenging questions rather than make instructional statements? How effectively have I been able to integrate the language arts, thus saving time and making learning more effective? How much more have I been able to use the language arts skills as an effective tool in the total school curriculum?

SUGGESTED FOLLOW-UP ACTIVITIES

1. Assist a child in selecting and preparing a story to read aloud to others. Remember that the choice of whether or not to read aloud

must be the child's. The choice of material to read must also be the child's.

2. Select written material of appropriate difficulty and on a relevant topic for a specific child. Follow the guidelines in the chapter to prepare and present a cloze test activity. Does this experience help the child become more aware of the importance of context clues? What did you discover about that child's use of context clues?

3. Observe children as they select books from a library. Note how they choose as they sort through collections. Try to determine what criteria or upon what basis they make their selections.

4. Help a child or small group find a purpose for writing which involves an intended audience. Assist the writer(s) to analyze the resulting work in terms of effective communication to that audience. If possible, arrange for the writer(s) to share their work with the intended audience.

5. Assist a child who wishes to polish something he or she has written. Follow procedures described in the preceding chapter.

6. Write something of your own using a word processing computer program. Use the program editing tools to polish your own writing. Contrast this editing process with the process you use for editing with a typewriter.

7. Learn how to bind books using cloth or contact paper-covered cardboard covers. Use taped or sewn bindings. Help a child create a book from some special writing.

8. Observe children reading silently. Note behavior and expressions which indicate comprehension and attitude toward the material.

9. One by one engage several children in private discussions about reading. The children should differ in reading abilities and levels. Ask each whether reading is enjoyable and why or why not. Ask each what kinds of reading materials he or she prefers. Ask how they deal with unknown words. Ask how they feel if they can't pronounce some words.

10. Engage children of differing writing abilities in private discussions about their writing. Ask what topics they usually write about and how they decide what to write. Ask if they write outside of school and for what reasons. Find out if they use any procedures for polishing when they share their writing with others. Ask what they like about their writing and what more they want to learn in order to write better.

11. Observe a teacher for a period of time. Note the ratio of thought provoking questions he or she raises versus the instructional statements made. If possible, tape record or video tape yourself teaching, and note the kinds of questions you use.

DISCUSSION TOPICS

1. A third grade student turns in a poorly written paper done hurriedly. The paper shows no thought or care for spelling, handwriting, punctuation, or even content. What should you do?

2. You are attempting to encourage creative writing in a second grade classroom. One of the children fears to write any word without knowing the correct spelling. She refuses to make a guess at spelling. Consequently, she writes very little and frequently interrupts the teacher to request correct spelling. How can this child be freed to learn through her own exploration of print?

3. Think about your own reading interests. How did they develop? What experiences have affected your choices of reading material? How do you decide whether or not you will read a particular book?

4. Families today seem to spend all their free time watching television and no longer read for pleasure. How can we motivate youngsters to do what their parents do not?

5. Many teachers' manuals provide check lists for assessing specific skills. How might these check lists be utilized by a teacher who was not following the program described in such a manual?

REFERENCES AND SUGGESTIONS FOR FURTHER READING

Books

Bond, G.L., Tinker, M.A., Wasson, B.B., & Wasson, J.B. (1984). *Reading difficulties: Their diagnosis and correction.* Englewood Cliffs, NJ: Prentice Hall.

Calkins, L.M. (1983). *Lessons from a Child.* Exeter, NH: Heinemann Educational Books.

Holdaway, D. (1979). *The foundations of literacy.* New York: Ashton Scholastic.

Goodman, K.S. (1968). *The psycholinguistic nature of the reading process.* Detroit: Wayne State University.

Goodman, Y.M., & Burke, C.L. (1972). *Reading miscue inventory manual; procedure for diagnosis and evaluation.* New York: Macmillan.

Graves, D. (1984). *A researcher learns to write.* Exeter, NH: Heinemann Educational Books.

Guszak, F. (1985). *Diagnostic reading instruction* (3rd ed.). New York: Harper and Row.

Lamme, L.L. (1984). *Growing up writing.* Washington, DC: Acropolis Books Lts.

Lee, D., & Rubin, J. (1979). *Children and language.* Belmont, CA: Wadsworth.

Newkirk, T., & Atwell, N. (1982). *Understanding writing.* Chelmsford, MA: Northeast Regional Exchange.

Pooley, R.C. (1974). *The teaching of English usage.* Urbana, IL: National Council of Teachers of English.

Pradl, G. (1982). *Prospect and retrospect: Selected essays of James Britton.* London: Heinemann Educational Books.

Rogers, J. (1985). *The secret moose.* New York: Greenwillow.

Scheffel, R.L. (Ed.). (1984). *ABC's of nature.* Pleasantville, NY: Reader's Digest Association, Inc.

Silvaroli, N.J. (1982) *Classroom reading inventory.* Dubuque, IA: Wm. C. Brown Co.

Smith, F. (1971). *Understanding reading.* New York: Holt, Rhinehart and Winston.

Smith, F. (1975). *Comprehension and learning.* New York: Holt, Rhinehart and Winston.

Smith, F. (1982). *Writing and the writer.* New York: Holt, Rhinehart and Winston.

Teale, W.H., & Sulzby, E. (Eds.). (1986). *Emergent literacy: Writing and reading.* Norwood, NJ: Ablex Publishing.

Temple, C.A., Nathan, R.G., & Burris, N.A. (1982). *The beginning of writing.* Boston: Allyn and Bacon.

Tiedt, I.M. et. al. (1983). *Teaching writing in K-8.* Englewood Cliffs, NJ: Prentice-Hall.

Veatch, J. (1968). *How to teach reading with children's books* (2nd ed.). New York: Citation Press.

Wilson, R.M. (1985). *Diagnostic and remedial reading for classroom and clinic.* Columbus, OH: Charles E. Merrill.

Woods, M.L. and Alden, J.M. (1985). *Analytical reading inventory.* Columbus, OH: Charles E. Merrill.

Periodicals and Documents

Agnew, A.T. (1982, January). Using children's dictated stories to assess code consciousness. *Reading Teacher, 35,* 450-454.

Anderson, P. (1984, December). Testing—testing—testing—testing—testing—testing. *Early Years,* p. 42.

Bailey, M.H. (1967). The utility of phonic generalizations in grades one through six. *The Reading Teacher, 20,* 413-418.

Blackburn, E. (1984, April). Common ground: Developing relationships between reading and writing. *Language Arts, 61,* 367-375.

Bradley, V. (1982, October). Improving students' writing with microcomputers. *Language Arts, 59,* 732-743.

Bristow, P.S., Pikulski, J.J., & Pelosi, P.L. (1983, December). A comparison of five estimates of reading instructional levels. *Reading Teacher, 37,* 273-279.

Cazden, C. (1977, October). Putting it all together. *National Elementary Principal, 58* (2), 40-44.

Chomsky, C. (1976, March). After decoding: What? *Language Arts, 53,* 289-294.

Clymer, T. (1963). The utility of phonic generalizations in the primary grades. *The Reading Teacher, 16,* 252-258.

Coon, G.E., & Palmer, G. (1985, January). Writing to be read. *Early Years,* pp. 49-54.

Dixon, C. (1977, May). Language experience stories as a diagnostic tool. *Language Arts, 54,* 501-505.

Dyson, A.H. (1984, December). N Spell My Grandmama. *The Reading Teacher, 38,* 262-271.

Dyson, A.H. (1985, October). Writing and the social lives of children. *Language Arts, 62,* 632-639.

Eckhoff, B. (1983, May). How reading affects children's writing. *Language Arts, 60,* 607-616.

Estabrook, I. (1982, October). Talking about writing—developing independent writers. *Language Arts, 59,* 696-706.

Fillion, B. (1983, September). Let me see you learn. *Language Arts, 60,* 702-711.

Goodman, Y.M., & Sims, R. (1974). Whose dialect for beginning readers? *Elementary English, 51,* 837-841.

Graves, D., & Hansen, J. (1983, February). The author's chair. *Language Arts, 60,* 177-183.

Hannan, E., & Hamilton, G. (1984, April). Writing: What to look for, what to do. *Language Arts, 61,* 364-366.

Hayes, D. and Cherrington, C. (1985, Fall). Children's early writing: Function and command. *Educational Horizons, 64,* 25-31.

Hosey, J.G. (1977). Oral reading—misused? *Elementary School Journal, 77,* 218-220.

Loughlin, C.E. (1980). *Reflecting literacy in the environment.* Unpublished manuscript, University of New Mexico, Department of Elementary Education, Albuquerque.

McCormick, S. (1981, October). Assessment and the beginning reader: Using standard dictated stories. *Reading World,* pp. 29-39.

Moore, D.W. (1983, November/December). A case for naturalistic assessment of reading comprehension. *Language Arts, 60,* 957-969.

Ohanian, S. (1984, September). Will you recognize the ready moment? *Learning, 60,* 62-71.

Pearson, C. (1980, November). The main event: Reading vs. reading skills. *Learning,* pp. 26-30.

Read, C. (1973). Children's judgements of phonetic similarities in relation to English spelling. *Language Learning, 23,* 17-38.

Readdick, C. (1984, July). A red marble! Guidelines for speaking to children. *Young Children, 39* (5), 67-73.

Rief, L.M. (1984, September). Writing and rappelling. *Learning,* pp. 72-81.

Roberts, F. (1984, May). Testing 1 . . . 2 . . . 3. *Parents,* pp. 44-46.

Smith, F. (1983, May). Reading like a writer. *Language Arts, 60,* 558-567.

Spiegel, D.L. (1983, Fall). Reading for reading comprehension. *Reading Horizons,* pp. 13-17.

Squire, J.R. (1983, May). Composing and comprehending: Two sides of the same basic process. *Language Arts, 60,* 581-589.

Stafford, W. (1985, January). Exploring the wild, surprising world of poetry. *Learning,* pp. 38-41.

Sulzby, E. (1985). *When kindergarteners compose: A developmental study of writing.* Paper presented at the annual meeting of the American Educational Research Association, Chicago.

Tierney, R.J., & Pearson, P.D. (1983, May). Toward a composing model of reading. *Language Arts, 60,* 568-580.

Yatvin, J. (1984, Nov./Dec.). Instead of waiting they could be working. *Learning,* pp. 76-79.

Children's Magazines Mentioned

Cricket

Odyssey

Scholastic Magazine

World

Computer Software

Chomsky, C., & Schwartz, J. (1984). *M-ss-ng L-nks* (Computer program). Pleasantville, NY: Sunburst Communications.

Hartley, C.A. (1983). *The Sensible Speller IV* (Computer program). Oak Park, MI: Sensible Software Inc.

5

Selecting Reading Programs and Materials

Tell a child WHAT to think,
and you make him a slave to your knowledge.
Teach him HOW to think,
and you make all knowledge his slave.

(Henry A. Taitt, 1982)

Constantly, we see advertisements for new and revolutionary approaches to reading instruction which assure success for all children. Many new or improved basal readers guarantee success by following their "recipe." With all these claims, how does the teacher or curriculum committee decide which approach to choose?

To make this decision more confusing, all programs have the same goal: for children to become proficient readers. Also, most make statements about the importance of helping children to succeed and to enjoy reading. Most offer attractive and colorful formats for children and time-saving, packaged teaching aids for teachers. In practice, the large textbook companies, with their array of readers, workbooks, drill sheets, flash cards, record keeping forms, and tests, tend to dictate how reading is taught in this country.

If educators select commercially published reading materials based on their beliefs about how children learn and about what is worth teaching, then using commercially published materials is both educationally sound and efficient. However, if educators choose programs based on whether the format is attractive, or by how easily the materials are to implement, or how well the materials provide accountability, then educators are making decisions based on nonprofessional criteria.

Philosophical considerations must guide judgement in selecting reading approaches and materials. Educators must first have a clear idea of what you believe reading is and how students develop reading competence; then, find materials that fit that belief. Materials should not determine the philosophy; the philosophy must determine the materials.

READING PHILOSOPHIES

Educators sometimes discuss reading philosophy as broad educational theories; for example, maturational, cognitive developmental, and behavioral theories are compared. We hear Gesell's ideas about time being the basic ingredient for learning and compare them with Piaget's ideas that action on the environment, social interaction, and equilibration (Almy, 1976) must be coupled with time. Skinner's theories contrast with the other two as they detail step-by-step learning through reinforcement. Although a view of the learner is inherent in each of these theories, sometimes teachers have difficulty relating any one of these broad theories to the specifics of reading.

More typically, reading philosophy discussion reflects the types of materials available. So, we hear debates about basal readers vs. self-selected reading materials, or basal readers vs. language experience stories. Actually, teachers may use each type of material so differently that the material reflects many different philosophies.

Once hotly-debated were the philosophical differences between phonics approaches and sight word approaches. Although proponents of each became opponents of the other, these two views are not far apart. Both operate on the assumption that after you teach children a sub-skill of reading, those children can then unlock the mystery of the printed page. Each method teaches specific facts by rote, whether they are the sound-symbol relationships of letters or the appearance of various words. Each assumes that youngsters can put these parts of the puzzle together to determine the whole of the meaning.

A more significant philosophical issue appears to be that characterized by the whole to part approach vs. the part to whole approach. As indicated, both the phonics approach and the sight word approach are essentially part to whole approaches. Of course, teaching letters separate from words would be a more extreme part to whole technique than teaching words separate from meaningful context. Nevertheless, whenever we teach word or letter recognition apart from context, we are teaching part to whole. The intent of the part to whole approaches is to break down the huge task of learning to read into child-sized chunks. The programs emphasize observable behaviors of saying letter sounds and identifying words. Teachers who use this approach assume that obtaining meaning occurs as a result of saying the words in a sentence.

Whole to part approaches are characterized by insistence upon context, or meaning, when teaching reading skills. So, when teachers present phonics, sight words, and other reading skills through whole to part approaches, they use written materials which communicate something. Children's dictated stories, their invented spelling compositions, or a book they have chosen provide the necessary content. The whole to part philosophy is based on the definition of reading as getting meaning from print. Since letters and even words alone have no meaning, for teachers to use isolated letters and words for reading is inappropriate. Whole to part advocates fear that an emphasis on the words and letters themselves will detract from children's abilities to concentrate on the meaning of what they read. They further believe that the whole of reading is much more than the sum of its parts. Since adults already understand the essence of reading, they are capable of putting the parts in their places and making sense of the total reading puzzle; children don't have that framework, and so they may jumble and confuse the pieces.

Part to Whole	*Whole to Part*
□ Directed instruction	□ Discovery learning
□ Teacher dispenses knowledge	□ Child constructs knowledge
□ Synthesis skill	□ Analysis skills
□ Behaviorist theory	□ Piaget theory
□ Phonics based	□ Language experience and literature based
□ Skills first	□ Writing first

Typically part to whole beliefs are compatible with an emphasis on directed instruction and the teacher as the center of learning. Whole to part beliefs are more compatible with an emphasis on discovery learning and the child as the center of learning.

Consider *Bloom's Taxonomy* of thinking skills (1956) in relation to this issue. Snythesizing, required for the part to whole approach, is listed as a more difficult skill than that of analyzing, which is required for the whole to part approach. This heirarchy provides one more argument against the part to whole approach for beginning reading. Additionally, part to whole approaches are incompatible with Piagetian descriptions of how children learn. Educators should have a firm understanding of child development theories in order to determine which ones are implicit in any given curriculum material.

An historical perspective of the field of reading and education in general reveals philosophical swings from one extreme to another. We can look back to the "look-say" period when phonics was considered passé and contrast that with the "back to basics" trend. We can contrast the quiet classroom of desks in rows with the "open-chaos" rooms which gave alternatives to traditional education a bad name. Although each new fad is generally based on some sound principles, too often the educational system loses a sense of balance and proportion in the implementation process. Also, too often we rush into new things without adequate preparation and therefore invite failure.

REVIEWING BASAL READERS

As a precaution against failure, school districts involve teachers in reviewing and recommending instructional materials before the district adopts them. Although personally opposed to purchasing one set of basal readers and uneasy about selecting one series for all teachers at all levels, the teachers we have been observing remain involved in reviewing reading materials for possible adoption.

From past experience, Mrs. Williams knows that each program has unique aspects and variations, but their concepts of the reading process are basically the same. She expects all the basal reading programs to include a series of readers, teacher's manuals for each book, and in most cases supplementary material such as workbooks and/or ditto masters, particularly at the primary levels.

Mrs. Thomas particularly dislikes one feature used by nearly all the basal programs—a *controlled vocabulary*. When texts introduce words systematically, and use no word that has not been previously introduced, the stories become stilted, and young readers get bored. Mrs. Thomas doesn't share the underlying assumption that reading is a process of identifying individual words, nor does she share the belief that children cannot recognize any word that they have not been formally taught. Also, she doesn't believe that if a child cannot read— or say—a word in a list of words, then the child doesn't know the word. Frequently, she has observed that children read words in context correctly before they can read them in a list (Goodman, 1973).

Particularly insulted by teacher's manuals which explain only the authors' concept of the reading process and present a sequence of specific skills that should be taught, Mr. Larson becomes irate when the manual suggests the actual wording for teachers to use in each of the lessons. He also dislikes manuals which suggest dividing the class into groups according to reading ability, three groups being the common practice. These detailed teacher instructions suggest to Mr. Larson that the author of the manual does not expect teachers to think.

Mrs. Williams realizes that reading programs using basals have changed very little since she was in first grade and bored to death in reading groups. In the majority of classrooms, we still find graded books with a controlled vocabulary from primer through sixth or eighth grade, short stories gradually increasing in length through the grades, and children in groups doing round robin reading.

Some changes have occurred. Much color now appears in readers, and pictures have increased in number and importance. Stories reflect ethnic and handicapped groups as well as a variety of lifestyles. Girls appear to be more active characters than they once were. The stories are somewhat more in tune with children's experiences, though whether more interesting is sometimes questionable. During the last ten years, however, the quality and appeal of the content has increased significantly.

The greatest difference between programs is the way each program handles phonics. Some reading series begin by introducing one or two words a day with picture associations. This is known as the *look-say* or *sight word* method which the Scott-Foresman Company used in "Dick and Jane" readers that Mrs. Williams remembers from first grade. Through this approach, children learn to recognize the words as wholes. Gradually, teachers introduce words a little faster, and most children soon build a word-recognition vocabulary of fifty to 125 sight words. At this point, the program begins to include phonics,

the sounds indicated by separate letters. Teachers then begin to expect children to recognize unknown words by blending these sounds.

Some reading programs start with phonics by teaching each letter, its name, and the sound it represents, in various sequences. In some programs, children begin reading words composed of the letters already taught, but other programs teach all the letter-associated sounds prior to any significant reading. Procedures then emphasize the "sounding out" of words not recognized. Mrs. Thomas stands opposed to this process since it involves the highly questionable procedure of attempting to isolate individual letter sounds and blend them together to sound like a word. Also, since so many of the most common and useful words don't follow the phonetic rules, this approach may cause young children to feel frustrated.

The first set of reading materials the group of teachers review, *The Headway Program*, published by Open Court, is a type of phonics-based program. The teacher's manual states that direct instruction and highly structured activities are important teaching strategies. A motivational strategy, *hot teaching*,—"a lively, fast-paced, and enthusiastic teaching presentation"—is recommended to help keep children interested. Mrs. Thomas thinks it sounds similar to the "Sesame Street" style. The teacher acts as the prime motivator as well as the source of information in this program. Mr. Larson comments that this approach ignores children's innate interest in reading as well as their ability to figure out reading rules as they figured out oral language rules.

This program concentrates on teaching not just one sound for each letter, but all possible spellings for each sound. Picture clues such as an angry goose for the *th* sound, both voiced and unvoiced, are used and reinforced with the prominent display of an illustrated card for each sound. The angry lion stands for the sound of *r* and *wr* at the beginning of words and for *er, ir,* and *ur* in the middle of words. The flat tire sound is for *s* and for *ce, ci,* and *cy*. Vowels appear on cards having a different format, called "block cards," which review the various rules pertaining to vowels. This program also systematically reviews many phonics generalization rules, such as the fact that the letters *e, i,* and *y* signal a change in the sound of nearby letters. Mr. Larson jokes that he could never learn all the rules. Mrs. Hanna joins Mrs. Thomas in being upset that the publisher recommends this content for the first half of first grade *or* the entire kindergarten year, and perhaps even for preschool. Both teachers agree that they would never use such an approach in their classrooms.

Some of the other teachers are attracted to the wide variety of teaching materials that come with the program. These materials provide children with a huge amount of drill and practice. Mrs. Thomas is interested in the process where the teacher dictates sounds, words, and sentences for the children to sound out and spell according to the rules they have learned. After further reviewing the materials, the teachers discover that although instructors may accept spelling inventions, these inventions are put on the board to be corrected in public and recopied by the entire class. Mrs. Hanna points out that the program recommends writing topics be related to stories in the booklets rather than to children's own experiences or interests. These teachers agree that this reading program ignores the important idea of children constructing their own knowledge.

At the next review session, the teachers study a series published by Houghton-Mifflin. Mrs. Williams expects that like most "best selling" basal programs, this series will attempt to combine some of everything in hope of pleasing everyone. This series uses a seemingly safe approach of teaching sight words, phonics, word patterns, whole words, and whole sentences and context clues, while constantly checking for comprehension. But, Mrs. Hanna says she has a friend who is having

trouble using this series in her kindergarten class. The friend complains that with the workbook covering so much content at once, her students are having trouble and don't want to use the workbook anymore. She says that the two children in her class who already know how to read are having a great time with the workbook, but those for whom it is aimed just can't understand it. This statement seems to validate Mrs. Hanna's belief that practice is useful for those skills already learned, but not as a tool for learning skills initially.

Directions such as "turn to the beginning of the book and put a line under . . . " are beyond the capabilities of many of the children in this teacher's class. She says they can't find the *beginning,* don't know which is *under,* and aren't even sure what a line is yet. With the program she formerly used, children could tell from the pictures what they were supposed to do.

Mrs. Hanna's friend compares her new Houghton-Mifflin program with one published by Lippincott which she used for several years. She didn't agree with the phonics approach of the Lippincott materials, but at least the children could do the work and enjoyed much of it. What they liked best were the cut and paste activities; they didn't care whether they pasted the right picture by the letter, but they loved pasting. This teacher prefers not to use commercially published reading materials, but her school policy mandates that all teachers will use the program formally adopted by the district.

Previously she had to use a program which didn't present material that she considers significant, and now is using one which turns kids off to what is significant. She struggles to make time in the short kindergarten day for the reading activities she considers valuable.

Next the Macmillan series arrives for review. Mrs. Thomas carefully reviews the pre-primers: *You Can, I Can Too,* and *We Can Read.* She feels convinced that many of her first graders would not be able to proceed at the rate presented in the books. Mrs. Thomas would have to use a pre-primer level book from another series when her slowest youngsters finish the Macmillan pre-primers in order for them to get the feeling of progressing without forcing them to move ahead to more difficult material.

In reading the books for first grade, Mrs. Thomas sees immediately that she would have trouble getting her students involved with these stories. Holding children's attention for stories with controlled and limited vocabulary (and consequently stilted and unnatural language patterns) always poses a problem. When little or no relationship exists between the story content and the children's own experiences and current interests, the problem grows. In the past, she has put a great deal of energy into building interest by bringing in items pertinent to story topics.

This tactic helped with the problem of topic relevance, but it did not always solve the problem of language relevance. Mrs. Thomas knows that when written sentence patterns are unnatural, children are unable to use what they know about oral language to assist with written language. With unfamiliar language styles and topics, a child cannot use syntax and context clues.

The Macmillan series, like most others, relies on pictures in beginning reading material to provide the context clues for many words. Sometimes there is no point in reading the words in these stories, since the pictures tell the story. During one lesson, the children were supposed to read in order to find where a pet lizard had disappeared; but, the picture clearly showed the lizard on its owner's back.

Another problem results from the basal reader tradition of round robin reading. Many teachers have abandoned the practice of having children take turns reading orally after observing kids reading ahead or day dreaming while another child reads. Mr. Larson feels especially sorry for the faster reader who sits in utter boredom while another child labors over a passage. He recognizes that oral reading is a skill separate from silent reading—one with its own set of criteria for excellence.

The multitude of questions and discussion topics suggested in the teacher's manual for each page of a story may also create an interest problem. A child may have trouble sustaining the flow or excitement of the story with these long interruptions. Mrs. Williams points out that if a teacher attempted to complete all or even most of the suggestions accompanying a story, the length of the lesson would guarantee loss of children's attention.

Mrs. Thomas wishes all reading series would abolish workbooks. Although some of her students like them, generally workbook assignments are met by groans. Just keeping the constantly changing directions in mind sufficiently challenges many children. Not surprisingly, Mrs. Thomas often observes children mindlessly marking response patterns without demonstrating understanding or thought. Most often the assignments themselves encourage this sort of mindlessness, such as when children are to mark all the words with a long vowel sound created by an *e* at the end of the word. Children needn't read to do this,—just watch for the *e* and mark those words. However, one page listed the word *come* along with *rope, bone, home,* and *mope.* Mrs. Thomas discovered her children were dutifully marking *come* as having a long vowel sound.

When workbooks try to cover comprehension skills, different problems emerge. Usually, children are either to match the reading selections with a picture or sort them into those which do or don't make sense. The problem lies in the inherently low interest level of the selections and the fact that many children come to associate reading with this type of work. If children must laboriously read these relatively meaningless passages, a high level of errors may result, especially for slower children. Naturally, children begin to have negative feelings about the whole process. One teacher reported having a group of children repeating first grade who had all been totally turned off to reading.

Yet, most basal series teacher manuals state that developing readers who confidently enjoy reading is their major goal. Although teachers cannot possibly argue with the goal, many question whether the prescribed processes can result in its attainment. They notice that most reading series also recommend desirable practices such as dictated or child written language experience stories and library books as supplements to the basal program. Yet, they know how difficult it is to find time for these valuable activities after children complete all the required reading and workbook pages.

Mr. Larson, Mrs. Thomas, and Mrs. Williams believe that the teacher's manual should serve as a guidebook, to be used at their descretion. They often thumb through manuals for exciting activities and for references to special directed lessons which they choose to teach. They see the manuals as useful aids to teaching, but never as "cookbooks" to follow precisely.

CREATIVELY USING BASAL READERS

As these teachers discuss and critique basal reading series, they discuss ways to use them constructively within their approach to reading instruction. Mrs. Thomas includes a few copies of various basal readers among the variety of materials available for her students. Some children are attracted to these books, and some are even attracted to the workbooks that can go with them. Mrs. Thomas keeps multiple copies of basal readers because they're valuable for the response to literature activities they include and the selections which students may find helpful for research activities. Many of the books contain excellent poetry, short stories, and plays. Mrs. Thomas knows exactly where to find her favorites.

Since none of these teachers use "round robin" reading, they look for educationally sound ways to give children practice in oral reading. Choral reading requires little preparation on the teacher's part and offers a safe situation for children to read aloud. Mrs. Thomas sometimes gathers a group of five or six children and reads them several short poems from various basals. After the children choose a favorite, she and the group read in unison several times. They discuss good expression and sometimes even decide to add props. They may read their poem to others. Mrs. Thomas knows that this enjoyable group activity meets the objectives of enjoyment of poetry and practice in oral interpretation.

Mrs. Williams often has students who love plays. The basals provide multiple copies of easy-to-read plays. Mrs. Thomas says that she has found plays in basal readers that most first graders can under

Alternatives to Round Robin Reading

There is little evidence that the traditional oral reading circle is of any educational value. However, many teachers still consider the ability to read orally an important skill. What are some ways to retain oral reading in the program?

Oral Reading for Diagnostic Purposes

☐ Have children read orally to the teacher in a one on one situation.
☐ Have children read orally to a tape recorder, parent volunteer, or older
☐ child.

Oral Reading for Information Sharing

☐ Children can read the lunch menu, daily bulletin, and newspaper items.
☐ Children can confirm an answer by reading it from a book.
☐ One child (a good reader) can read out loud while others listen with their text books closed.
☐ Children can read passages from reference books or trade books.

Oral Reading for Entertainment

☐ "Chinese Reading:" Two children share one book, reading to each other
☐ Choral reading
☐ Reading poems or essays for audience
☐ Radio drama, play reading, or readers' theater
☐ Sharing original, creative writing or reports

Tips about Oral Reading

☐ Anything read for an audience should be prepared in advance.
☐ Oral reading decreases comprehension.
☐ Teach children how to read punctuation and inflection.
☐ Give children the opportunity to listen to good readers (tapes and records).

From unpublished paper by K. Spangler, 1986, Juneau, AK: University of Alaska, Center for Teacher Education. Reprinted by permission.

stand and easily read. When a group of youngsters have become tired of creative dramatics and express an interest in putting on a real play, the basals come in handy.

Sometimes a class integrates their current studies around a certain theme. The class may study pets, or sea animals, or families for several weeks at a time. In addition to the relevant library books a teacher may bring into the class reading area, she may find many appropriate stories in basal readers. Sometimes children use the basals to do research on special topics. For example, when Mike shared in a "show and tell" group that he wanted to be a policeman when he grew up, Mrs. Thomas directed him to a basal story about a policeman.

By the time children are in first or second grade, they begin to recognize authors they especially like. Mr. Larson features one children's author each month for his literature corner. His class knows Peter Spier, Beatrix Potter, Ezra Jack Keats, and Arnold Lobel. Many of the basal eclectic readers published in the 70's and 80's feature excerpts from esteemed children's authors such as these. Mr. Larson also uses multiple copies of basals so his students can share stories by favorite authors.

Mrs. Williams often cuts out the stories she especially likes from the old basal readers and asks a parent volunteer to laminate and file them. After the volunteer files these special stories, she discards the outdated books.

LOOKING AT OTHER APPROACHES

Selecting a program after reviewing the mass of available material and accompanying advertisments is overwhelming. Mrs. Williams proposes that the district consider other possible choices, such as the programs which use only library materials and children's own writing. Because these programs have no reading materials for the publishers to advertise, they are easily overlooked. Too often the "newness" of material, the cost, or the effectiveness of a salesperson determines the selection.

Individualized Reading

The teachers whose classrooms we have been describing all use some form of *individualized reading,* a general term that covers a wide range of programs. Individualized reading means that *a teacher plans with each child in a classroom and for each child individually,* not that all teacher-pupil interaction is conducted on a one-to-one basis. The material children read takes into account their general stage of reading development, interests, and desires. Therefore, each child chooses materials to read from among those available. A teacher or school using this program provides material having a wide range of difficulty, content, and format. The teacher notes each child's progress and whether to provide any direct instruction through small groups with common needs, through individual or small group activities and experiences, or during the teacher-pupil reading conference. The frequency of conferences varies with the stage of development and the particular needs of each child, from four or five times a week to once every week or so.

Several factors work together to deter teachers from individualizing their instruction. Often schools do not have a wide range of materials. Their supply has remained limited through purchasing sets of thirty-five or forty copies of the same book. Some teachers have only learned to work with children as a group and rely on being able to say, "Take out your books and turn to page sixty-seven." Many teachers lack confidence that children do learn by constructing their own knowledge rather than from direct instruction. "How can they know something, if I don't teach it?" they say. Some teachers misunderstand both individualized instruction and how children learn when they say, "I just don't have time to teach material to each child separately."

Certain schools continue their basal programs but use individualized reading as a supplementary library program. Others use the basal readers but allow the advanced readers to read ahead as fast as they can and in any sequence they wish. Another procedure, erroneously called individualized instruction, has each child use the same materials in the same sequence and carry out the same assignments in the same way. Each child moves along the path at his or her own rate. Of course this method only individualizes in terms of rate of progressing through specified material, and ignores all else that is individual about a child.

When the concept of individualized instruction was the "in" approach, publishers jumped onto the bandwagon and marketed extensive sets of materials and keyed tests. Teachers placed each child at the point indicated by the test scores. Then, children worked at their own rate. Because of the volume of material available, they stayed busy throughout the year. Few teachers recognized that these programs violated all but one of the basic principles originally established for individualized instruction, the rate of going through the material. Individualizing in terms of learning style, personal interests, background, or specific instructional needs were all ignored. The implicit assumption, often unrecognized, is that the more capable the child, the more of the same type of material the child should cover. This approach is not particularly rewarding to the children. As one boy said, "It's no fun being smart; you just have to do more work."

Language Experience Approach

Earlier chapters in this book describe teachers and parents taking dictation from children, using those materials and that process to help youngsters become literate. This method is called the *language experience approach* to reading and writing gradually evolves into individualized reading and creative writing.

The language experience approach grew out of the teaching of reading with experience charts that began in the late 1930's and early 1940's. At first, charts were all group charts (Figure 5.1). Then, educators discovered that children were more interested in their own individual dictations and learned more from them. As the interrelationship of all aspects of the language arts became more evident and teachers became more aware of the importance of children's own experiences to their learning, the language experience approach developed.

Through experiences with children as long ago as the 1930's, Lamoreaux and Lee (1943) found that the stories children dictated were

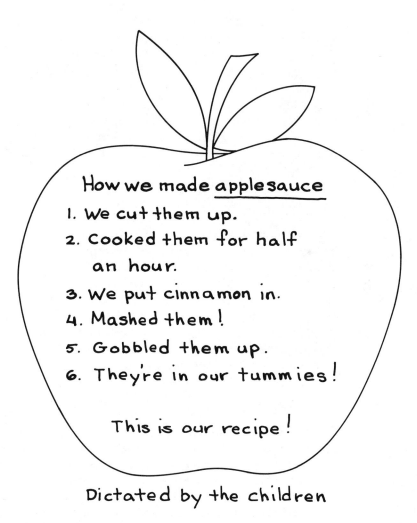

How we made apple sauce

1. We cut them up.
2. Cooked them for half an hour.
3. We put cinnamon in.
4. Mashed them!
5. Gobbled them up.
6. They're in our tummies!

This is our recipe!

Dictated by the children

Figure 5.1   A language-experience chart dictated by a group of children to their teacher.

easiest for them to read. In a revision of their book, Lee and Allen (1963) extended the program to include substantial use of individually dictated stories, independent writing, and self-selected reading. Sylvia Ashton-Warner (1963) developed a program based on a similar rationale. In New Zealand, working with Maori children, she used an individualized program with a *key vocabulary.* Unique to each child, this vocabulary was developed from the one word that each child most wanted to know each day. Dr. Ashton-Warner wrote each of these words on a card. She found that when the word was truly important to the child, he or she never forgot it. Mrs. Thomas's students also cherish their own special words. Each child in her class has a set of word cards with words like *rocket* or *love* or whatever that child has requested. They delight in showing their own words to class visitors.

Educators generally accept the value of the language experience methods of teaching reading in the early years. Most basal reader programs encourage language experience activities as supplements for enrichment. Many persons writing about beginning reading emphasize the importance of language experience activities to show children the connection between spoken and written language (Durkin, 1980; Flood and Lapp, 1981).

A true language experience program is built on the child's natural ways of learning—through experiences. The basic premises of this approach are expressed in the following: "What a child thinks about he can talk about. What he can talk about can be expressed in painting, writing or some other form. He can read what he writes and what other people write" (Lee and Allen, 1963).

Chapter 3 includes a description of how a language experience program encourages each child to talk about a personal experience or idea. Each child dictates a statement which the teacher records and reads back to the child. After a number of talking and dictating experiences with a small group of peers, children can read back the sense of the stories themselves. Writing through dictation encourages children to write by themselves, using many resources available around the room. Children can read their own stories as well as many of those written by their friends. They soon begin to find they can read some of the books in the room library.

Misunderstanding has resulted in confusion about how to use the language-experience approach. In some classes teachers use only group dictation, and everyone copies it. Sometimes an instructor teaches a dictated story with all the rigor and mechanics of a basal program. Some teachers expect children to work alone having no interaction with other children and books, reading only what they themselves dictate or write. Occasionally, children are even grouped for language-experience lessons on the basis of achievement.

PRE-PRIMARY AND INFANT-TODDLER PROGRAMS

Now that the general public has become aware of the importance of learning in the early years, instructional materials are available for very young children. Concerned about children's learning, many adults have come to feel they must provide these instructional materials for them. Parents are also faced with important decisions about educational programs for their children and want more information for making educational decisions.

Reading Readiness Programs

Parents frequently ask Mrs. Reynolds to look at materials designed for "reading readiness." She must respond to the parents from her cooperative preschool who think she should be using these types of materials.

Literacy Development and Pre-First Grade

A Joint Statement of Concerns about Present Practices in Pre-First Grade Reading Instruction and Recommendations for Improvement

☐ **Association for Supervision and Curriculum Development**
☐ **International Reading Association**
☐ **National Association for the Education of Young Children**
☐ **National Association of Elementary School Principals**
☐ **National Council of Teachers of English**

Prepared by the Early Childhood and Literacy Development Committee of the International Reading Association

Concerns

1. Many pre-first grade children are subjected to rigid, formal pre-reading programs with inappropriate expectations and experiences for their levels of development.
2. Little attention is given to individual development or individual learning styles.
3. The pressures of accelerated programs do not allow children to be risk-takers as they experiment with language and internalize concepts about how language operates.
4. Too much attention is focused upon isolated skill development or abstract parts of the reading process, rather than upon the integration of oral language, writing and listening with reading.

5. Too little attention is placed upon reading for pleasure; therefore, children often do not associate reading with enjoyment.

6. Decisions related to reading programs are often based on political and economic considerations rather than on knowledge of how young children learn.

7. The pressure to achieve high scores on standardized tests that frequently are not appropriate for the kindergarten child has resulted in changes in the content of programs. Program content often does not attend to the child's social, emotional and intellectual development. Consequently, inappropriate activities that deny curiosity, critical thinking and creative expression occur all too frequently. Such activities foster negative attitudes toward communication skill activities.

8. As a result of declining enrollments and reduction in staff, individuals who have little or no knowledge of early childhood education are sometimes assigned to teach young children. Such teachers often select inappropriate methodologies.

9. Teachers of pre-first graders who are conducting individualized programs without depending upon commercial readers and workbooks need to articulate for parents and other members of the public what they are doing and why.

Recommendations

1. Build instruction on what the child already knows about oral language, reading and writing. Focus on meaningful experiences and meaningful language rather than merely on isolated skill development.

2. Respect the language the child brings to school, and use it as a base for language and literacy activities.

3. Ensure feelings of success for all children, helping them see themselves as people who can enjoy exploring oral and written language.

4. Provide reading experiences as an integrated part of the broader communication process, which includes speaking, listening and writing, as well as other communication systems such as art, math and music.

5. Encourage children's first attempts at writing without concern for the proper formation of letters or correct conventional spelling.

6. Encourage risk-taking in first attempts at reading and writing and accept what appear to be errors as part of children's natural patterns of growth and development.

7. Use materials for instruction that are familiar, such as well-known stories, because they provide the child with a sense of control and confidence.

8. Present a model for students to emulate. In the classroom, teachers should use language appropriately, listen and respond to children's talk, and engage in their own reading and writing.

9. Take time regularly to read to children from a wide variety of poetry, fiction and non-fiction.

10. Provide time regularly for children's independent reading and writing.

11. Foster children's affective and cognitive development by providing opportunities to communicate what they know, think and feel.

12. Use evaluative procedures that are developmentally and culturally appropriate for the children being assessed. The selection of evaluative measures should be based on the objectives of the instructional program and should consider each child's total development and its effect on reading performance.

13. Make parents aware of the reasons for a total language program at school and provide them with ideas for activities to carry out at home.

14. Alert parents to the limitations of formal assessments and standardized tests of pre-first graders' reading and writing skills.

15. Encourage children to be active participants in the learning process rather than passive recipients of knowledge, by using activities that allow for experimentation with talking, listening, writing and reading.

The idea of readiness materials is based largely on the concept of a particular and necessary sequence of learning, a concept Mrs. Reynolds does not accept. She finds that when children can exercise choice in their learning, readiness, ceases to be an issue. They learn what they are ready to learn, because they select that which is meaningful to them. Research in the field of beginning literacy has made the term reading readiness outmoded. We now know that young children constantly construct important knowledge about written language, not just get themselves ready to learn (Dyson, 1985; Goodman, 1985; Sulzby and Teale, 1985).

Even preschool children already have had experiences resulting in significant knowledge about reading and writing. The only realistic way for a teacher to find what a child is ready to learn next is to provide that child with opportunities to begin writing and experiencing print, without pressure, and see what happens. Only when a child is placed in a highly structured program, need we worry about whether the child is "ready."

Nevertheless, "readiness workbooks" have become a tradition in many kindergartens and even in some preschools. They use pictures and discussion to teach such facts as the difference between various colors and shapes, between big and little, up and down, loud and soft. They present picture patterns, sequences, and letter forms. Discussions about what is happening in pictures are designed to increase oral language ability. Formerly, Mrs. Hanna used this type of workbook in kindergarten by school district mandate, but now explains that she would much rather be teaching these concepts in a more effective way: through first-hand experience. After several years of gaining confidence in her teaching, she uses the workbooks very little. Instead, she substitutes hands-on activities which she knows will meet the workbook objectives far better than the workbook.

Superbaby Syndrome

Parents also frequently ask educators about commercial programs advertised for teaching toddlers and even babies to recognize words and letters. The "teach your baby to read" type of programs are having a definite impact on achievement oriented parents. According to these programs, parents must hurry and teach letter sounds and word recognition to babies two and under to be sure that they achieve their potential. Although these programs invariably deny that youngsters are to be pressured, pressure is inevitable when materials tell parents that a high proportion of children who are taught to read at the age of six or seven fail, but that all children can learn to read at age two or three (Hopson and Hopson, 1981).

Mrs. Reynolds gets upset because these programs tend to quote research which is valid in itself, but irrelevant to what the program is doing. For instance, no educators question the research on the importance of early stimulus, but many do question whether looking at letters on flashcards provides that stimulus. No educators question that the first three years are language acquisition years either, but they know that research refers to oral language acquisition rather than written language. Sometimes a researcher will be quoted out of context in support of an approach, such as when Carol Chomsky was quoted

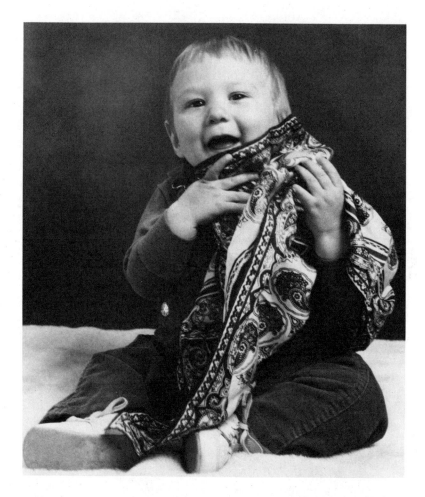

as part of a rationale for a phonics approach to reading. Anyone who had read the original research report would be aware that Chomsky actually ridicules phonics instruction (Chomsky, 1971). Mrs. Reynolds worries about parents being mislead.

Montessori Approach

Mrs. Hanna frequently is asked for advice about preschool experiences that will best prepare youngsters for kindergarten. A new Montessori program has just opened in town, so parents have asked for her opinion about the Montessori approach to early childhood education. Mrs. Hanna explains that most Montessori materials are highly concrete and most subject areas strongly emphasize learning through personal exploration. She believes that most of Montessori education is quite compatible with Piaget's research about how children learn, except for the reading lessons. The heavy emphasis on phonics and blending words in the Montessori reading approach make it abstract, despite its use of small objects in boxes to represent various sounds. The Montessori reading program is another example of a part to whole phonics approach. These factors make it contradictory to Piaget's findings which describe how children learn.

Mrs. Hanna thinks that the Italian language, which Maria Montessori spoke, with its extremely consistent sound-symbol system, was more suited to a phonics-based approach than English. She also knows that Montessori worked with impoverished children at the turn of the century; a situation in which the adult illiteracy rate was high. Possibly, if the children for whom she developed her curriculum had come from a literate society and a print-rich environment, Montessori's reading program would be based on experiences in that environment and be quite different.

The rest of the Montessori curriculum firmly reflects the importance of experiences to promote discovery learning, which Mrs. Hanna thinks is appropriate for preschoolers. The math materials are delightfully concrete, as exemplified by the golden beads, and remain compatible with current thinking about how young children learn math. The *practical life activities* help children learn through their own actions, with acceptance of errors and misjudgment along the way. Only the reading curriculum, which does not transfer well to this time and place, makes Mrs. Hanna hesitant about a Montessori curriculum.

COMPUTERS, KIDS, AND LITERACY

Another area of decision making has arisen with the advent of computer-assisted instruction. Computers are the current rage. Parents feel compelled to buy home computers and educational software for their youngsters, and teachers are taking crash courses in order to keep up with the children. Major manufacturers encourage school districts to adopt their machines by donating computers for trial programs, and the multitude of software being produced to tap into the lucrative education market boggles the mind. Amid the hype, how do we decide if young children can profit from working with computers, and if so, what type of computer materials are best for them to use?

Do we automatically accept the advertising claims, or do we take the time to exercise professional judgment regarding the most appropriate learning activities for young children? Many attractive materials claim to teach almost any reading skill; and school districts seem willing to spend the money to acquire these materials. Further, kids are fascinated by the magic of fast moving, colored graphics responding to their slightest touch and they vie for time on the computer. Teachers feel pressured to teach with computers by the administration, by parents, by students, and by the media. The teacher who wants to stop and examine just what computers offer to students seems rather a spoilsport.

Let's do it anyway. First, we must decide on our criteria for determining educationally sound materials for young children. Do we change our criteria when examining electronic educational materials, or do we continue with the same criteria? Unless we keep a clear vision of effective learning activities, no matter what the medium, we leave ourselves in danger of accepting computer versions of workbook drill or other approaches we have already determined to be ineffective. Unless we keep a clear vision of young children and how they learn, we may feel tempted to offer them abstract learning they are not ready for, just because it is computerized abstraction.

Criteria for Developmentally Appropriate Material

☐ **Does the material allow children to explore and discover?**
☐ **Does it present the whole before the parts?**
☐ **Does the concrete precede the abstract?**
☐ **Is it relevant to the child's experience?**

Mrs. Thomas is trying out some software produced by Children's Television Workshop with her first grade class. Several children are crowded around the Apple computer installed in a corner of her class-room, watching the child on the keyboard and waiting their turn. *Instant Zoo* (CTW, 1981) appears to be lots of fun. In the game by that name, a partial representation of some animal appears on the screen and the children guess which one it is. Everyone can participate to that point, but then only those who can read the names of the animals are involved in selecting the appropriate word from those listed on the screen. No doubt those who can't read the animal names are motivated to memorize those words; but once that task is mastered, the game probably has little additional value.

On the same disk the game, *Scramble,* requires children to take a nonsense listing of letters and put them in the right sequence to spell a word. Children found the set of letters *O W N,* which of course already made a word, and could either become *now* or *won.* Yet, only one selection was rewarded by the computer as correct. This game was great fun for the girl who could read at fifth grade level, but confusing to the other first graders. Advertisements for the game described it as useful for teaching children to read, not for those who already read well. What is the purpose of such a game? It doesn't teach children to recognize a word on sight; it actually obstructs the visual memory process by presenting an inaccurate version of words it attempts to teach. The game doesn't help children gain meaning from printed symbols, since words are presented in isolation and therefore have no meaning. It does force children to attend to individual letters in a word, a practice which can produce slow readers with lower comprehension ability.

These games have animated graphics which entertain the young-sters much the way that Sesame Street animations do on television. Although Mrs. Thomas does not have a color monitor, the designs are intended to be seen in color and are more attractive that way. Interest-ingly, although manufacturers promote these games as tools to teach children basic reading and prereading skills, the directions for playing and the indicators of correct or incorrect responses mostly appear in writing and must be read. The basic directions don't present too much of a problem, since the children seem to remember them after having them read to them a few times.

The *ATARI* computer in a near-by kindergarten has a color mon-itor for added reinforcement. Adults as well as children are captivated by the colorful and fast moving displays that appear on this screen. The teacher has been experimenting with a program called *Kindercomp* (Early Learning, 1983). This program provides six game options which are printed on the screen at the start, and children are to choose the number corresponding to their choice of games. Robert needs an adult to read the choices to him, but after he selects his game, no reading is required. In the matching game, a clown face appears

either with a wink or a tear to tell Robert whether his response was right or wrong. To play, Robert must determine which of three shape sequences matches the model and then type the corresponding number. Since he is successful with this task, we can assume that Robert has had sufficient concrete level experiences with visual discrimination tasks. A younger child would probably need to first match shapes of real objects, such as silverware, shells, or leaves. A less mature child would also need to duplicate sequences with beads and blocks before the more abstract symbols on the screen would be appropriate.

Although Robert can find out immediately if he is right or wrong with the computer, and using the computer is fun because of the color and movement, his task is similar to traditional workbook or worksheet material. His teacher realizes this but chooses to use the program to reinforce learning which has occurred through other modes because the children enjoy working with the computer. The teacher makes an important distinction between teaching and reinforcing learning.

Other options on the program—completing a number sequence or typing a letter to match a letter on the screen—are equally mundane, except for the immediate feedback feature. Several programs are fun but of doubtful educational value. One makes a whole line of any letter hit, and another makes a delightful display of a child's name (or any set of letters) after a child types it in. Using a joystick instead of the keyboard, children can also draw designs of various colors. Because the joystick is difficult to use for drawing, Robert likes to use the *Koala Pad* (Koala Technologies) instead. It allows him to draw with a pencil type tool onto a pad while his drawings are shown on the monitor screen. He especially enjoys choosing the *mirror option,* which makes a mirror image as well as the original of whatever he draws. This results in amazingly complex designs which he can color in a variety of ways with just the touch of the keyboard. The *Mousepaint* program (Apple Computer, 1984) allows similar drawing, but the "mouse" type of control appears more difficult to control. Questions of frustration or fun aside, what do children learn by using such computer programs?

Mrs. Reynolds keeps this question in mind as she previews software for possible use in her preschool. She has borrowed several educational game disks and is trying them out on her computer at home. *Juggles' Rainbow* (Learning Company, 1982) which is aimed at ages three through six has great color and entertaining sound effects. Although the instructions and responses are in writing, touching any key makes something happen. Mrs. Reynolds discovers that playing this game as designed requires that the keyboard be divided in half with a blue strip of cardboard inserted between the second and third rows of keys. The child is supposed to learn the principles of above and below by touching keys either above or below the strip. The game similarly presents principles of left and right by dividing the keyboard up and down. Aside from the fact that this game for prereaders requires constant reading, Mrs. Reynolds thinks it is totally inconsistent with what she knows about how children learn. If she decides to spend time helping an individual child learn those principles, she will do so at the concrete level and in a personally meaningful way rather than by reading computer game instructions to the child. Mrs. Reynolds finds that activities in which children experience above and below or left and right with their own bodies are more meaningful to them. She plays follow the leader games and helps children verbalize the words above, below, over, under, inside, and outside while they experience them. She teaches her preschoolers how to dance the "Hokey Pokey" and put their left leg in the circle, then their right elbow out.

Tanya's father has just bought a piece of hardware designed to make a computer more accessible to youngsters. An alternative to the regular keyboard, it is called Muppet Learning Keys (Koala Technologies, 1984). He is excited about it and brings it to show Mrs. Reynolds, hoping to get her opinion regarding the educational value. Mrs. Reynolds admires the attractive colors and layout of the keyboard. Sections of keys denote colors, numbers, and letters plus keys for "oops" and "help" indicated by cartoon illustrations. Directional keys are marked by arrows.

Children don't have to be able to read to enjoy the Muppet Learning Keys software "Discovery Disk." Any key pressed results in some change on the screen, provided the child uses a color monitor. If Tanya presses a letter key, a cartoon picture corresponding to that letter appears: an alligator for *A*, a bird for *B*, and a camel for *C*. The number of alligators, birds, or camels showing on the screen changes according to what number key she presses. Similarly, the color of the figures on the screen changes according to which color key is pressed. The characters dance or hop in different directions which children can control

by pressing the arrow keys. Mrs. Reynolds likes the fact that what happens on the screen is controlled by the child. She also notes that a child can learn by discovery how to operate the keyboard. She watches Tanya as she explores the various keys and quickly learns which keys get which results.

Obviously, Tanya is enjoying her new toy, and her parents are enjoying watching their three-year old use the computer. The question of educational value still exists. Mrs. Reynolds fears that some parents will think this device can teach their children reading and arithmetic since it presents letters and numbers. She thinks that it might prove valuable for matching numerals and visualizing quantity, but only for those children who have developed the one-to-one correspondence concept already. Unless a child has had sufficient experience with counting actual objects, counting ability will be not be sophisticated enough to determine how many little figures are dancing around and relate that quantity to a numeral. Mrs. Reynolds worries that adults may try to substitute this abstract level counting for the concrete level experience required first.

Mrs. Reynolds is concerned that adults have unrealistic expectations for the educational value of the letters on this keyboard. These concerns are intensified when she sees an advertisement for more Muppet Learning Keys software, which is called "Kindergarten Curriculum" (Sunburst Communications, 1986). It isn't educationally sound to present letter sounds out of the context of words, nor even possible to isolate sounds. This Muppet Keyboard program apparently is based on a set of assumptions which she rejects. Even if she did believe that letter sounds could or should be taught in isolation, she doubts that "The Muppet Discovery Disk" could teach those concepts. She bases her doubts on the content and quality of the pictures selected to represent letter sounds. When the letter *I* is represented by something so foreign to the experience of today's children as a bottle of ink (labeled *ink* and requiring reading ability), a child can't be expected to understand. When *E* is represented by an elephant for which the *E* sound is obscured by the *L* sound, a child can't be expected to understand. When *H* is represented by a hopping thing with legs and eyes, how can anyone know without being told that this is a hamburger? Several other figures were so difficult to identify that Mrs. Reynolds needed her own knowledge of letter sounds as a clue to what the picture could be. Additionally, she found the cartoon quality of several pictures offensive to her personal aesthetic sense.

The *Talking Screen Textwriting Program* (Computing Adventures, Ltd., 1984) utilizes another computer attachment which attempts to assist preliterate children. In this program, the Echo II Speech Synthesizer (Street Electronics Corp.) is teamed up with an Apple computer and a word processing program designed for beginning writers. The speech synthesizer is supposed to say aloud what the child writes on the computer keyboard. The program is based on educational assumptions which Mrs. Reynolds shares: that children learn to read through their active exploration of print as it expresses their own ideas and experiences. She feels pleased to find a computer program which attempts to teach reading skills in the context of meaning, and which acknowledges that children learn about reading by writing as well as the reverse. She is also happy to read in the program manual that the speech synthesizer does not say the sounds of the separate letters, but will only try to say complete words. The Echo will say the name of the letters as typed, but does not try to isolate their sounds.

Having been excited about trying this program, Mrs. Reynolds feels disappointed when she discovers that the quality of speech sounds from the synthesizer is so poor that she cannot understand the sounds. Further, she finds that the synthesizer "reads" words phonetically, and naturally, many words sound distorted. The program attempts to remedy this problem with a "Yuk" key (Y) which provides an opportunity for a child to change standard spelling to phonetic in order to have it sound right. The example given in the manual is *tomatoe* and the revised spelling suggests is *toe mai toe*. This example seems backwards to Mrs. Reynolds, who knows that children progress from phonetic spelling to standard spelling rather than the other way around. She also sees problems for the child writing at the letter naming stage, which precedes the phonetic spelling stage. She likes the word processing part of the program, but prefers it without the sound. She would like to suggest to the program designers that they substitute a natural voice device for the speech synthesizer and that they design the program to respond to known words as wholes, rather than to combine phonetic sounds of separate letters. Mrs. Reynolds sees a parallel in the problem the synthesizer has with combining letter sounds and the problem children have when they are taught to read that way.

The *Writing to Read* program (IBM, 1984) has been widely publicized as a new approach to teaching literacy. Mrs. Hanna and Mrs. Thomas went to the presentations explaining how the program would work if adopted in their school district. They were surprised to discover that this "new" program was actually an updated mixture of three old approaches. They agreed with the proposition that children can most easily learn to read what they themselves have written and that invented and phonetic spelling grows naturally into standard spelling: They have been teaching reading according to these guidelines all along. Even IBM acknowledges that the writing component of the program doesn't require a computer, and it is separate from the computer directed lessons. Mrs. Hanna and Mrs. Thomas know children can read their own writing first because it is personally meaningful and intrinsically interesting, as well as familiar. The *Writing to Read* program seems to embrace the importance of meaning, but at the same time contradicts that principle with a component which isolates sounds and asks children to reconstruct them into words without any context.

Children use the computer for this phonics portion of the program. Initially, the computer shows a picture to teams of youngsters plugged into the computers via earphones. If the picture is a cat, the tape recording tells the children to say *cat*. Then, each letter of the word appears on the screen separately, with accompanying taped instructions to say the sound of each letter (although most educators agree that it is impossible to isolate most sounds) and to press the key that corresponds to the letter. This computer exercise is in effect a talking, animated workbook exercise. No matter how attractive, it still violates the research showing the importance of meaningful context in teaching reading (Pearson, 1984). Mrs. Hanna and Mrs. Thomas think this is an example of what Donald Graves, a writing expert, means when he told an interviewer "Kids have never liked workbooks and they never will, so people are using the computer in gimmicky ways to make the workbook more palatable" (Green, 1984, p. 22). These teachers prefer to help children learn phonics from words in sentences, especially those sentences the children have written or dictated themselves.

Another strand of the program does not involve computer use and consists of commonly used kinesthetic exercises to help children become familiar with letters. Mrs. Hanna has always made many of these available for her kindergarteners, such as making letters from clay and drawing letters in cornmeal. She finds that some children's learning styles and developmental stages require this type of reinforcement and that other's do not. Therefore, she questions the value of having all

children involved in this component of the program. An audiocassette listening library in which children read along as a recorded voice reads a story is another component of this program. Mrs. Hanna and Mrs. Thomas have used this approach to sight word vocabulary for years.

After hearing the explanations of how the program works and seeing the materials in action, Mrs. Thomas and Mrs. Hanna decided that they were already implementing the parts of the program that had value and didn't understand why buying computers suddenly made this reading program exciting. After they discovered that a typical *Writing to Read* installation to accommodate 120 students would cost a school about $17,000 (Howitt, 1984), Mrs. Thomas and Mrs. Hanna wished they might be allowed to use some of the money they would not be spending on the program to buy more blocks or to go on field trips.

Both teachers began thinking about how they could use the computer's capabilities to help children focus on reading skill concepts demonstrated in their own writing. Mrs. Thomas already has some commercial computer programs which allow the teacher to insert the words with which children play a word game, such as unscrambling words in *Word Editor* (*Instant Zoo,* Children's Television Workshop and Apple Computer Inc., 1981) or a variation of the old *hang man* game called *Raise the Flag* (*Mix and Match,* Children's Television Workshop, 1981). However, these games present words in isolation and/or in scrambled versions and have no more validity for helping children learn than when the words are suppled by the computer program. Mrs. Thomas continues to think about computer capabilities which she is discovering in the computer class she is currently taking; she suspects that the computer can do more than has been shown, and that someone must be creating programs which are educationally sound for young children.

Mrs. Hanna and Mrs. Thomas are not opposed to using computers for helping children learn reading and writing, if they can use the computers as they see appropriate. They like having a computer in their classroom, but not a set of them apart from the classroom in a separate *Writing to Read* laboratory. These teachers enjoy having the computer with its word processing capabilities available for children whenever they feel like writing but don't want to labor over forming letters by hand. Each teacher has noticed that the effort required to make the letters uses up much of the writing energy of some youngsters—those who consequently put few ideas onto paper. Both Mrs. Thomas and Mrs. Hanna want the computer to be a tool for expression of ideas in writing, through which children can explore phonics and composition principles just as they do when writing on paper. These teachers believe work on the computer should not be limited to responding to commands to say the sounds of letters in isolated words. They were surprised that the *Writing to Read* program suggested children use typewriters instead of computers for their writing. The typewriters make letter formation easy, but still require children to totally rewrite their work for revision. This program ignores word processing, which

they think is the most exciting use of computers for helping children read and write (Figure 5.2).

Word processing has proven a remarkable boost to writing skills in Mrs. Thomas's and Mrs. Hanna's classrooms. They find that even beginning writers are willing to revise, edit, and polish compositions for an audience when they can do it so easily. Where formerly, rewriting involved totally recopying a piece, now it only involves editing the parts that need change. Especially helpful for youngsters with immature handwriting skill, the finished copy comes out crisp, with no smudges or erasures. Children are proud to bind these finished products into books and place them for others to enjoy in the library corner.

Sometimes Mrs. Hanna takes dictation from children at the computer keyboard rather than writing by hand. She thinks modeling both kinds of writing is important, since the children she teaches will probably use both methods throughout their lives. When a child indicates a desire to edit a handwritten piece, Mrs. Thomas sometimes first enters it into the computer. This eases the revision process for the child even when he did not originally write the piece on the computer.

Although excited about the potential of computers, these teachers are not willing to accept just any educational material simply because it utilizes a computer. As careful consumers, they protect their students from unsuitable educational products. Unfortunately not all teachers are so discriminating. Glorified workbook materials seem to be selling at a rapid pace and are therefore encouraging production of more of the same, rather than mandating increased sophistication (Komoski, 1984).

```
                  ABOUT MY TRIP



To Tony we are going to  go fouar a chrip in too mor years. Me

and mi grapo wr tocin ubuot not havin a hors cus you hafto clen

up aftr thim. But I im gunu hav a thre wellr.      BYBY

Tony N.    5-20-85
```

Figure 5.2   A child's language-experience story written on a word processor. (To Tony, We are going to go for a trip in two more years. Me and my grandpa were talking about not having a horse cause you have to clean up after them. But I'm gonna have a three-wheeler. Bye, Bye. Tony N. 5-20-85)

Even if educators could find more suitable programs and get rid of "drill and kill" computer programs, early childhood teachers still might not wholeheartedly embrace computer education. They may think that computer assisted instruction suitable for older kids, but still reject it for their students. Early childhood teachers know their students are different and require different modes of learning. Early childhood educators never forget that intellectual skills unfold according to a definite maturational sequence and that each stage of intellectual growth is nurtured by specific forms of learning. Therefore, most preschoolers and many primary grade students are not yet able to profit from the abstract level of learning presented by a computer. Children whose stage of development requires first hand sensory experiences with real objects do not have those needs met by figures on a screen—even by adorable, animated figures. Although many adults recognize that letters and numbers are abstractions, sometimes they perceive pictures as real rather than as another form of symbolic representation. Children cannot gain the same type of knowledge from a picture as from interaction with the real thing, whether the picture is in a workbook, picture book, or on a computer screen. Teachers must always keep in mind this innate limitation of the computer, no matter what the program.

Mrs. Williams thinks that some available software might be fine for her third graders, since they are more able to think abstractly. Many of the educational games are similar in format to video arcade games. She has watched her own youngsters' intense interest in video games and noticed some definite values. At first she thought eye-hand coordination and practice in quick response was the main value. But as her children continued to be engrossed in various levels of the games, she knew intellectual stimulation probably was involved. She watched her youngsters play and saw how they had to plan ahead and develop strategy in order to do well. Sometimes they had to analyze several sets of information in making choices for their strategy. Mrs. Williams soon became convinced that many video games, whether played in an arcade or on a computer, involved thinking skills. Now she is comfortable both with games for fun and similar games for education for her third graders. Actually, youngsters themselves soon weed out materials that are less valuable because they lose interest in them. Then Mrs. Williams returns these materials to the computer software library where she borrowed them. She only purchases the software that grabs and holds kids' interests due to challenging content.

Some materials she orders are just glorified workbook activities, but Mrs. Williams has made the conscious decision to sugar coat drill for her slower students who need that repetition. "Besides," she says, "the computer has more patience than I do." But she doesn't confuse drill with thinking or with actual learning.

All these teachers are making difficult decisions about how to spend instructional dollars and how to spend childrens' instructional time. The question we need to ask ourselves is whether having the computer in schools will allow us to meet children's learning needs in innovative ways, or will it just extend electronically what were poor education practices in the first place?

UNDERSTANDING OURSELVES AS DECISION MAKERS

Parents and teachers share the common concern of seeing that children succeed at learning to read. Their shared desire that children have the best possible experience makes them vulnerable to claims of advertisers. As more reading programs proliferate, adults must make decisions for children based an understanding of child development theories and an ability to analyze teaching materials accordingly. As manufacturers produce more workbooks and drill cards, educators need to consider more carefully the philosophy of education which each set of materials exemplifies.

Those making decisions about reading programs must have an understanding of both the part to whole and the whole to part approaches. For those whose value system and beliefs about children and learning are compatible with part to whole approaches, that is the right choice in order for them to be authentic teachers. But for those whose values and beliefs are not compatible with part to whole reading instruction, they should be aware that another approach to reading instruction does exist. All teachers need to be aware of the philosophy behind the materials they use and should match that philosophy to their own.

Jeanne Chall (1984) takes credit for textbooks using the part to whole approach more today than in the past. Yet, her research and experience base stems from a remedial reading viewpoint. She is associated with a reading clinic for problem readers and is not a classroom teacher. Chall says that running a classroom the way Mrs. Hanna, Mrs. Reynolds, and Mrs. Thomas do is an impossible task. But, should a remediation philosophy permeate reading instruction for children who have no difficulty moving from oral language to written language skills?

Sometimes Mrs. Reynolds and Mrs. Thomas sit down together and try to figure out why some people find it so hard to understand and accept a developmental approach to literacy. They have come to the conclusion that educational philosophy is related to personal life philosophy. Mrs. Reynolds suggests that maybe people with a generally upbeat and optimistic view of the world tend to perceive children as capable and growth seeking. They expect them to succeed. Those people would then be more able to accept Piaget's research on children's construction of their own knowledge, more apt to allow youngsters time to learn their own way, and more comfortable with children's trial and error approach to learning.

Mrs. Thomas agrees and imagines that those with a generally pessimistic view of the world would tend to see children as having difficulty learning or as not wanting to learn. They would worry about children failing. Those people would be more apt to feel compelled to try and break down complex concepts into the small pieces they hope will be easy to feed into children's minds. Their worries about failure would make them feel pressured about the pace of a child's learning and cause them to get nervous about incomplete learning or temporary misconceptions. Since they don't believe in childrens' innate desire to learn, they have trouble accepting that children will actively work to construct their own understandings. Such a view of life and learning could leave no alternative but the belief that children won't learn unless adults somehow put knowledge into their minds. Mrs. Reynolds and Mrs. Thomas can see how this viewpoint would get in the way of accepting the belief that understanding cannot be transmitted to oth-

ers: only facts can be given, whereas understanding must be constructed from within.

As the discussion between the two teachers deepens, they consider why some people tend to be optimistic and others pessimistic. Having a background in child development, they believe everyone is influenced in their view of reality by their own personal experiences. Mrs. Thomas thinks that if you yourself experienced difficulty learning, you would have a more negative view of the learning process. Perhaps those who work with children who are having learning problems, such as remedial teachers, develop a similar pessimistic outlook.

Mrs. Thomas's ideas remind Mrs. Reynolds of criticism aimed at Freudian psychology. Many psychologists claimed that Freud's constant interaction with troubled people led him to view the mind's operation based on a sickness model rather than on a wellness model. Freud was thus criticized for trying to extrapolate general principles about human functioning from his disturbed patients and applying them to all persons. Mrs. Reynolds wonders if some educational programs don't do the same thing: Programs designed for remediation or intervention with "high risk" students often seem to find their way into general use for children with no problems. Skeptical about the traditional remediation approach for kids with learning problems, Mrs. Reynolds feels certain that this approach is extremely inappropriate for other children. She thinks approaches which force-feed irrelevant minutiae to children can actually destroy their natural love of learning, can interrupt their natural search for understanding, and can damage their confidence in themselves.

Before we get too depressed, let us take comfort in remembering that most children eventually learn to read regardless of how they are taught. With enough print, and literature, and language in their natural environment, most children take advantage of a whole to part approach outside of the classroom, counterbalancing the part to whole instruction they may receive at school. Children's natural interest and desire to learn causes most of them to explore the world of print until they discover the keys to its mystery. It is also important to remember that loving, caring teachers enrich children's lives regardless of how they teach reading. But knowledge of how young children learn and of what the reading process entails will surely add to any teacher's success rate.

SUGGESTED FOLLOW-UP ACTIVITIES

1. Observe a school reading program in a primary grade. Focus upon the following:
    a. What is the basic philosophy behind the reading program?

     b. What type of materials do students use?

     c. Who assumes responsibility for what takes place?

     d. How do youngsters function—in groups, in teams, as a total class, or as individuals?

     e. How is student achievement or progress evaluated?

2. Visit a school where teachers use readiness workbooks with pre-readers. Become familiar with the materials in the program. Observe how the program is used. Focus on points listed in Question 1.

3. Visit a Montessori classroom and observe a reading lesson. Become familiar with the materials teachers use to teach reading and compare to those with materials they use to teach math.

4. Interview a public school teacher about the use of officially adopted texts. Does this teacher feel obligated to use them? Does he or she use them as directed? If not, how does he or she adapt the texts?

5. Observe children using electronic learning materials and/or try some computer educational software yourself. Evaluate the material in terms of the developmental guides presented in this chapter.

DISCUSSION TOPICS

1. Discuss reading programs you have observed in terms of the child development and educational philosophies explained in this chapter.

2. How can teachers and parents be helped to have faith in the child as an active learner and to believe that the child constructs knowledge rather than receives it?

REFERENCES AND SUGGESTIONS FOR FURTHER READING

Books

Almy, M. (1973). *Young children's thinking.* New York: Columbia University Teachers College Press.

Ames, L.B., & Ilg, F.L. (1979). *Your six year old.* New York: Dell Publishing Company. 1979.

Ashton-Warner, S. (1963). *Teacher.* New York: Simon and Schuster.

Bloom, B.S. (1956). *Taxonomy of educational objectives.* New York: David McCoy Co. Inc.

Botel, M. (1981). *The Pennsylvania comprehensive reading communication arts plan.* Harrisburg, PA: Pennsylvania Department of Education.

Cochran-Smith, M. (1984). *The making of a reader.* Norwood, NJ: Ablex Publishing Corporation.

Chall, J. (1983). *Stages of reading development.* New York: McGraw-Hill.

Durkin, D. (1980). *Teaching young children to read* (3rd ed.). Boston: Allyn & Bacon, Inc.

Flood, J., & Lapp, D. (1981). *Language/reading instruction for the young child.* New York: Macmillan Publishing Company.

Frank, M. (1982). *Young children in a computerized environment.* New York: Haworth Press.

Geber, B.A. (Ed.). (1977). *Piaget and knowing: Studies in epistemology.* Boston: Routledge & Kegan Paul Ltd.

Gesell, A., Ilg, F.L. & Ames, L.B. (1974). *The child from five to ten.* (Rev. ed.). New York: Harper & Row.

Goodman, K.S. (1973). *Miscue analysis: Applications to reading instruction.* Urbana, IL: National Council of Teachers of English.

Graves, D. (1983). *Teachers and Children at work.* Exeter, NH: Heinemann Educational Books.

Greenfield, P.M. (1984). *Mind and media: The effects of television, video games, and computers.* Cambridge, MA: Harvard University Press.

Hopson, M., & Hopson, M. (1981). *Little people can read: A synchronized verbal and visual language acquisition curriculum for the very young.* Anchorage, AK: Reprographics Center.

Huey, E.B. (1968). *The psychology and pedagogy of reading.* Cambridge, MA: M.I.T. Press.

Lamoreaux, L., & Lee, D.M. (1943). *Learning to read through experience.* New York: Appleton-Century-Crofts.

Lee, D.M., & Allen, R. V. (1963). *Learning to read through experience.* New York: Appleton-Century-Crofts.

Lee, Dorris, & Rubin, J. (1979). *Children and language.* Belmont, CA: Wadsworth.

Lee, B. & Rudman, M.K. (1982). *Mind over media.* New York: Seaview Books.

Montessori, M. (1965). *The Montessori method.* Cambridge, MA: Robert Bentley, Inc.

Morrison, C., & Austin, M.C. (1977). *The torch lighters revisited.* Newark, DE: International Reading Association.

Papert, S. (1980). *Mindstorms.* New York: Basic Books.

Pearson, P.D. (Ed.). (1984). *Handbook of reading research.* New York: Longman.

Rey, H.A. (1941). *Curious George.* Boston: Houghton Mifflin.

Rogers, J. *The Secret Moose.* (1985). New York: Greenwillow.

Rudolf, M. & Cohen, D.H. (1984). *Kindergarten and early schooling,* (2nd Ed.). Englewood Cliffs, NJ: Prentice-Hall.

Skinner, B.F. (1971). *Beyond freedom and dignity.* New York: Alfred A. Knopf.

Periodicals

Artley, A. (1980, May). Reading: skills or competencies? *Language Arts, 57,* 546-549.

Bruce, B., Michaels, S., & Watson-Gegeo, K. (1985, February). How computers can change the writing process. *Language Arts, 62,* 143-149.

Burg, K. (1984, March). The microcomputer in the kindergarten. *Young Children, 39* (3), 28-33.

Charlesworth, R. (1985, Spring). Readiness: Should we make them ready or let them bloom? *Day Care and Early Education, 12* (3), 25-27.

Chin, K. (1984, February). Preschool computing: Too much, too soon? *InfoWorld,* pp. 24-27.

Chomsky, C. (1971). Write first, read later. *Childhood Education, 47,* 296-299.

Deardorff, B. (1982, November). Confessions of a former skills teacher. *Learning,* pp. 42-43.

Dyson, A.H. (1984, December). 'N spell my grandmama': Fostering early thinking about print. *The Reading Teacher, 38* (3), 262-271.

Dyson, A.H. (1985, Fall). Puzzles, paints, and pencils: Writing emerges. *Educational Horizons, 64* (1), 13-16.

Elkind, D. (1967, Fall). Piaget and Montessori. *Harvard Educational Review, 37* (4), 535-545.

Freire, P. (1985, January). Reading the world and reading the word: An interview with Paulo Freire. *Language Arts, 62,* 15-21.

Goodman, Y. (1985, Fall). Developing writing in a literate society. *Educational Horizons, 64* (1), 17-21.

Green, J.O. (1984, March). An interview with don graves. *Classroom Computer Learning,* pp. 20-23.

Howitt, D. (1984, October 29). Experimental software boosted. *InfoWorld,* pp. 29-30.

Kamii, C. (1985, September). Leading primary education toward excellence. *Young Children, 40* (6), 3-9.

Komoski, K. (1984, December). Educational computing: The burden of ensuring quality. *Phi Delta Kappan, 66* (4), 244-248.

Martin, A. (1985, August). About teaching and teachers: Back to kindergarten basics. *Harvard Educational Review, 55* (3), 318-320.

McLanahan, J.F. (1984, Winter). Software for young children. *Day Care and Early Education, 11* (2), 26-29.

Noble, D. (1984, October 3). Jumping off the computer bandwagon. *Education Weekly,* pp. 24-25.

Ohanian, S. (1984, March). What does it take to be a good computer. *Learning,* pp. 31-40.

Rubens, T., Poole, J., & Hoot, J.L. (1984, Spring). Introducing micro-computers to micro-learners through play. *Day Care and Early Education, 11* (3), 29-31.

Sandberg-Diment, E. (1984, November). Buying software: The best and worst learning programs. *Parents,* pp. 180-190.

Schickedanz, J. (1981, November). Hey, this book's not working right. *Young Children, 37* (1), 18-27.

Scouler, M. (1979, June). Beginning reading through language-experience. *Australian Journal of Reading,* pp. 66-71.

Shannon, P. (1982, November/December). A retrospective look at teachers' reliance on commercial reading materials. *Language Arts, 59,* 844-853.

Shannon, P. (1985, October). Reading instruction and social class. *Language Arts, 62,* 604-613.

Smith, J.A. & Gray, J.M. (1983, November). Learning about reading, writing and fish with the help of the word processor. *Australian Journal of Reading,* pp. 186-192.

Sulzby, E. & Teale, W.H. (1985, Fall). Writing development in early childhood. *Educational Horizons, 64* (1), 8-12.

Taitt, H.A. (1982). Training materials. *Thinking-Learning-Creating: TLC for Growing Minds.*

Tierney, R. & LaZansky, J. (1980, September). The rights and responsibilities of readers and writers: A contractual agreement. *Language Arts, 57,* 606-613.

Tierney, R.J. & Pearson, D.P. (1985, April/May). New priorities for teaching reading. *Learning,* pp. 14-17.

Walton, S. (1984, September 5). And after the reign of Dick and Jane? *Education Weekly,* pp. L10-L11, L52-L53.

Winkeljohann, R. (1980). Queries: How can basal readers be used creatively? *Language Arts, 57,* 906-907.

Zacharias, J.A. (1983, November/December). Microcomputers in the language arts classroom: Promises and pitfalls. *Language Arts, 60,* 990-995.

Index

About the Authors

Marjorie Vannoy Fields is coordinator of the early childhood teacher education program at the University of Alaska in Juneau. She has combined her early childhood education background and experience with a previous specialty in the area of teaching reading. Dr. Fields has taught kindergarten and first grade as well as working with younger children. She also has two teenage sons. Dr. Fields is currently serving on the Board of Directors for the National Association for the Education of Young Children.

Dorris M. Lee was a member of the Portland State University faculty for 16 years. Prior to that time, she taught at Washington State University and was an education consultant for the White House Conference on Children and Youth in 1960. Her elementary teaching was at the fourth- and fifth-grade levels. Dr. Lee authored or co-authored ten books on education and published dozens of articles for teachers over a 40-year period of time. Two books with special significance for this book are: *Learning to Read Through Experience*, 1943, with Lillian Lamereaux, and the 1963 edition with R. V. Allen; and *Children and Language: Reading and Writing, Talking and Listening*, 1979, with Joseph Rubin. Dorris Lee passed away in October 1985, before the current text was completed.